THE RESEARCH COMPENDIUM

REVIEW AND ABSTRACTS

1942-1962

This book represents an important contribution by the School of Social Work at the University of Toronto. It is a record of a carefully designed plan to include a worthwhile research experience in the educational programme of every student engaged in graduate education for the profession. In the introductory essay Dr. Albert Rose explains the methods by which this educational objective has been attempted and traces the evolution of the research requirement as a valid learning experience.

The abstracts of 398 student projects provide a varied and interesting illustrative record of the students' work. These are not definitive studies but they are fertile in suggestive ideas; and the reported findings, though limited, are studded with clues for further and more intensive study in a wide range of welfare services and in different forms of social work. The result should be a valuable source of ideas for intending researches in this field, both of what is known, and perhaps equally important, of how much is not known.

The abstracts have been prepared by Margaret Avison, who has also provided an evocative introductory review.

MARGARET AVISON has recently completed research or editorial assignments for the Canadian National Commission for UNESCO, the Royal Ontario Museum, the Canadian Association for Adult Education, and the Indian School of International Studies. She is also a poet, and her first collection, *Winter Sun,* received the Governor-General's Award for Poetry in 1961.

ALBERT ROSE is Professor of Social Work and Co-ordinator of Research, School of Social Work, University of Toronto. He is the author of *Regent Park: A Study in Slum Clearance.*

FLORENCE STRAKHOVSKY is Research Secretary, Harry M. Cassidy Memorial Research Fund, School of Social Work, University of Toronto.

THE RESEARCH COMPENDIUM

Review and Abstracts of Graduate Research 1942-1962

Abstracts by MARGARET AVISON
Introductory essays by
MARGARET AVISON and ALBERT ROSE
Editorial Consultant, Florence Strakhovsky

Published in celebration of the
Fiftieth Anniversary of the
SCHOOL OF SOCIAL WORK
UNIVERSITY OF TORONTO

UNIVERSITY OF TORONTO PRESS

© UNIVERSITY OF TORONTO PRESS 1964

Reprinted in paperback 2014
ISBN 978-1-4426-5152-4 (paper)

Foreword

This publication takes an important place in our celebration of the School's Fiftieth Anniversary. No proposal advanced received greater support or aroused greater enthusiasm. Expectations have been fully realized. The Research Compendium is at once a contribution to our still scanty knowledge of social need and social welfare and a tribute to twenty generations of students who have undertaken, as a modest but effective part of their professional education, to apply the disciplines of scholarly research to some of the human problems that confront them in their chosen vocation. Teaching and research are complementary tasks of a faculty member, and his researches are concerned largely with the advancement of knowledge. Student research has a somewhat different function, described with some care in Dr. Albert Rose's essay in this volume. Student research, however, also makes its special contribution to knowledge, and here in this volume is the winnowed harvest of many hours of devoted labour, and not a little insight and imagination, to which the students of the School have given themselves as part of their progress from neophyte to beginning professional competence. Margaret Avison, in her impressions, in the other essay which this volume includes, has caught in a subtle, imaginative, and tantalizing way something of the rich store of knowledge, something of the sensitive human understanding, and something of the new perceptiveness of the kaleidoscope we call the condition of man that have been uncovered, if not in full or in definitive form, by the graduate students whose reports she has abstracted with such skill. We believe that this Compendium is not only an impressive record and itself a useful reference for research workers, but a timely reminder of how much we do not know about social welfare, social policy, and social work. It can be a source for questions as much as, if not more than, a source for answers.

The classification of the abstracts themselves has given us a great deal of trouble. Our objective has been to put each abstract under a heading where it will be most easily found by the reader. Where it appeared an abstract could be classified under more than one heading, a cross reference has been provided. The index has been arranged by author, agency, and subject matter. We trust that this will make the abstracts readily available to those who wish to use this volume for purposes of reference. It is our hope and intention, at regular intervals of from three to five years, to publish supplements to this initial Compendium. The School will continue, also, as is customary among universities, to make available original research documents through inter-library loan.

There have been many authors to this book. The students themselves have provided the substantive work from which it has been drawn. Miss Avison has tried to do justice to each of their reports within the brief compass of an abstract. From the beginning of the student research program Professor John S. Morgan has played an important role, as has Mrs. Sadie Gerridzen, School librarian and secretary of the Research Committee, which in recent years has been chaired by Professor Edgar Perretz, and during the preparation of this publication, by Dr. John Spencer. Florence Strakhovsky, Research Secretary, has co-ordinated all these efforts into a single piece of work and overseen the technical problems of publication. Special thanks are due to Mrs. Beverley Brookes for her painstaking and efficient typing of the manuscript.

The finances required for the preparation and publication of this Compendium have been supplied by the Cassidy Memorial Research Fund, the Welfare Research Grants Administration of the Department of National Health and Welfare, and the University of Toronto. Grateful appreciation is hereby recorded.

To all of those whose work and support have contributed to the publication of the Compendium the School owes a debt of gratitude. It is, I believe, an exciting and encouraging record of one part of the School's educational task which has meaning and usefulness to all who are interested in professional education and the continued application of disciplined study of human needs leading to the fuller discovery and development of our human resources.

Charles E. Hendry
Director

CONTENTS

Foreword   v
    By Charles E. Hendry

Impressions of a Lay Reader   3
    By Margaret Avison

The Research Requirement   9
    By Albert Rose

Abstracts

  Doctor of Social Work   29

  Master of Social Work or Its Equivalent

    Health and Welfare Services
      addiction   35
      aged   45
      child welfare - general   52
                      adoption   65
                      day nurseries   70
                      foster homes   71
                      institutions   79
                      unmarried parents   83
      crime and delinquency   90
      employment   113
      family welfare   117
      group services   131
      housing   136
      immigrants and ethnic groups   143
      medically and physically handicapped   154
      mental health   168
      public assistance   195
      schools   198
      transients   201

    Social Work
      administration   206
      casework   216
      community work (community organization)   220
      education   230
      group work   233
      research   243

    Community Attitudes to the Social Work
    Profession and Social Welfare   246

Unclassified   255

    List of Reports Not Abstracted   258

Index of Authors   263

Index of Agencies   268

Index of Subjects   271

THE RESEARCH COMPENDIUM

REVIEW AND ABSTRACTS

1942-1962

IMPRESSIONS OF A LAY READER

The Committee charged with planning this publication asked me to read and make abstracts of all doctoral dissertations and masters' theses, and to plan a "trend report" when the reading had been completed. It was their deliberate choice to have someone unfamiliar with social work literature come fresh to the task. And I attempted to give a clear picture of each report -- of not only its argument but its approach and tone as well. The tracing of "trends" would have called for awareness of more than the material I had to work with, however. And in the end the Committee asked me instead to gather the general impressions I had formed while engaged in the reading.

The studies presented in this twenty-year period cover a wide range of concerns. They indicate a disturbing number of communal responsibilities for which no part of the community yet acknowledges steady obligation. Increasingly, too, they reflect the difficulty of pinning down (for the sake of continuity and coherence) one ripple in Heraclitus's ever-flowing river. Through the war and postwar decades here represented, teachers and research programs in the School, Canadian experiences, and the "climate of thinking" in general have altered. The effect of such differences is evident in the reports across the years.

Yet surprisingly, although the tone of voice in almost every thesis is lively and individual, the conceptual climate struck me at first as oddly artificial and uniform. Almost every writer seemed involved in some form of one exercise: to apply a doctrine without becoming dogmatic. Then it appeared that the definitions of man and social relationships commonly implied and often quoted from "authorities" were "answers" carefully worked out and agreed upon in advance simply to expedite practice in a puzzling and problem-filled world. Moreover, the play of individuals' intuition between the bars, as it were, often proved freer than intuition that operates on the loose. The range of ease in this formal climate varied with the quality of the work: thoughtful treatises usually took their shape freely within the doctrinal framework without insisting upon it; where a student used the accepted terms glibly, his thought usually had a low evaporation point; on the few occasions when the formulations were spoken through clenched teeth, there was also evidence of a stall at the verbal level, a freeze-up in the thinking.

My initial uneasiness changed as I turned more pages

of more studies on more dimensions of communal life than I
had ever known existed. A fixed way of looking at the human situation, I began to realize, is seen as a practical
necessity by anyone who values deliberation and planning,
for if viewpoint ranges as widely as the variousness of
the human situation, everything but the immediate moment
is out of focus, a non-existent blur. Apparently social
workers have to project a future state of affairs and establish a widely-acceptable and professionally-accepted
value system -- and moreover they have to act, often drastically and on a moment's notice.

Action brings in all the other "fields" of human concern, too, directly or by implication. Thus social work
meets biology, comparative languages, political economy --
and drama! -- by engaging with the human creatures who are
focal to these and many other disciplines. Many theses
referred to work done in other "fields", but again, largely
within doctrinal limits. One student quoted William James's
statement that "the whole modern scientific organization of
charity is a consequence of the failure of simply giving
alms". These words clarified a trend which many students
had suggested or illustrated in their reports: social work
emerging as a distinct profession when services were sec-
ularized, deriving its earlier insights more from sociology
and its later ones more from psychiatry. Also notable
throughout is the predominance of the "scientific method".
The approach, in other words, is far oftener like that of
an ecologist, for example, than like that of a novelist.
Dreiser's American Tragedy is unlikely to be cited by any
student writing on delinquency, nor Scott Fitzgerald on
alcoholism, nor Kerouac on homeless transients or putative
fathers. Why is this so?

Is it in part because of the strict forms and pre-
established terminology already mentioned? And is the
preference for scientific objectivity of method and language part of the process of disciplining feelings and
attitudes? Nobody approaches the sore spots of our social
life without wincing and bracing himself. Using strict,
scientific language is a human gesture, an admirable way
of neither evading a human claim nor intruding upon it with
an irrelevant private emotion. This combination of distance
and warmth of understanding often impressed me and sometimes
touched me in these studies.

An exact terminology is occasionally a kind of short-
hand that only other specialists can read: the group worker's
sense of "formed" groups is one instance; the child-care

concept abridged in the one word "placement" is another.
("In adoption, 'infant' means under three months," one
student explained.) Sometimes the word given special
meaning is later missed in its general, popular sense;
e.g., when "need" becomes a particular noun in social work
writing, the simple verb "to need" is soon missed, and for
want of it writers fall into circumlocutions ("It is requisite" etc.). Sometimes language seems by its very nature
to resist scientific exactness. For example, a student may
avoid the noun "cause" — for modesty and precision prefer-
ring "one occasion of ..." — and then find himself using
the verb "occasioned" as a synonym of "caused" and uncon-
sciously retaining the conjunction "because".

The "jargon" I had been led by self-depreciating
social workers to expect was scarcely ever obtrusive in
these papers. Language that is used to mask feeling or
exact sense, to obscure something the writer feels to be
suspect in his sense of his subject, or words vaguely
waved like faded flags in an uncertain breeze: such language is not particular to any occupational or academic
group.

During preliminary discussions of this work, a staff
member told me about a mentor who had early pointed out to
him the advantage to incisive writing of active rather than
passive expressions. The comment stuck in my mind as I
read. "When there is a 'large turnover' who turned over?"
I found myself rephrasing one student's title. These "data"
— by whom are they given, to whom, and in what context?
If a person is a "delinquent", who delinquished him, or
what did he delinquish? And when an alcoholic is not
"healed" or "improved" but "rehabilitated", for what is he
re-hable? It is a good game to play, turning passives into
the active thus, even if not invariably useful! (The last
illustration, for instance, shows thoughtful and honest
begging of a question, i.e., by using "rehabilitate" the
worker at least sheds medical or moralistic pre-judging of
a little understood condition.)

Even in objective, scientific prose, the emotional
colouring of words is worth watching. Why is "preventive"
a friendly word, and "deterrent" a stern one? When did
"deranged" fall into disfavour, and does "disturb" (from
turba, crowd) seem better now because of modern acquaintance
with masses in agitation? Is "well adjusted" preferred to
"well balanced" because it suggests more complex points
and kinds of contact? Why do "sympathy" and "words of advice" describe nineteenth century practice, where the

5

contemporary worker substitutes "warmth" and "counselling" (but not "counsel")? Is today more concerned about "tone" than yesterday was? And if so, is it newly stout in facing disaffections, or is it gradually substituting salesmanlike manoeuvres for open-ended speculation?

Several searching historical theses apart, these studies generally showed a coldness of historical imagination, it seemed to me. Many reviews of institutional history showed up the ladies bountiful, paternalistic administrators, and smug dictators of standards and morals, whose narrowness inhibited service and demeaned clients in the past; but few went on to note the polar difficulties that dog present practice -- professionalism sometimes excluding laymen's contributions; mechanical notions of efficiency; and such careful flexibility in value judgments that a basis for action can be hard to define.

Historical sense, as others of these studies demonstrate, can help to make a living discipline of the formal limits necessary to professional discussion. Thus, identifying the disciplinarian's harshness in a earlier day's institutions can reveal the dangers of reflecting excessive parental anxiety about children in those of today. Or the social scientist's breaking down of problems into component factors may be seen as a method analogous to the factory method of the era of assembly lines, and due caution perhaps should be taken from flaws in that era's methods; e.g., the short-sighted calculating which omitted from work units, or cost items, the expensive morning and evening transportation the worker paid for, until the unplanned growth of cities and concentration of traffic that ensued made a whole society reconsider the cost. Or the psychiatric insights that enrich awareness of interaction may mean on occasion such entanglement in interactions that nothing gets done.

In a short period with many influences at work the trend of these studies cannot be read aright by an outsider. Yet it seemed to me that the immediately postwar students showed greater zeal for legislative action and agency reorganization, whereas students recently show far greater caution in defining expectations or in speaking out as representatives of the whole community. Is a subdivision within the profession and among specialists responsible for less "con-science" nowadays?

But such a drift into discouragement can quickly find counteraction in the theses themselves. One student cites an 1857 report on practices that "deprave (i.e., make crooked) the minds of convicts by enforcing division of

labour in the interest of completing contracts, to the
detriment of enabling the convicts to learn a trade" which
was supposed to be the point of the institution's occupational program. This focus on human beings and their individual well-being is continually renewed. Vocational
guidance geared to a manual of occupations is seen as unlikely to satisfy the pressure of endlessly varied potentiality in people. The "homeless transient" is seen in
the perspective of the traditions of Canada's frontier and
its northland. The dissatisfaction of the aged is seen in
association with that of other people who find themselves
suddenly "redundant". The class-dimension of values and
preferences is sensitively explored among children in a
city's recreational agency. And so on.

Again and again the real experience that individual
writers convey both illuminates the research they completea
for their degrees in the School and enhances the understanding among us all, and the understanding by each of us
of the social life that is bewilderingly projected out of
the past, seems to function beyond our reach, and yet is
answerable to our engagement with it.

Margaret Avison

THE RESEARCH REQUIREMENT

The School of Social Work of the University of Toronto achieved full graduate status during the academic year 1946-47. In retrospect it seems inevitable and entirely natural that the terms of this achievement would include a requirement that each successful candidate for a graduate degree must complete a piece of research and write an acceptable thesis.

Harry M. Cassidy, who had returned to Toronto as Director of the School in the latter months of 1944, was no novice in the process of negotiation with university bodies such as the Senate and the Graduate School. In the years 1938-42 he had struggled successfully in Berkeley to lead the educational program in social work at the University of California from its modest position within the social sciences to graduate status. He became the first Dean of a graduate School of Social Welfare in California.

This process was duplicated at the University of Toronto where Dr. Cassidy was by no means a newcomer. In the early 1930's he had joined the staff of the Department of Political Economy as a young lecturer, fresh from a doctoral program at the Brookings Institution. His course in "Labour Problems" was open to students in the Department of Social Science, forerunner of the School of Social Work. This latter program also fell under the administration of the Chairman of his Department, the late Professor E.J. Urwick.

When Dr. Cassidy came to a meeting of his staff in the winter of 1946-47, following a series of sessions with the Executive Committee of the Senate of the University of Toronto, his colleagues knew that the terms of graduate status represented a reasonable balance between the expectations of both graduate study and professional preparation. The arrangements were in large measure a product of the Director's experience, his knowledge of the University of Toronto and its historical evolution, his personal background as a scholar, and the traditions of the University of Toronto. An individual research project and a thesis were to be required of each candidate for the Degree of Master of Social Work.

In the course of the negotiations Dr. Cassidy had assured the members of the Senate that a graduate curriculum in social work was more extensive in its breadth and in the time required for its completion than most, if not all, of the curricula leading to a Master's Degree in other graduate divisions of the University. Clearly there was not sufficient time within two academic years, of eight or nine months each, to enable students to initiate, develop, and complete a Master's thesis. The second year of study in social work, the critical year of graduate study in the view of the University, was extended, therefore, to a full eleven months, to begin in early September and finish at the end of the following July. Candidates for the degree of Master of Social Work would be enrolled in a Summer Term (of ten full weeks) commencing late in May, to be devoted to the writing of a research report under the guidance of a faculty consultant.

The stipulation of a research requirement for a graduate degree was accepted as an entirely normal procedure at the time. This was surely the practice of most universities in North America and in Western Europe, and a well-remembered part of the educational experience of most members of the staff of the School of Social Work.

Objectives of a Research Requirement
in Graduate Professional Education

No profession worthy of designation as a learned vocation can earn the respect and support of the society of which it is a part unless its members embark consciously upon a process of continuous study and evaluation of its professional practice. The problems for research in social work arise in the performance of social work or in planning to perform it. In the last analysis, improvement of practice can be achieved only through research carried out in whole or in part by members of the profession itself.

The research component in graduate professional education for social work has as its basis a realization of the objectives of research in social work itself, namely, improvement of practice and assumption of social responsibility by members of the profession. While professors in any school would be delighted if as many as one or two students each year embarked upon a career in research after graduation, this is not the prime objective.

The educational objective, in its universal application, is to ensure that the student becomes a reasonably intelligent "consumer" of research findings. In his professional career the social worker will receive and read many more documents which purport to be reports of research in the field than did his counterpart of one or two decades ago. He must have a sufficient knowledge of the research process (scientific method) to be able to read and judge the value of current research findings for the practice and policy of his agency or social work operation. He must be able to distinguish between sound, adequate methodology and the inadequately planned and executed study which is to be dismissed without serious consideration.

At a more sophisticated level the objective is to provide the student with an opportunity to understand and use the research method, through reading, discussion, and active participation in a research project. In the course of these studies the student will become acquainted with the techniques of research (often described as research methods), particularly in the social sciences -- the social survey, the case study, historical, statistical, and experimental research. It is one thing, however, to make a study of research already completed or underway in various settings or communities; it is another matter to assume personal responsibility for a piece of research work. The academic research course cannot, by itself, in the view of most graduate schools, achieve the objectives of a research requirement.

In another approach, an additional objective of the graduate research requirement is the instillation of an attitude usually described as "research-mindedness" within the spirit of the emerging member of a profession. No one is interested in the development of cynicism or destructive criticism, but intelligent skepticism and critical analysis of professional practice and research findings are qualities worthy of inclusion in the personal value system of each graduate. The research requirement can play an important role in the development of these qualities, since it offers an opportunity for personal study and reflection not available in quite the same way elsewhere in the curriculum.

Finally, the objective of the research requirement in a graduate curriculum is the further provision of an opportunity for the student to integrate various aspects of his knowledge. The research project and the research report give many students an occasion to bring knowledge from the social sciences and from the practice of social work to bear upon the process of seeking meaningful answers to questions posed for objective study. Not only is it often possible to utilize knowledge gained in all other aspects of the social work curriculum, but knowledge in other disciplines may also be relevant to the solution of the problem in hand. The research requirement provides, for the graduate student, the major opportunity for private study and personal speculation, for the use of logical judgment, without the constant supervision of an instructor or supervisor. The student is more nearly "on his own" than he is in any other aspect of the educational program.

The Teaching of Research

At the end of the Second World War and for many years thereafter there were very few university courses in "research methods" _per se_, either within the social sciences or elsewhere in North American universities. It was generally assumed that a graduate student would comprehend the nature of scientific method from his undergraduate studies and related reading; he was likely to have been exposed to an introductory course in statistics, at least. It was generally assumed, as well, that a university professor who had undertaken a research project in his own graduate studies would be competent to advise graduate students with respect to their research work, particularly since he would be carrying on further research in his own fields of interest.

These assumptions are tenuous at best, but they broke down quickly in graduate schools of social work under the pressure of relatively large numbers of students. In the first place, most students came to graduate studies in social work without much comprehension of the nature of scientific inquiry and without even an elementary acquaintance with statistical methods. It was necessary for the schools to provide these. In the second place, it could not be assumed that a background of training and orientation to professional practice would equip many members of the faculty in a school of social work to serve comfortably in the capacity of research consultant. It was necessary for the schools to equip some staff members through a form of in-service training and through experience, or to dichotomize its faculty into wings, a research-oriented and a non-research-oriented group. In most universities, however, the original assumptions continued to be held and there was little or no acceptance of the notion of a non-research-oriented group of professors.

At the University of Toronto School of Social Work a successful attempt has been made during the past fifteen or more years to involve every member of the teaching staff in the implementation of the student research requirement. In the role of student advisor most members of the faculty play a part in assisting students to identify a problem for research, to explore the problem with appropriate colleagues in the University and elsewhere, and to meet responsible persons in social agencies or government departments where relevant data might be secured. In the role of university teachers many members of the faculty serve as research consultant to one or more students each academic year, and a number of persons have served as group research project leaders (since 1959), either alone or in collaboration with a colleague. As well, every member of the teaching staff is required, as one of two readers, to read one or more research reports each year and to grade them for acceptance in partial fulfilment of the requirements for the Master's degree. At one time or another, many members of the staff have served on the Research Committee of the School, a committee charged with the development of educational policy in this area of the curriculum.

In these various ways, it is fair to say, the major responsibilities for the teaching of research and the administration of the research requirement have been widely diffused throughout the faculty. This has been true whether the professor was a product of the social sciences and primarily interested in social policy, or a product of the curricula in social work and primarily interested in social work practice. This is not to suggest, of course, that responsibilities have been equally divided in the Toronto School. It is apparent from participation in sessions on research at Annual Program meetings of the Council on Social Work Education or in Workshops on Research under Council auspices, that in some schools of social work, concentration of responsibility for research initiation, teaching, implementation, and grading has been placed in the hands of one or two members of the faculty.

The formal teaching of research began at the University of Toronto School in the fall of 1946 with a course for second-year students entitled "Social Statistics", roughly the equivalent of a one-semester sophomore or junior course in statistics in the social sciences. A year later, with the introduction of the research requirement for the graduate degree, this first course was followed by a spring-term seminar in Research Methods. As the years passed, the fall-term course changed gradually in orientation and in content. Emphasis on statistical method was reduced both in nature and scope, and emphasis upon the nature and practice of research in social work was introduced. This course has been known for some years now as an "Introduction to Research in Social Work" and is offered in the second term of the first year.

The seminar in the second semester of the second year was carried on in a unique form for more than a dozen years. It was assumed that by late January each second-year student would have submitted an acceptable proposal for an individual research project and been assigned a research consultant from among the several available. The only exceptions would be those few students who might be

13

experiencing serious difficulties in other areas of the curriculum, particularly in field practice, and these would be advised to postpone the research activity until the summer months or some later time.

Fifteen or twenty students were customarily enrolled in each section of the Research Seminar and, in fact, they reinforced one another in the learning experience, which is, of course, a basic objective of the discussion seminar as a teaching method. In this case, however, about half the time was devoted to formal instruction by the instructor. In the remaining time each student was expected to present his research problem to the seminar and explain the origin and development of his interest in the research question, its specific formulation, his hypothesis, and his progress to date. Inevitably, since students were at different stages in their individual research, it was almost always possible to schedule the student class presentations in the familiar sequence of the research process. One or more students had merely completed a satisfactory formulation of a research question as the seminar began; others had developed and tested instruments for data collection; still others were in the early stages of collecting data. By the late spring, a few students were in the midst of data collection as a preliminary step in the analysis of evidence and one or more students had written first drafts of certain chapters of their thesis and could present preliminary findings for class consideration.

It is the concensus of the instructors involved that the research seminar was generally a lively and interesting class period (two hours per week). Although it was sometimes necessary to stimulate discussion and constructive criticism of one's peers by the students, and sometimes necessary to intervene to ensure that criticism was essentially constructive, for the most part the students in research gave careful consideration to the experiences of their fellows and learned from them. It was a pleasure to note the transmission of knowledge and the results of experience from student to student in the seminar.

With the introduction of the faculty-led group research project in 1958-59 as an alternative method of fulfilling the research requirement, the research seminar as it has been described was no longer possible. A second-year course in "Research Methods" is now almost entirely didactic, and much of the teaching of research takes place within the group research units or between the individual student and his consultant.

14

The Student Research Program
     For the first twelve years each candidate for the de-
gree of Master of Social Work at the University of Toronto
was required to identify a question for research of his own
choosing, although, of course, suggestions by teachers,
supervisors, agency workers, and colleagues may have supplied a fair proportion of the fundamental "leads". Whatever the source of the idea, the major responsibility for
each stage in the research process lay squarely upon the
shoulders of the student. The faculty research consultant
provided as much guidance and assistance as possible within
the limits of his time and competence and the demands of
the individual student. Student demands varied widely, and
were related not merely to the personality and competence
of the student but to the nature of his research question
and the ease or difficulty in securing the required data.
     Some students displayed a very considerable measure
of independence in the research work together with qualities
of perseverance not always evident in other areas of the
curriculum. Although, in general, most students who achieved
high standing in other areas also achieved high standing in
research, there was by no means a perfect correlation between achievement in academic and field work and excellence
in research. Many "poor" students did reasonably well in
research; some "good" students did not succeed in meeting
the research requirement. One of the critical factors in
any research project is what has been called "the finishing
quality".
     The statistical results of the experience at the
Toronto School have not previously been presented with full
clarity and the presentations which have been published
have been somewhat less than just. For example, in the
Social Worker for October 1956 Colette Lecours presented
figures which indicated that only about 19 per cent of the
students at Toronto earned the Master's degree from 1951-55.[1]
Studies by the Council on Social Work Education indicate that
only a modest proportion of the students who enroll in the
Toronto School in a particular year graduate with the Master
of Social Work degree two years later.[2]
     These publications, and other less formal comments by
colleagues in other schools or in the profession, begin with
the acceptance of a premise which might have substantial
validity at the University of Chicago, or the University of
California (Berkeley), or at Washington University (St.
Louis), namely, the assumption that most students who enroll in the social work program will continue directly
through two successive academic years to the attainment of

the Master's degree. At Toronto this premise could never be accepted,because a basic condition of graduate status was the completion of requirements for a Degree of Bachelor of Social Work at the close of the first academic year.

It must also be emphasized that a good many of the students during the first postwar decade had completed not merely thirteen grades of elementary and secondary education (as compared with twelve years normally completed by students in the United States and in most Canadian provinces) but also four years of undergraduate work in an Honours Course in the social sciences or other studies at the University of Toronto or at some other university in Ontario.

Contrary to intention, the Bachelor of Social Work thus tended to become a terminal degree for approximately half the Toronto students in social work, or at least a point of distinct interruption in their studies. The continuous and critical need of the social agencies for employees with even partial training brought pressures in the same direction. It is conceivable, of course, that the existence of the research requirement might have led some students to defer or abandon plans for a second year of graduate education in social work. Many young women were motivated simply by plans for marriage, the need to assist in supporting young husbands in the midst of professional studies of their own, or the desire to test their motivation for full professional training through a period of full-time employment. The problem of student finances through a sixth year of University education scarcely needs mention.

Enrolment in the second year at the Toronto School could be expected to be at least one-half, perhaps two-thirds, that of the previous first year. About half of the first-year students continued their studies immediately and others returned from a work experience or transferred from other universities. It is this enrolment as the second year began each fall, therefore, that is the critical base figure, namely, the number of candidates for the Degree of Master of Social Work then enrolled for the first time in the Graduate School at the University of Toronto. It is their performance which alone has statistical relevance.

When these base figures are examined for the years 1947-58, inclusive, it is noted that there were 435 candidates for the Master's degree. By 1962, when the class of 1958 completed its four-year period of grace for completion of all requirements, 316 had received the degree. Some 73 per cent of the candidates for the Degree of Master of Social Work had in fact received it.[3] The writer has been assured by colleagues in several schools of social work that this is an enviable record for a school with an individual research requirement, and that, in fact, the proportion of successful candidates in most schools maintaining the individual thesis was substantially less than in Toronto.

It is true, of course, that the proportion of candidates who actually received the degree at the close of the eleven-month second year of study, varied from year to year. In 1959, for example, 25 of 31 candidates who enrolled in September 1958 (80.6 per cent) received the degree; in 1954, only 7 of 42 candidates who enrolled in September 1953 (16.6 per cent) received the degree. Since the policy was that the student had four full years from the time of first enrolment in the Graduate School to complete all the requirements for the degree, three years remained for each of the unfinished candidates. Extensions of time for cause were granted for some students at the close of four full years from the date of enrolment in the second year. By 1959, for example, 93 per cent of the class of 1955-56 had received the degree; yet, by 1955, only 59.5 per cent of the class of 1951-52 were in this fortunate position.

It must be understood that the reasons for non-attainment of the Master's Degree by 27 per cent of the candidates of 1947-57, rested by no means entirely in the domain of the research requirement. As was noted previously in this essay, some students were encouraged to defer their research work in order to provide more time for other subjects in which they were experiencing difficulty. Some students, of course, failed in field work or in other areas of academic work. Some students, in fact, never did initiate a research proposal and left the school with only as much work for credit as they could reasonably complete in the second year.

Some students did not progress with the research requirement beyond the submission of a formal proposal. Some students completed a modest amount of research work and disappeared during the summer term to reappear some years later, if at all. The number of students who actually submitted a thesis which was failed by faculty readers and not revised for later submission, numbered 13 in these twelve years. Attrition, not outright failure, is the most common factor among those without the degree.

New Approaches in the
Research Requirement
By the middle 1950's three major weaknesses in the

student research program were apparent in the Toronto school's approach, which was almost sole reliance upon the individual research project and thesis.[4] These weaknesses were clearly identified as the major pressure points experienced by most students, yet beyond the capacity of some students to overcome.

The first pressure point lay in the serious difficulty experienced by some students in identifying and formulating a question for research. It is indeed conceivable that as the years passed many of the most obvious questions suitable for research at the Master's level had been studied. Students, on the whole, are not too keen to undertake replication studies, despite their importance in the process of research. Also, as the student body changed drastically in age and sex composition after 1951 (younger persons and fewer men) there could have been a difference in the attitudes of students towards the research projects. Certainly students in general seemed less capable of independent work and more fearful of technical statistics than the students of the early postwar years.

A second pressure point lay in the question of the "size" of the sample of cases, or respondents, or the number of groups or community leaders, for example, which might be studied in a research undertaking. Students were often more concerned with statistical reliability, with "proving something", while their mentors were more concerned with the educational experience and the basic curriculum objectives. Many students undertook studies that were "too large", despite faculty warnings and objections, collected masses of data and were unable to complete the analysis and the research report in the time available. It was not uncommon for students to read fifty or sixty voluminous case records in an agency or complete a like number of personal interviews with respect to a complex research problem.

The third pressure point lay in the length or size of the research report which some students produced, and the months and years required to complete 150 or more pages of text (not to mention appendices) to the mutual satisfaction of student and consultant. Although the research instructors and consultants affirmed repeatedly that there was no optimal length which might be cited as a firm guide to students, and that the educational expectation was quality and a logically ordered argument rather than quantity, many students were delayed or failed to obtain the degree because they could not seem to complete the document they felt they had to produce.

These were the principal points of pressure with

respect to the students. On its part, the faculty faced
very severe pressures in meeting the demand for research
consultation by new and former students alike, in advising
students, in negotiating with agencies, in reading completed
theses, and in developing an appropriate and widely accepted
evaluation (grading) procedure. Such familiar pressures
upon the teaching staff have been well documented by leaders
in the teaching of research, such as Gordon,[5] Greenwood[6] and
Macdonald[7] and need not be repeated here. The situation in
the Toronto School, however, differed in at least one major
respect from that in many American and Canadian universities.
At the University of Toronto the strong traditional patterns
of graduate work, including the individual Master's thesis,
were and are sufficiently strong that the faculty in social
work cannot assume any ready acceptance of new approaches
to the research requirement in a graduate professional
school. The School must proceed with more deliberation
than speed in its efforts to modify the research requirement
as a realistic part of the totality of demands upon the student.

The group research project, as it was conceived at the
University of Chicago in the late 1940's and described by
Professor Mary Macdonald, appeared to promise a solution to
the several important pressure points faced by students and
some relief to the pressures faced by hard-pressed faculty
members. As Greenwood put it:

Three major characteristics distinguish the group project from the thesis: (1) Instead of the single student, several students work on one study problem
interdependently toward a collaborative product.
(2) Instead of students, the supervisor determines
the subject for investigation. (3) Finally, the
supervisor, not the student, controls the direction
and pace of the research.[8]

It is the group project leader who, in assuming responsibility for development of the question for research and in assuming control of the process of data collection and the
eventual reporting of research, relieves the student of the
most serious pressures at the cost of adding greatly to his
own. Insofar as he assumes responsibility for six to twelve
students he relieves his colleagues of some pressure as well.
At the same time these new responsibilities may be no more
demanding, and perhaps less difficult, than the process of
advising a like number of students with respect to a series
of different individual research problems.

As early as 1953 a few members of the faculty in
Toronto experimented with a prototype or forerunner of the

group research project. It was not until 1958, however, that the Toronto School formally adopted the policy that student participation in a group research project was an equal but separate alternative to the individual research undertaking. During the academic year 1958-59 two faculty members led three groups of students; the following year three professors were so engaged; and by 1963-64 nine faculty members working alone or in pairs have proposed ten group research projects (some are alternatives) for consideration by incoming second-year students. These groups will afford research opportunities for approximately two-thirds of the sixty candidates for a graduate degree.

The choice of individual work or participation in a group effort remains with the student. While it is assumed in some schools that the individual thesis is beyond the capacity of all but the exceptional student, this has not been the Toronto experience either before or after 1958. Although the proportion of second-year students who elect to work on a group research project has increased, as a larger number of group projects and student research places were made available, nevertheless, the proportion of individual research projects attempted during the years 1958-62 was 48 per cent and even in 1963-64 will be about one-third.

Current Position of the Research Requirement in the Schools in North America

In 1957 the University of Toronto School participated in a modest study developed by Professor Arthur Fink, Dean of the University of North Carolina School of Social Work. Dr. Fink sought the experience of 44 schools with the individual or group project requirement and received responses from 34 schools. He summarized the over-all numerical findings as follows:

> There appeared to be 10 schools (Group I) that gave primary emphasis to the group research project; 10 (Group II) with primary emphasis on the individual thesis; 14 schools (Group III) to permit choice. However, there is an identifiable preference among these 14 for the group research project even though the "choice" appears to be a "free" one.[9]

The use of quotation marks around the words "free" and "choice" appears to indicate that Dr. Fink recognized that in many schools the choice of an individual research project is permitted so rarely and the reasons for joining a group project are so compelling that very few students have a real choice.

The University of North Carolina report of July 1958 includes a valuable digest of the points made by each of the three groups of schools (listed in the above quotation) concerning the values and disadvantages of each of the three approaches. In the case of the so-called "Group Project Method" the values related both to the research itself and to the students. The schools argued that group research projects "are most nearly like research experiences which students will encounter in professional practice", that is, a team approach. A larger body of data is accumulated and studies of greater significance to the field can be undertaken (surely not a primary objective at the Master's level) with a reasonable opportunity for the determination of statistical reliability and consequent generalization. It is argued that the experience of working together is of great value for the students.

Nevertheless, the key to the puzzle lies in the North Carolina statement that "There is greater assurance /in the Group Project Method/ that students will finish their research requirement, just as they do other school requirements." This may be the case where each student writes a modest contribution to be edited, or otherwise used, as a part of a single document emanating from a group project. In fact it is difficult to understand any student's failure to complete the research requirement under these conditions, barring illness or emotional breakdown. In the University of Toronto, however, where an individual report is required of every student enrolled in a group project, the record has been good but not startlingly different from that of the past when groups did not exist. During the years 1958-62, 116 students were enrolled in group projects and 94 will have received the degree by November 1963, that is, 81 per cent. Of course, only the class of 1958 has run out of time and other students may yet finish.

Some students still require the full three years after leaving the School to complete the written document. Apparently, the approach to the research requirement is not necessarily the basis of success or failure. The main stumbling block is the problem of writing a clear, grammatical, sensible, logically ordered argument -- a task for which many graduate students seem remarkably badly prepared. They are not in the habit of writing, and the demands in graduate professional education for written work both in the academic courses and in research are devastating for some.

Professors McPhee, Magleby, and Otto of the Graduate School of Social Work, University of Utah, undertook a further survey in 1961 of "Thesis and Research Requirements

of Schools of Social Work". They believed that marked
changes had taken place since the report of the study by
Professor Fink. This time a questionnaire was mailed to
each of the 62 graduate schools of social work in the
United States and Canada. Fifty-seven (92 per cent) of
the schools completed the questionnaire.

The Utah surveyors found that in most schools both
group and individual research projects were permitted.
However,

> only 41 per cent of the schools (23 schools) reported
> that more than half of their students were writing
> individual theses, and 60 per cent of the schools
> (34 schools) indicated that more than half of their
> students were doing research on group projects.[10]

> ... 28 per cent of the schools had no students in
> group research compared to 12 per cent with no stu-
> dents doing individual research.[11]

The value of these findings is unfortunately weakened
seriously in that the survey report does not in any way
indicate the relative significance of these groups of
schools in terms of enrolment. We are still uncertain
about the relative proportions of students graduating
under the two major approaches to the research requirement.
It is known, however, that several of the largest schools
(University of Chicago, University of California at Berkeley,
University of Southern California, Tulane) are entirely on
a group research basis.

Concluding Comments

The research requirement in graduate schools of social
work in North America has clearly not been an unchanging
demand. Similar pressures upon the various schools have,
however, been met in quite different ways. At the University of Pittsburgh, for example, the research component in
the Master's curriculum has in recent years been entirely
didactic or academic, that is, the formal research project
has been eliminated. At Washington University (St. Louis)
one very substantial group research project is developed
each year and forty or more students may participate in
the single research undertaking. There are many variations
in the schools within the familiar pattern of the individual
or group research project requirement.

At the University of Toronto the determination to offer
each student the choice of identifying an individual problem
for study or of participating in a faculty-led group project
coincided with the School's decision to adopt a program of

"block field practice" in the second graduate year. This
fundamental resolution which involved the placement of
students in teaching centres some distance from Toronto
(from 40 to 165 miles apart) provided additional pressure
to change the School's approach to the student research
program.

In the essential discussion of every facet of the
second-year curriculum with a block field practice component, the faculty was presented with five alternative pro-
posals for the research requirement. These were described
with a convenient label in each case, as follows:

1) Research as an academic course, without an individual research requirement.
2) The individual research requirement -- the current
   system.
3) The individual research requirement -- modified.
4) The individual requirement as part of a group project.
5) The group project qua group project.

From the earlier presentation in this essay it will
be recognized that the Toronto School adopted the third
and fourth of these alternatives as equally acceptable
approaches to meeting the research requirement. It did
not favour the fifth proposal which failed to require a
demonstration of individual capacity from each student.

Considerable effort has been devoted to the task of
assisting students who wish to undertake individual research projects to formulate their questions for research.
This has to be done in such a way that the implementation
of the research design is sharply delimited, and the research activity of the student is feasible within his
limits of time, money, and personal effort. An attempt
has been made to clarify expectations of the School in this
area of the curriculum as a qualitative educational experience rather than a quantitative exercise in data collection
and writing.

The block field practice requirement occupies four
days per week for twenty weeks from late November until
early April. During this period of nearly five months the
fifth day of the regular work week is devoted substantially,
if not entirely, to the research requirement. (Consultants
travel regularly to distant teaching centres.) It is on
this day that students meet with the research consultant
or with the research group and its leader; it is on this
day, primarily, that data collection and data analysis take
place in the appropriate sequence. The new curriculum has
in fact provided more clear-cut time for the research

23

requirement than was evident in the earlier years. By the time students return from the field placement, the data must be collected in full and provision made for data analysis and the writing of the research report, for which an eight-week summer term (reduced by two weeks from the earlier years) is provided until the end of July. Faculty consultants remain on duty with their individual students or research groups throughout the entire eleven-month year.

From the point of view of the students the changing nature of the research requirement could scarcely be appreciated in full measure, since the individual student (with a few exceptions) had no experience with the earlier system. It has been noticed by instructors that the individual research problems of the early postwar years were far more likely to involve studies of social problems and social policy than the problems of recent years, which were more often oriented to professional practice and the administration of social work. It is difficult to say whether or not this is a reflection of the differences in age and experience between the two groups of students and, in particular, whether it represents in part a difference between the students who lived through the years of depression and war and those who are too young to remember those fifteen years of chaos and suffering.

One set of impressions is certainly clear in the minds of those who have had major responsibility for research instruction. For some students (perhaps a third of the entire group over the years) the research requirement has been a source of great satisfaction and, indeed, intellectual excitement. For some of these students this has been the most satisfying portion of the entire course. On the other hand, perhaps another third of the candidates have found the research requirement the most frightening experience of their several years of educational preparation. The fear and anxiety generated by the need to undertake a systematic study of a research problem have been well beyond the level which might normally be expected in the average student. These feelings were reinforced, of course, by the knowledge that many past students had completed all requirements for the degree but the research, and by the fact that the research project was the last requirement in time, at the end of two years of graduate professional education and a formidable hurdle to surmount when one is tired and perhaps emotionally drained.

The abstracts presented in this Compendium are, therefore, a reflection of all these tendencies and influences connected with the research requirement during the past fifteen years. They illustrate the wide range of choice of subject matter, the efforts of the brilliant and the weak students as well as the vast majority of those who fall between these extremes, the varying capacity of graduate students to write a logically ordered argument, and the strengths and weaknesses of a formal research requirement at a level below the doctoral. In a real sense these abstracts reflect the postwar history of the profession of social work and the development of social work education in Canada.

References

1. Lecours, Colette, "Some Aspects of Recruitment for Social Work", The Social Worker, Vol. 25, No. 1, (October 1956) 30-34.

2. Council on Social Work Education, Statistics on Social Work Education 1960-61, New York, 1962.

3. A special effort was made during the academic year 1962-63 to offer those without the degree one last opportunity to complete the requirements. Thirty-four students re-enrolled under two alternative schemes, and by November 1963 an additional 24 candidates from the years prior to 1958 will have received the degree.

4. It should be noted that on three occasions the faculty did permit two students to work together on a single problem (a joint project) and to produce one research report only. In each case the participation of each student in data collection and in writing was made entirely clear to the consultant and to the readers.

5. Gordon, William E., "The Research Project: Its Educational Value and Its Contribution to Social Work Knowledge", Social Work Journal, XXXI (July 1950), 110-116.

6. Greenwood, Ernest, "Social Work Research: The Role of the Schools", Social Service Review, XXXII (June 1958), 152-166.

7. Macdonald, Mary E., "The Use of Group Study in Teaching Research", Social Service Review, XXIV (December 1950), 427-441.

8. Greenwood, Ernest, op. cit., p. 157. Greenwood states that, "Along with supervised field work, the group project may be considered social work's contribution to graduate education."

9. Fink, Arthur E., Memorandum to Respondents of Survey of July 25, 1957, regarding Thesis or Research Projects, School of Social Work, University of North Carolina, July 15, 1958 (mimeographed), p. 1.

10. McPhee, William M., Magleby, F. LeGrande, and Otto, Herbert A., Thesis and Research Requirements of Schools of Social Work - A Survey, School of Social Work, University of Utah, undated (mimeographed), p. 1.

11. Ibid., p. 6.

Albert Rose
Co-ordinator of Research

DISSERTATIONS

ACCEPTED FOR DEGREE OF

DOCTOR OF SOCIAL WORK

1. GRAHAM, Lloyd B. (1958). The adoption of children
    from Japan by American families, 1952-1955.
    From 956 passports issued in Japan during 1952-
    55 to children bound for the United States, and through
    official records provided in Japanese home districts,
    779 cases were identified for study involving 674 fami-
    lies to which the Japanese-born children were not con-
    sanguinously related and in which neither American
    adoptive parent was a first-generation immigrant of
    Japanese ancestry. Case records on a few children
    were available in Japanese institutions and agencies.
    Material was gathered in the United States through
    two questionnaires (the preliminary one answered by
    223 families, the intensive one by 105, and both by
    65 families with 79 of the study's children), and
    through interviews with 41 families involving 50 of
    the children. In the context of inter-country adop-
    tions as progressively developed through International
    Social Service channels, and against the historical
    background (servicemen discouraged from "fraternizing"
    in Japan, Japanese mothers without means of support,
    children blocked from immigrating into the United
    States, except for specially arranged individual cases
    or small quotas, until 1953's legislation), the proc-
    ess of adoption and the children's situations follow-
    ing entry into their new homes are examined, their pre-
    placement experiences reviewed generally, and the homes
    and children's adjustment given a brief, exploratory
    evaluation. Five criteria for adoptions are cited.
    Only one — legal recognition — seemed satisfactorily
    met here through the procedures of the Japanese Family
    Courts. Some children were relinquished under economic
    pressure, some abruptly transferred from natural
    mothers to adoptive families without explanation or
    preparation, some withheld by institutions because
    they were favourites there or had minor disabilities.
    Homes, accepted mainly on material qualifications,
    were assessed as inadequate in terms of motives, atti-
    tudes, and realistic understanding in almost one case
    out of four examined. The lack of professional methods
    -- home finding, probationary placement, casework --
    was less dangerous for adopting families in Japan, who
    knew the child's pre-placement setting and conformed
    to age and military rank regulations, than for the few
    families in America on whose behalf institutions ar-
    ranged adoptions by "proxy", by a legal loophole by-
    passing the internationally arranged investigations

provided for in such cases. Two years after adoption
few children showed symptoms of disturbance, according to responding parents' reports. But the hazards
of adoptions can be and should be kept to a minimum
by ensuring as far as possible the use of established
social work methods.

2. SPLANE, Richard B. (1961). The development of social
    welfare in Ontario 1791-1893: the role of the
    province.
       The province's first century saw some impressive
    accomplishments in social welfare, although various
    needs, to varying degrees, remained unfilled. Consti-
    tutional weaknesses and political unrest hampered pro-
    gress at the outset, with a provincial executive
    limited in its capacity to administer and local govern-
    ments little able to administer or finance social wel-
    fare measures. Both the official use of special boards
    and commissions and the organizing of voluntary private
    agencies and institutions began before 1841. In the
    Union period, Upper Canada had a more efficient execu-
    tive, and a provincial Board of Inspectors was ap-
    pointed in 1859 to co-ordinate and extend various pro-
    grams developing by then. The Municipal Act of 1849
    encouraged the increasingly active local governments.
    After Confederation progress was remarkable. The first
    Provincial Inspector of Asylums, Prisons, and Chari-
    table Institutions, J.W. Langmuir, had outstanding
    administrative capabilities, and provincial funds were
    available for carrying out many of his recommendations.
    But integrated leadership was lost by bifurcation of
    the inspectorship at a time when industrialism, and
    social problems,were growing apace. In 1890 the Royal
    Commission on Prisons undertook an assessment of social
    welfare in general; its 569-page report contained ex-
    tensive recommendations about specific programs but
    failed to propose a strong, flexible administrative
    structure.
       The degree of responsibility acknowledged by
    the province varied, as the kind and extent of its
    activities reveal. Was public responsibility for the
    care of the poor denied when in 1792 the English Poor
    Law was rejected? Loyalist settlers afterwards re-
    ceived generous public assistance. But though some
    municipalities provided limited outdoor relief by the
    1840's and contributed to privately-supported Houses

of Refuge, provincial encouragement lagged even after the Charities Aid Act (1874) systematized provincial grants. In corrections, developments were notable: a provincial penitentiary and special institutions for boys, girls, and women were established. The mentally ill were removed from catch-all local gaols to a system of hospitals which was admirably developed by the 1850's. Public health programs, except during cholera and typhus epidemics, remained sporadic until 1884. Children's legislation was scarce until 1893 when the semi-private system of Children's Aid Societies under provincial supervision was established and a non-institutional approach encouraged.

Welfare achievements by 1893 were notable, despite the inchoate administrative framework.

(This dissertation is the basis of a book entitled Social Welfare in Ontario 1791-1893--A Study of Public Welfare Administration to be published by the University of Toronto Press during 1964.)

REPORTS ACCEPTED IN PARTIAL FULFILMENT

OF REQUIREMENTS FOR DEGREE OF

MASTER OF SOCIAL WORK

OR ITS EQUIVALENT

ADDICTION

3.   DASTYK, Rose (1959). The relationship between the
       drinking pattern of alcoholic patients and their
       employment pattern before and after treatment.
            The 42 married men here studied by interview
       had all been inpatients at least six days and had had
       at least three contacts as outpatients of the Brook-
       side Clinic in 1951-53. The 24 unemployed when ad-
       mitted for treatment showed a mean gain in abstinence
       of 43 per cent compared with 63 per cent for those
       with jobs. A few, mainly from the latter group, had
       relatively stable work histories -- men with private
       businesses or seniority in large companies, or strug-
       gling to support families. For the rest, factors in
       frequent moves were drinking on the job, absenteeism,
       inefficiency, and from the patients' viewpoint, rest-
       lessness and frustration. Since employment records
       did not improve after treatment in ratio to gains in
       abstinence, and since overwhelmingly the patients
       cherished unrealistic employment goals or none at all,
       and all but one preferred solitude and experienced
       varying degrees of difficulty in working with others,
       a sheltered workshop is suggested as part of the thera-
       peutic service for alcoholics.

4.   HOLGATE, Elizabeth (1958). Interpersonal relation-
       ships in a group of single male alcoholics.
            From the data recorded by Brookside Clinic's
       social workers, psychiatrists, doctors, and nurses in
       the 33 available case records on unmarried men first
       admitted as inpatients during 1957, the writer ex-
       tracted information for this exploratory study. Of
       the 20 living alone, all but one were rooming; 12
       lived with relatives but only 8 had designated these
       on their admissions forms as "persons interested".
       Although three-quarters had had both parents at home,
       almost all reported cold or demanding or rejecting
       parental attitudes. Many felt inadequate, shy and
       lonely as adults, 6 had problems of identification,
       and the most frequent relationship, a common-law union,
       seemed dependent on the woman's mothering -- and her
       unmarriageability. During treatment only 3 had rela-

35

tives who involved themselves by visiting the clinic.
After discharge, these unmarried patients will need
some support and sense of belonging. The writer pro-
poses group therapy for such men in the rehabilitation
period.

5.   JACKSON, Mary Jane (1958). A follow-up study of the
      relationship between drinking behaviour and par-
      ticipation in child-care activities of a sample
      of alcoholic patients, before and after treatment.
      The writer selected 54 men with children from
the Alcoholism Research Foundation's 1956 study (of
102 cases of the total 235 who had received extensive
treatment and after-care). They proved an elusive
group: 9 were not located, 9 others refused to participate, 10 let another person be interviewed in their
stead, and 4 used interviews to express hostility.
Wives tended to focus on children's symptoms of disturbance rather than on their own grievances, often
acknowledging their own psychological problems. Many
men talked volubly about their drinking difficulties
but avoided discussing the parent-child relationship
or dismissed children's concerns in vague, often unrealistic terms. Their attitudes were characteristically those of a rival child rather than of a father.
In all but 2 cases male and female roles in the family
were reversed to some degree. Wherever the family's
strong support had helped a man to marked gains in
abstinence, he tended to show renewed involvement with
children's discipline, education, and recreation.
Wives' and children's participation made for the most
valuable interviews.

6.   NEILSON, J.A. (1956). The association between moti-
      vation for seeking treatment and treatment out-
      come in a sample of alcoholic patients treated at
      Brookside Hospital and Clinic.
      Data here analyzed were gathered in 1956 by the
Alcoholism Research Foundation in its follow-up study
of former inpatients who had returned as outpatients
for at least three visits. Do the reports on 67 such
cases support certain hypothetical associations between treatment outcome (measured in post-treatment
months of abstinence) and a patient's motivation and
degree of participation? Patients have to participate
more in the psychiatrically-oriented treatment at this

36

clinic than do patients in the conditioned—aversion
therapy at another. However, comparable groups from
the two clinics showed similar treatment outcome.
Perhaps social pressures motivated the majority rated
as "socially stable" to seek and respond to treatment
inasmuch as 76 per cent (as against 21 per cent of the
socially unstable) stayed sober seven months or longer
after treatment. However, to reach those whose only
security is among Skid Row associates, the writer suggests, may mean a different appeal in every individual
case.

7. SCHMIDT, Wolfgang (1957). <u>A study of the relation between social participation and drinking before and
after treatment in a sample of alcoholic patients.</u>
As a basis for measuring change during rehabilitation, the writer interviewed the approachable 15 of
21 married men admitted for treatment at least two
years previously (from the 69 interviewed during an
Alcoholism Research Foundation follow-up study on 555
patients treated during 1951-54). Using sample statements from interviews, he illustrates his method of
analyzing content and assessing the patient's change
in terms of what others in his sub-culture expect of
him. Change ratings in seven areas of social functioning are examined in relation to comparative post-
treatment abstinence ratings. Negatives, whether
drinking or isolation, are interpreted as continuations
of the pre-treatment trend, i.e., as "no change".
Least change was noted among these patients in their
role as breadwinners. Gains in abstinence tended to
correspond with more harmonious domestic life, shared
household responsibilities, and even increased participation in child care, although prolonged abstinence
seemed necessary to restore a child's trust. The
methods used "seem capable of validation and extension
by analogous studies".

8. STERN, William I. (1952). <u>Young adult drinking habits.</u>
Scores of young adults in one University Settle-
ment group, the Club Cosmo, were interested when the
writer informally broached the subject of drinking
habits with them. From their comments, and the literature, he then devised questions, and interviewed 30
members. They could speak freely, he felt, because
he had become familiar with Club Cosmo boys while a

student-staff person at Settlement House, and because he conducted 23 of the interviews as fellow worker on a crew preparing a campsite for the neighbourhood's children. All but 3 respondents said they drank, about half of them drinking weekly or oftener. Two were in danger of alcoholism. Almost all considered drinking bad for health, and over half said they would forbid their children to drink. Sociability, dash, group pressures, and pay-day treating were cited as motives, although recreational satisfactions from drinking seemed meagre. The writer recommends alcohol education in public schools, and the encouragement of such discussion as these young adults seemed to want on the subject.

GROUP PROJECT. Social factors in the causation of alcoholism.

Two groups of students undertook this study. They shared their ideas in planning a schedule of questions for semi-structured interviews and then each student met twice for a two- or three-hour session with each of six subjects. Half of the 72 respondents were voluntary inpatients in the Toronto hospital (the "Clinic") of the Alcoholism Research Foundation (a body founded by provincial legislation in 1949). The other 36 respondents had been arrested on weekends in 1958–59 and, failing money or somebody to pay the fine, had been sentenced to Don Jail, on at least the fourth such conviction for drunken offences within the year.

9.   BOUSCHARD, Phyllis (1959). Parent-child relationships and alcoholism.

Information was lacking about the mothers of 4 of the 72 subjects. Records on the other 68 were examined for anything pertinent to one research worker's suggestion that personality factors related to sex identification may be important in determining the acceptance or rejection of parental teaching about drinking. When figures gathered by this group were compared with statistics compiled for the Alcoholism Research Foundation (as published 1958), markedly more abstainers and non-drinkers appeared among subjects' mothers than among the comparable age group

of Canadian women, and slightly more among their
fathers than among the comparable male group. Respondents tended to a childlike dependence on their
mothers and dislike or dread of fathers. Some apparently identified imbibing with mother love; others
tried through heavy drinking to identify with the
masculine sex. However, the many exceptions established primarily how complex the problem is, and how
much research into alcoholism needs to be done.

10. DUNLOP, Julia E. (1959). Alcoholism and employment.
    Nine factors related to employment are analyzed
in the life histories of the 36 jailed alcoholics.
Interviewers' records built up a picture of the men's
work histories: the number of jobs increasing, occupational status declining, and periods of unemployment
lengthening. These men tended to have broken off
schooling or vocational training without forethought,
to have continued with few social involvements or
responsibilities -- half were single, and despite
earlier ties all the others were living alone at the
time of arrest -- and increasingly to be offered only
jobs conducive to a mobile or convivial or rootless
life. Every incarceration means less aplomb in seeking work; no agency or employment service helps finance
or place men released after minor sentences. For the
physical care and the strong, constant supervision
needed, a "half-way house" system is suggested to offer
such men some hope of and chance for rehabilitation.

11. FARRY, John B. (1961). Drinking behaviour of the
    relatives of alcoholics.
    The powerful effects of parental attitudes and
behaviour, and the possible relevance to drinking of
the choice of a wife or her subsequent influence, determined this writer's focus. Two-thirds of the 72
respondents' mothers were negative towards drinking,
with a predominance of abstentionists among the prisoners' mothers. More than two-thirds of the fathers
were positive, however, with social drinking predominant among patient's fathers and heavy drinking among
prisoners'. One or both parents of 72 per cent of
the prisoners had been extreme in their behaviour towards alcohol, often with intense -- and anxiety-
producing -- disagreement in the home on this subject.
Many, especially among the prisoners, remained un-

married. Broken homes abounded in both groups among
men who had married. Most of the wives reportedly
used alcohol, especially as social drinkers; might
their husbands' post-marital problem drinking indicate
"contagion"? Only study of a carefully selected group
of alcoholics' wives could assess this effect or the
alternative, that the men chose wives who would "drink
with them".

12. FRIESEN, Miller A. (1959). Alcoholism and inter-
        personal relations.
          What do the reports on the 72 interviews suggest
    about the extent and nature of the men's problems in
    social relationships? What common factors in their
    childhoods might be noted in connection with the com-
    mon outcome, alcoholism? Most of these men described
    their childhood and their mothers in terms indicating
    that they had never developed the capacity to form
    relationships owing to early emotional deprivation.
    Only 17 had worked at one job for the full year pre-
    ceding the study. Very transient living arrangements
    predominated, and there were few instances of success-
    ful marriage or of good social adjustment in general.
    Such findings suggest that excessive drinking can be
    a method of trying to cope with unmet personal and
    social needs. Thus whatever encourages healthy family
    life helps prevent alcoholism. And social agencies
    and organizations helping alcoholics to find a social
    niche will also help to minimize the pressures to ex-
    cessive drinking.

13. GROVER, Ione E.H. (1959). Differences in prognosis
        between two groups of alcoholics.
          Of the 36 men in the prison group only 4 had
    sought any form of treatment. Unlike the clinic
    group, many of whom were in treatment due to threat
    or duress from families or employers, the prisoners
    seemed not to have anyone urging them to seek treat-
    ment and little left to lose. All were single, sepa-
    rated, or divorced when arrested; almost all were long
    since parted from parental families; 28 were homeless(as
    compared to 4 in the clinic group); and with the pre-
    dominance of seasonal labour and odd jobs few had
    any long-term relationships with any other human being.
    Their comments revealed a characteristic suppression
    of anxiety about the future and an awareness of public

rejection. To break the vicious spiral from early
school-leaving to rootlessness and resignation will
involve a change of attitude on the part of the community towards these men and the development of rehabilitative facilities.

14. LEIA, Shirley F. (1959). Alcoholism: a pattern of
    social adjustment.
    Among reports on the 36 clinic respondents the
    hypothesis is examined that initially the alcoholic
    is attempting to use drink to alleviate some inner
    need and thereby to attain some form of social ad-
    justment. Case histories might suggest that those
    who depend upon alcohol to help them function socially
    are basically people who need alcohol to feel socially
    adequate and secure (16 here); who seek in drink a
    mothering gratification (the 9 "passive-dependents");
    who seek anaesthesia from stresses too great for them
    (6 cases); who in drinking both feel they demonstrate
    their virility and find themselves in male company
    (4 with homosexual tendencies); and who become physi-
    ologically addicted after years of drinking with busi-
    ness associates (1 instance). Initially a means,
    drink had become an end in itself involving for these
    men new maladjustments and increasing social rejection.
    Preventing alcoholism, then, apparently means encourag-
    ing whatever is conducive to healthy personalities and
    a congenial environment.

15. MAEERS, Donald D. (1959). Drinking patterns of male
    alcoholics.
    Drinking patterns were studied in relation to
    the men's constitutions, environments, and associations.
    Among the prisoners periodic drinking had predominated,
    and among the patients continuous drinking. A minor-
    ity in both groups switched between bouts and steady
    drinking, with the switching usually occasioned by
    circumstances of stress after long years of problem
    drinking. Four-fifths of the respondents remembered
    their first drink clearly, nearly always as a dramatic
    experience (involving drunkenness, sickness, punish-
    ment, etc.). Children of non-drinking parents usually
    began with drinking bouts. Sporadic drinkers had very
    unstable employment and marital records and, surpris-
    ingly, seemed less hopeful about recovery. Inter-
    viewers assessed a significantly larger proportion of
    solitary drinkers as mentally disturbed. The evidence

contradicted a widespread theory that problem drinking tends to become solitary drinking. Further study
might highlight the first drink among alcoholics and
a control group, social drinkers compared with solitary
drinkers, and the point of change when drinking patterns switch.

16. NEVIDON, Patricia T. (1959). <u>Cultural conflict in the</u>
    <u>genesis of alcoholism.</u>
        Through the case records the effect on the jail
    group is studied of the views on drinking of various
    groups -- religious, ethnic, and social. Disparities
    in habits and attitudes between home and community at
    large apparently affect problem drinkers as adversely
    as disagreement between the parents about alcohol:
    the same high proportion reported non-Canadian back-
    grounds as mentioned conflicting parental views.
    Consistent views, such as the Jewish culture's associ-
    ation of drinking with religious observances exclus-
    ively, or the Italian culture's acceptance of drinking,
    make for moderation. Inconsistencies -- between what
    is preached and what is done, or, for example, between
    society's indulgent legend of hard-drinking lumbermen
    or servicemen, and its rejection of the man who lives
    the legend -- make for excess. Many who suffered from
    cultural conflict or inconsistency and could not con-
    form ultimately found acceptance only among other iso-
    lates who shared their drinking problem. Their histor-
    ies indicate that this aspect of "conditioning" is
    worth thorough study.

17. REED, Mary Pauline (1959). <u>A study of the relations</u>
    <u>between ego-need and parental attitudes in a</u>
    <u>sample of alcoholics.</u>
        This study focuses on 25 men, the 34 per cent
    of the 72 interviewed who, according to interviewers'
    judgments, were attempting through alcohol to compen-
    sate for their own sense of inadequacy. They spoke
    of "a warmth never experienced before" from drinking,
    or release from worry, or of unaccustomed self-
    confidence. Mistrust, insecurity, and lack of realism
    appeared throughout their records: "My ambition and
    my bank book never went hand in hand" or "You have to
    fight for anything you get." Strict, remote or hostile
    attitudes had conveyed to 48 per cent rejection from
    both parents, to 88 per cent from at least one --

"Ever since I had been able to dress myself I had been thinking of leaving --- to get away and never to come back." Family relationships, more than alcohol, seemed the root of the trouble for these men. Larger groups should be studied, for links between child-parent and marital problems, contrasts between drinkers with over-indulgent and with rejecting parents, and so on.

18. SCOTT, Arthur Mitchell. (1959). <u>The chronic inebriate offender and the correctional system</u>.
Some 89,235 Canadians are convicted annually on drunken offences. Judging by the 36 studied here who among them had so far served at least 25,500 days, the problem is chronic and progressive. Characteristically "lone men," under-educated, unemployed, almost all knew the "deteriorated living" that involves trying "to keep clean when you end up with no place of your own ... and your only clothes are the ones you stand in". Men feel their already damaged self-respect further undermined by "the process": the disinfectant spraying; humiliation in court when nobody listens to their statements in their own defence; boredom and resentment about com-pulsory maintenance jobs in prison -- even though they welcome prison routines and shelter. Almost one-third had applied for the Alcoholic Clinic, Mimico, where those judged amenable to treatment in the reform in-stitutions are transferred. Its educational and treat-ment service is a step at least towards rehabilitating these men whose "crime" has been "impaired mobility in a public place".

19. TELA, Carlo (1959). <u>Marital patterns among alcoholics</u>.
The records showed that 35 of the 36 patients had been married, but only 18 of the prisoners; that over one-third of the patients' marriages were broken, and all of the prisoners' marriages. Were the jailed al-coholics, then, markedly less able to take on the adult responsibilities of marriage? The opposite conclusion, that the "personality pathology" is more marked among the patients, is suggested by the number showing re-jection or dependency in the marital relationship. Sexually some alcoholics seemed to be inhibited, some showed strong guilt feelings, and a few seemed latent homosexuals. Promiscuity was greater among the prison-ers, and the patient group was more prolific, but there

43

were evidences of a basic sexual problem throughout
both groups. In early childhood men in both groups
had had insufficient or inconsistent emotional nurture
and as adults they showed correspondingly unsatisfactory
interrelationships.

SEE ALSO Entries 34, 113, 117, 127.

20. DORGAN, H. Jean (1949). The Old Age Pension applicant.
      To study pensioners' needs the writer read the
Toronto Department of Public Welfare files for all
365 applicants of December 1948, analyzed 144 records
more closely, and interviewed 30 individuals selected
proportionately from three groups (those living alone,
with a spouse, or with relatives). Shelter cost dearly,
often in comfort and morale as well as money. Ages and
circumstances on application suggested that women often
need pensions before age seventy and many men over
seventy are healthy enough for at least light work.
"Pensionability" should therefore be flexibly defined.
Although an agreement between the Province and the
Ontario Medical Association entitles pensioners to
medical care and certain drugs (but not to dentures
or glasses), several pensioners reported that doctors
had refused their cards. Judging by the records, regular medical attention might forestall many serious illnesses in this age group. Public Health Nurses or
social workers could help many pensioners now immobi-
lized by ignorance or anxiety. Visits by volunteers
could improve morale.

21. FALCONBRIDGE, John A. (1951). Living arrangements of
elderly people.
      This study begins with the hypothesis that "the
need to be as independent as possible and the desire
to remain independent for as long as possible are important factors in the living arrangements of elderly
people". Facts were collected through interviews with
100 members -- every fourth name on the rolls -- of
the Second Mile Club, Toronto, a non-residential centre
for men and women aged sixty or over; the respondents
also met later for group discussion. Despite grudging
landlords and such hardships as lack of central heat
(9), or of a comfortable chair (30), or sharing a toilet with six or more (45), privacy and independence as
choices of "the one thing desirable" nearly outweighed
all others put together. Study is recommended of the
old in relation to changing family structures. That
many interviewed here had moved to be near relatives
or friends indicated the balancing need for security.

But evidently even those who are alone, on low fixed incomes, fighting a step-by-step retreat to the four walls of "residual housing", cherish their independence.

22. FERGUSON, Mary (1961). <u>An exploratory study of the way in which the social needs of a group of elderly Jewish clients have affected their participation patterns in a day-care program.</u>
The Day-Care program of the Toronto Jewish Home for the Aged was launched in 1959, the first of its kind in Canada. Its experiences will be instructive as attitudes and social institutions adjust to increasing life expectancies. Hence this analysis of data from case histories on, and interviews with, 13 men and 17 women, half selected proportionately by sex of a random sample of 60 medically fit participants. Predominantly older widowed persons, about half living with children, all conceding their dependence on a protective environment, they found establishing human contacts more difficult the more they needed such contacts. Most preferred passive entertainment, although a minority remained open to learning and exercising initiative. All were responsive to the program's unlimited acceptance and genuine concern. Further study of these participants a year later would be useful, as would similar studies of different ethnic and cultural groups, especially in relation to the old persons' family settings and backgrounds.

23. HAHN, Eva Brass (1958). <u>Admissions to the New Jewish Home for the Aged, Toronto.</u>
Since many more apply than the home can accommodate, the Admissions Committee's principle is that those in financial need should be served first. In the light of avowed admissions policies, the writer studied case records on the 65 persons admitted to the 138-bed section for the "well aged" between June 1956 and June 1958 -- in the home's third and fourth years when conditions and social service staff had both settled into normal operation. Most residents had become unable to manage alone because of inadequate living conditions or strained family relations or poor health. None of the 14 with liquid assets could pay for more than three-and-a-half years of maintenance; 31 had no pre-admission income except Old Age Security; and 13 had no children who could contribute. A later study might be made of this group's adjustment and

46

their financial arrangement with the home over an extended period. Admissions policies, apparently upheld in their cases, need better publicizing in the community.

24. HUNSBERGER, Wilson A. (1951). A history of the Ontario County House of Refuge and Industrial Farm, Whitby, Ontario (now known as the Ontario County Home).
At least three decades of research and discussion preceded the home's opening in 1903. The practice of placing "lunatics" and indigent old people in jails, since it was cheaper than paying cash maintenance allowances, had aroused humanitarian concern. The home was sorely overburdened long before its peak population of 134 in 1943, mainly because inadequate alternatives had dictated catchall admissions practices. Yet few bought independence when pensions permitted after 1929. Its good staff was this home's good fortune. Comparable concern with residents, and the provision of trained personnel especially to help develop social and recreational programs, will be needed when the modern facilities currently under construction replace the outmoded building and farm. Supplementary boarding-home and foster care and the seeking out of the right accommodation for varied individual needs will promote the best use of the new resources.

25. KAGAN, Gitl (1961). Social factors influencing the excessive use of outpatient facilities by a group of elderly patients.
The writer studied records in Toronto's New Mount Sinai Hospital, and interviewed 30 outpatients aged sixty-five or over, 15 having paid five or fewer visits during 1960, and 15, twenty or more visits most of which were medically needless. In the latter group — two-thirds women -- 13 lived alone, 14 were widowed and one a bachelor, only one-third had good relationships with their children, 8 had no relatives and no friends, and twice as many were in contact with social agencies as in the other group where men and persons married or in rewarding contact with several friends predominated. Marked hypochondriac behaviour was thus always associated here with loneliness and dejection. Almost all outpatients appreciated the serving of mid-morning coffee and biscuits, but the frequent visitors were much more intensely and personally interested in

clinic personnel and procedures. From older people's
needs for material help and sociability our focus must
shift, the writer feels, to the needs for friendlier
living arrangements and for usefulness.

26. KATZ, Sidney (1952). <u>A sheltered workshop for older</u>
<u>people</u>.
        The Women's Patriotic League Emergency Workroom
(Toronto), initially an offshoot of a 1914-18 organization to provide servicemen's comforts, is now supported by the City and the Community Chest. Mr. Katz
interviewed, in March 1950, 25 of the 41 workers there:
some women, squeezed out of other jobs, supported themselves by a five-day week at needlework; others supplemented pension or other income by a few hours' work.
"Living in a room is like a box when you have to be in
it all day," as one worker put it. To go out among
people, to be usefully employed ("I'm just in my glory
working"), and to receive at noon the kind of meal few
single women have energy, motivation or facilities to
provide for themselves, had meant improved health for
over two-thirds and happier living for almost all.
Clarified policies, more such services, and vocational
training (which almost all up to their late seventies
would welcome) are recommended.

27. KENNEDY, Margaret F. (1952). <u>Recreation for the aged;</u>
<u>a study to determine the program needs of old</u>
<u>people</u>.
        The writer sent 125 questionnaires to all known
Canadian centres serving the social needs of the aged,
and interviewed a random sample (50) of the 410 members of the Second Mile Club (Toronto). The 40 per
cent questionnaire responses showed that in Ontario
and the west, communities are beginning to accept responsibility for their aged and to help them towards
self-enrichment and usefulness. In general, clubs,
being newer resources with voluntary memberships, provided more adequate recreation than old people's homes.
The Toronto club's members, on average, most enjoyed
cards, music, and visiting in the lounge. People living alone participated more in almost all club programs. While staff effectiveness and members' physical
strength conditioned some preferences, most participation arose from outgoing, sociable impulses. The
slowest programs to develop are those designed to

help members to learn more about, and work with and
serve, other sections of the community.

28. LOWERY, Richard (1959). <u>The satisfaction the old</u>
      <u>person finds in the use of recreation services.</u>
      The writer interviewed, in the central branch
of Toronto's Second Mile Club, 41 members who had a
relative in the Toronto area, selected proportionately by sex. Many were lonely despite the relative:
sometimes their brother or sister was ill, or a child
was in the suburbs tied down by a young family; and
even the 28 contented with their family association
often sounded resigned -- "We live in two worlds" or
"They're young; I don't expect them to be interested."
Those with meaningful family contacts made better use
than did the more deprived members of the Club's opportunities for meeting people, learning, and participating. Women tended to enjoy organized programs; men,
informal activities. Only a minority developed new
skills, interests, or outside activities because of
membership, although several reported themselves "friendlier now". Friends most commonly had brought members
into the Club, and new friendships were overwhelmingly
its most valued contribution, especially to the 25 in
light-housekeeping rooms.

29. MACKLIN, Olive M. (1956). <u>Aged veterans deferred for</u>
      <u>domiciliary care.</u>
      In 1952 one Toronto hospital began accepting as
residents certain elderly veterans needing some medical
supervision, but the number of applicants for this accommodation who were deferred reached 115 within eighteen
months. Their circumstances and attitudes, especially
as indicative of the problem of older people generally,
are here studied through the files of the Department
of Veterans' Affairs and in personal interviews with
22 of the men deferred between July 1952 and December
1954 who were accessible. Housing was given oftenest
as the reason for applying, although suitable living
quarters in the community were judged preferable to
the institution. With families often dispersed, employment gone, income barely adequate, and companionship increasingly elusive, the need was often uncovered
for "right social as well as individual adjustment".
Follow-up casework service is recommended for all deferred veterans. For the old generally it is urged

that individual differences and preferences be more
fully respected and used as a guide in planning.

30. MAIN, William (1951). <u>Lambert Lodge Home for the
Aged</u>.
The postwar pressures on jobs and housing compounded by the lengthening life span necessitated
emergency measures in 1949, when Toronto began preparing the homes for the aged required by that year's
Act. Hence this reconstituted veterans' hospital was
opened for the infirm or chronically-ill aged, who
contributed if possible although City and Province
jointly provided support. This extensive study in
mid-1951 assesses the institution, judged by visits,
consultations, and records, in terms of standards as
defined in the literature and practised elsewhere.
Over two-thirds of the 690 residents shared rooms for
six or more, although only 20 were fully bedridden
and only 77 were senile. Lack of privacy, no professional occupational or physiotherapy, and want of integration with public libraries or other community
resources, magnified the difficulties of this temporary expedient, despite the staff's high quality.
Better staff benefits are recommended and more than
one social worker for residents, their relatives, and
the 589 on waiting lists.

31. TAYLOR, Eleanor D. (1954). <u>Social and economic circumstances of the mentally-ill aged</u>.
Postulating that adverse social and economic
circumstances may in themselves, or together with
physiological decline or disease, be related to a
greater increase of mental illness among the elderly
than among other age groups, out of all proportion
to their increased numbers in the general population,
the writer studied records in the Ontario Hospital
(Toronto) on 40 of 125 patients aged sixty and over
who were first admitted in 1949. Choosing cases with
adequate data (i.e., facts supplied by friends or relatives) meant over-representing the less isolated.
Even so, only one-quarter had living spouses, some of
these now remote or disinterested. The majority had
never been active socially. At least half had had
good physical and mental health, although half the
men were malnourished on admission. All but 8 had inadequate or marginal incomes by then, often having

50

suffered fairly recent reversals. Surprisingly often, certifying physicians mentioned as the "precipitating factor" not chronological age, but changes, uprootings, deaths, or financial worry.

32. WARRINER. Walter L. (1950). <u>Medical services for old age pensioners in Ontario: a study of the extent and character of the medical services afforded the old age pensioners in Ontario under the Ontario Medical Welfare Board</u>.

From general study, and particular examination of the monthly reports of the 1,914 doctors who rendered service during March 1949 to beneficiaries served through the Ontario Medical Welfare Board's plan, under professional jurisdiction, Mr. Warriner describes the plan, its operations for one month, and its administration. The province provides funds, at that time assessed at 83¢ for each of the 78,413 old age pensioners whose cards were signed by one of the approximately 3,300 participating physicians; these received payment (then about 85 per cent of rendered fees) pro-rated according to statistical formulae. About 22 per cent of pensioners received care in March 1949, with cities least served, perhaps because of available free clinics or because general practitioners in the cities are less available. Utilization and participation rates compare well with those for comparable schemes elsewhere. For general application this plan providing home and office visits will need integrating with hospital care, etc., and probably the scope of the medical profession's responsibilities should be redefined so that records and supervision would be handled by administrative authorities.

SEE ALSO Entries 153, 154, 189.

General

33. BAIN, Ian (1955). <u>The role of J. J. Kelso in the</u>
<u>launching of the Child Welfare movement in</u>
<u>Ontario.</u>
Two things stand out in this historical study:
the social ferment of Kelso's times; and his ability
"by the carrying on of a steady educational propaganda"
to win "a gradual acquiescence in a movement that fully
demonstrates, in operation, its own rationality" (to
quote his own 1897 report as Ontario's Superintendent
of Neglected and Dependent Children). Details of
Kelso's early career, to 1911, are drawn from private
papers as well as from official and published sources.
His skill in mobilizing support for a wide range of
services and in delegating volunteer work is evident
in the continuity of those services. In child welfare, organizations were already active in Ontario
in the 80's. It was Kelso's part to bring these various community efforts into a co-ordinated plan under government supervision, and to extend this unique
private-public undertaking throughout the province.
An administrator often coping with his problems in
the flesh, short of paid staff, fighting for appro-
priations, Kelso kept his focus steadily on the child's
right to develop in his own family or, when that failed,
with the help of a responsible community.

34. BARNES, John (1957). <u>The protection client who drinks</u>
<u>to excess.</u>
This study uses 209 long-term cases still active
with the Protection Department, Children's Aid and Infants' Homes (Toronto), in mid-1956 to investigate the
low referral rate from social agencies in general to
the Alcoholism Research Foundation. Workers identified 79 of the cases as involving an alcohol problem.
The author read 39 of these records and agreed in at
least 29 that the evidence suggested excessive drinking by parent(s). He found that workers had identified 7 of the 8 (among 209 clients) also registered
with the Alcoholism Research Foundation. He dis-
cusses problems of identifying alcoholism in a

protection case (the focus on the children, parents'
defensiveness about drinking, etc.) and possible
reasons for not referring alcoholic clients (for example, the difficulty of enlisting parents' co-
operation in a referral). Records showed that the
39 clients had had contacts with an average of four
social agencies each, with alcoholism perhaps seen
as peripheral to the focal problem in every instance.

35. BELL, Marion M. (1949). The history of the Catholic
Welfare Bureau of Toronto.
To trace the evolution of a professionally-
staffed agency based on Christian concepts of charity
and the nature of man, the writer interviewed leaders
and searched official files and publications on both
the eighty-one years of local Catholic welfare work
prior to the founding of the bureau in 1922 and its
subsequent development. In 1921 a survey had established that a constellation of parish services, developed by Bishop de Charbonnel, Archbishop Neil
McNeil, and through the Catholic Charities Office
under Father Bench, were ready for co-ordinated professional reorganization. The bureau initially supervised organizations and provided direct family, child,
and probationary services. Other agencies soon took
over its non-caseworking functions. By 1944 it was a
member of the Community Chest of Greater Toronto, with
representation in four Divisions. Its relations with
public welfare and specialized agencies, and voluntary
parish services, support and define its direct concern
with protection work, temporary child care, and care
for unmarried mothers and their infants.

36. BRANT, Marlene J. (1959). Parental neglect in Indian
families.
Social workers can understand an Indian client's
objectives and difficulties only if they have insight
into what his cultural heritage means to him. The
writer seeks to interpret 20 records -- admittedly
extreme cases -- of families with at least one Indian
parent whose children were permanent wards of the
Children's Aid Society (Toronto) in January 1959. In
14 cases dissolution of the union precipitated social
intervention. Common-law marriage is acceptable in
Indian culture, but it seemed to have a special function for women in the city: protection while they

53

learned to fit into, or refuge from, white society (albeit often unsatisfactory). Some of the Indian fathers in migratory or seasonal jobs were constantly away; others had "dependent, inadequate personalities". Between workers and parents, passivity, some hostility, and poor communication seemed the norm. Background facts indicated emotional deprivation for some, raising the question of whether all might not be experiencing comparably crippling cultural deprivation.

37. CULHAM, Lottie J. (1953). Wards of a Children's Aid Society.
    To assess how responsibly an agency fulfills its guardianship role, the writer studies the general pattern of adjustment of a group of permanent wards who were not placed for adoption. Her 29 examples, drawn from the records of the Toronto Children's Aid Society, are all of the nine- and ten-year-olds who had been made permanent wards in 1941-42 (before the Society and the Infants' Homes amalgamated), i.e., all 29 had been taken into care during their first year of life. Each child's history is given: his relation to his foster home, the school, his playmates, and his own circumstances. In 48 per cent of the cases social adjustment was less than satisfactory, with a correlation between maladjustment and changes of foster homes and of social workers, but with wide variations between I.Q. ratings and individual patterns of adjustment. The study challenges an assumption that children are "unadoptable" because of below-average intelligence. It also points up the importance of the social worker's obligation to help a child to understand and accept his status as a ward.

38. GRIFFITH, Gwyneth (1956). The meaning of wardship to a child.
    The permanent wards who attempt to leave agencies at age sixteen, when compulsory schooling ends but not legal guardianship, are studied through records on the 25 cases in this category in one agency between 1945-54 and through interviews with 5 of the young people concerned. Then three workers helped select 25 records on permanent wards who had not tried to strike out on their own prematurely, of whom 6 were interviewed. Many of the latter group found it hard to "live other people's lives" in foster homes, as one adolescent put it, but yet accepted wardship. The

group who tried to assert their independence of the agency's authority were predominantly boys, of aggressive (rather than submissive) personalities. Where did they go? In every case where contact with the natural mother had been maintained during wardship, the sixteen-year-old had sought her out; others who had brothers or sisters in town had used them as "home base" while job hunting. These histories indicate that social workers should continue, whenever feasible, to work with natural families, even after wardship has proved inevitable.

39. GRIFTON, James (1958). <u>Education and occupational training of a Children's Aid Society's wards</u>.
    Despite the obvious responsibility of schools and foster homes, it is the responsibility of the Children's Aid Society, according to Ontario statute, to make provision for a ward's education and occupational training "such as a good parent would make for his own child". To assess what the agency here undertakes and how effectively it has functioned, the writer studied a sample of Children's Aid Society (Toronto) case records on 50 boys, all permanent wards between eight and twenty years of age in 1954. The proportion with less-than-average intelligence was larger than in a normal group; too often such wards were in rural placements where the appropriate special training was unavailable. Workers tended to focus on the child's general welfare rather than his educational needs, and to take no part in decisions on courses and curricula. Half of the psychologists' recommendations on school matters were not acted upon, and little use was made of the community's resources for vocational counselling. If wards were to develop according to their natural endowments, a new emphasis on education in agency program was seen as needed, as well as more adequate funds for higher education and special classes.

40. HOWSON, Carol (1957). <u>The division of casework services between family and child during temporary agency care -- does it affect the preservation of family unity?</u>
    How effectively applied is today's knowledge that children need their own parents, however inadequate, and parents need to develop in response, however

impeded by their own life experiences? To help assess
the practice in a large departmentalized Toronto agency,
workers participated through questionnaires on cases
involving 67 children admitted to care between September
1952 and August 1953 who were temporary wards in April
1954. Most Child Care workers said they usually knew
answers to questions children asked about their parents
but, although they frequently met parents during visits,
they seldom discussed children's concerns with them.
Fewer protection workers knew the children. Parents
usually were cut off from information about foster-
family relationships, or children's illnesses or school
progress. Close informal contact among workers would
be needed, supplementing formal communications between
departments, to unify service to the total family or
better still, "one worker for parent and child". (A
parallel study is recommended of the agency during a
1954 experiment with the latter method.)

41. JANES, William G. (1953). The rehabilitation of the
family.
The families under review were all charged with
neglect between 1941 and 1949, and in all cases the
parent(s) were permitted to resume guardianship in
1949-50. The release date and the age of the children
(between four and sixteen) defined the group of 24
families selected from the records of the Children's
Aid Society of Toronto. The agency had opened cases
with 11 of the families twice or oftener before the
court hearing. The commonest basis for the charge
was "delinquency or incorrigibility", with apprehen-
sion necessary in only 6 cases. By the release date
parental relations were judged improved in 9 cases;
6 of the 9 mothers who were then alone had separated
since the wardship period began. On final contact 5
families only evinced hostility and poor readjustment.
Apparently court action provides a salutary jolt in
some cases. And protective work, co-ordinated with
the services of other agencies, can support parents'
potentiality for change.

42. JOLLIFFE, Russell (1952). History of the Children's
Aid Society of Toronto, 1891-1947.
The socially prominent citizens who first established the Society were concerned with crime prevention rather than with child welfare. From primary

sources such as the minutes of the Board of Management, Mr. Jolliffe documents their dread of "government interference". Entitled to provincial grants by 1894 and accepting city support by 1900, the Society long continued to operate with one paid administrator, Lady Visitors for investigations and home finding, and a small staff at the Shelter. For a time the Shelter doubled as a Detention Home. Only in 1920 when the Board membership changed radically was the drift to institutional care arrested. During the 1930's community services were better co-ordinated, trained staffs developed, and functions were diversified, although for an interim the Board assumed too little responsibility for policy. After the war, when a housing shortage threatened family continuity, the agency significantly reaffirmed that children's welfare is its focal concern.

43. KOBAYASHI, Jean H. (1962). A descriptive study of children in the Residence of the Metropolitan Toronto Association for Retarded Children.
   The group studied, the 21 residents in June 1962 who had been in the residence for at least a year and a half, was too small to make statistical analysis meaningful. Moreover, 15 of the boys and girls studied were Children's Aid Society wards, and thus were exceptional in social history as well as in mental capacity. Although the parents of the remaining 6 children were interviewed, most of the information was gathered from case records supplemented by direct observation and discussions with the residence's staff members. The description of the group included background material on the parents, the children's age and sex, age on admission, religious affiliation, developmental history, reasons for present referral, and plans for the future. Four cases are decribed in detail. The group's characteristics are also compared with those described in the literature on mental retardation, a relatively new but increasingly challenging concern of social workers.

44. McCLURE, Kathryn H. (1956). Services given by the Children's Aid and Infants' Homes of Toronto as seen by a group of ex-wards of this agency.
   Probing questions are likely to elicit subjective answers: many ex-wards who had been old enough

"did not remember" their court hearings, for example,
and many understated or exaggerated their number of
placements. The recipients' views of an agency's
services, then, should be looked to for a general impression, not as any kind of appraisal. The writer
interviewed 25 persons who had been permanent wards
and had come of age between November 1951 and July
1953 -- all who were accessible and willing of a
total of 91. Those who had been over five years of
age on admission to care showed, on average, a better
adjustment than the 10 who had become wards in infancy.
Even in the best foster homes most agreed that "something was missing", and many expressed anxiety about
their identity and the status of a ward. Positive
feelings about the agency prevailed, despite some con-
fusion about the worker's role. The new individualistic clothing policy met with strong approbation.

45. MORLEY, Margaret (1951). Social work in the Child
Guidance clinic.
From the viewpoint of Canadian social workers
interested in the establishment of such clinics in
Canada, materials are here studied on the history
and practices evolved in recent decades, especially
in demonstration clinics initially sponsored by the
Commonwealth Fund (in 1920 in the United States, and
in 1928 in Great Britain). American services varied
according to the emphasis of the auspices under which
they developed (hospital, court, school, etc.) and
the orientation of their directors (Rankian or Freudian,
roughly speaking); their primary concern was a client's
adjustment. The state-operated clinics in Britain
tended to be predominantly Freudian but concerned with
environmental modification too. In both countries
specially-trained social workers met parents while the
children were being seen by therapists, and co-operated
with other community services. Canadian cities contem-
plating such agencies can ensure sound development by
careful preliminary research, readiness to adapt any
applicable features of these earlier clinics, deliberation in appointing the clinic director, and then support for whatever orientation of service he establishes.

46. O'CONNOR, Catherine J.M. (1949). History of the Board
of Directors of the Catholic Children's Aid Society
of Toronto.

58

Changes are traced in the functions of this
public-private agency's Board of Directors, 1894-1945.
Originally the Board members placed children and visited
the homes as well as financing province-wide activities.
By 1911 when 481 children were involved in cases reported, the one staff member was given an assistant,
and in 1932 the first trained social worker was appointed. But in the early 1930's the Board was still
making decisions about tonsillectomies and school plans
at its monthly meetings. With weekly staff conferences,
legislation introducing temporary wardship, court work
and the Shelter's administration, the Board's function
changed. After 1936 its composition was altered too:
membership was reduced, terms of office and duties were
defined, and advisory and executive functions were separated. By 1945 standing committees were working out
policy details, and the director was authorized to perform many agency functions. The volunteers, once essential to the agency's existence, then to its growth,
now maintain its lifelines with the community.

47. PAGET, Norman W. (1949). A statistical analysis of
    Family Allowances expenditure by forty-eight
    Ontario Children's Aid Societies.
         In 1945, when the government authorized payment
    of Family Allowances for all children in care, it
    ruled that agencies might use a stated maximum to
    raise boarding-home rates, but the remainder was for
    "additional advantages and benefits" for the children.
    The Ontario office ascertained by questionnaire how
    the funds had been spent between July 1945 and
    December 1947, and national directives in 1948 and
    1949 then further regulated allocation. The writer
    analyzed official questionnaire returns from all the
    semi-public agencies, and investigated agency atti-
    tudes and staff knowledge through his own question-
    naires and interviews. Over three-fourths of the
    expenditures went to increase boarding rates, he
    found, reflecting the shortage of homes in cities;
    and more was spent on, for example, cub uniforms in
    districts with no service clubs. But no significant
    correlation emerged between area, quality of agency
    service, and need for "extras". Some workers did
    not know that these funds could be passed on to long-
    term foster parents. Interest of several agencies in
    building up education funds or "nest eggs" for wards

could account for some of the large unspent accumulations of the period.

48. PARSONS, Allan F. (1949). Voluntary social maintenance in the Child Welfare field in Toronto.
Besides two semi-public agencies caring for children on a wardship basis, Toronto has six private agencies giving short-term care to dependent children and receiving "Charitable and Institutional Grants" from the City. Their development is here illustrated from historical documents, and their current preventive service is described through case records of 91 families from the City's Department of Public Welfare files for 1947. The Department decides on applications within the leeway allowed by maintenance grants. Since Toronto's private agencies serve only residents, would provincial legislation, to establish maintenance, help other areas to provide better alternatives to wardship care? These resources for children can give parents a chance to reconstitute broken homes. When children are placed because a parent is ill, would Visiting Homemakers serve instead? And might not private agencies help more than Training Schools in many cases of behaviour problems? Administrators and social workers alike weigh such questions, despite the inherent budget difficulties.

49. RAMSEY, Dean P. (1949). The development of Child Welfare legislation in Ontario.
The province, by 1840 relatively populous with a mobile labour force and communal responsibilities, early regulated apprenticeship and institutional custody, often in the interests of employers and lawmakers rather than of the children. But in 1893 a new Act made cruelty punishable, defined "neglect", provided for the establishment of Children's Aid Societies, and even recommended a special court for juvenile offenders. In 1920 the Adoption Act and the Children of Unmarried Parents Act cleared up further damaging anomalies. By 1926, 26,557 children had come under protection. However, theory advanced more rapidly than practice, with persistent lacks in supervisory structures, financial enabling, and trained workers. Following a 1930 Royal Commission investigation, order and authority were brought into a reorganized welfare administration. Preventive

work increased steadily. Further consolidation occurred by the 1940's as wartime services proliferated; then, too, the province accepted responsibility for a substantial share of the costs of child welfare. (The contributions of individuals, from J.J. Kelso to B.W. Heise, are everywhere evident.)

50. ROBINSON, Mona (1957). A study of reopened protection cases in the Children's Aid and Infants' Homes of Toronto in 1953.
   In an agency obligated to investigate every complaint received (although decisions are a court responsibility) one department tries to help a child's family to modify his environment so as to preclude his removal. To assess this preventive aspect of the work, the writer studied the 40 available records on all cases previously closed not earlier than 1950 and reopened for continued service in 1953. Over half the complaints were of general neglect, originally referred by other community agencies or concerned citizens, and on reopening referred mainly by agencies. Parental desertion, mental illness, or imprisonment led to 7 initial and 10 second requests for foster care. Juvenile courts referred most of the balance -- cases of problem behaviour or emotional neglect. Perhaps initial service was too brief (under three months in 10 cases). However, effective preventive action must come earlier for families with problems of irregular or inadequate income, overcrowded or unhygienic quarters, marital discord, or alcoholism.

51. RUSSELL, Donald A. (1962). Permanent wardship.
   Despite greatly developed resources for helping, and skills in enabling families to change, some children's physical and emotional needs are still being so persistently and drastically neglected that final removal to agency care is judged unavoidable. Why? The answer is sought in 31 records from the 44 protection cases where children were made permanent wards of the Toronto Children's Aid Society in 1957 after a period in temporary care. Only 6 homes had both parents, with only one couple living in anything approaching marital stability. Most of the children in care were younger than seven and had suffered emotional deprivation. Facts about parents were unexceptional or, as with mental instability, too

irregularly recorded for generalization. Children
suffering mishandling from one parent in a broken
home far outnumbered children alone through death,
desertion, or institutionalizing of parents. Where
family groups still existed, complex internal difficulties had proved resistant to casework. Wardship
seems the only present solution in such cases.

52.   SMITH, W. Reginald (1957). A study of reopened pro-
          tection cases.
          The incidence of reopenings -- 12 per cent of
the 984 cases coming to the Children's Aid and Infants' Homes (Toronto) in 1954 -- struck the writer
as high in an agency empowered to intervene until
children's protection needs are achieved in family
or community. Records on all 47 cases where previous
agency contact occurred since the agency amalgamation
of 1951 showed that over three-quarters of the families were broken, and even oftener parents were identified as mentally inadequate or emotionally disturbed.
The 18 cases where parents' backgrounds were noted
showed a history of mental deficiency in the only two
brought up by their own parents. Situations were the
same or worse at reopening for 35 families. In 33
cases initial service had been completed or families
had moved, and recurrent opening arose unforeseeably,
sometimes unnecessarily. In the other 14, including
even the 8 where parents rejected service, authority
might have been asserted rather than hope (wherever
possible) for a child's own home.

53.   SPLANE, Richard B. (1951). Administration of the
          Children of Unmarried Parents Act of the Province
          of Ontario.
          This 1921 Act reflects a contemporary concern
with the welfare field's exceptional vulnerability to
political uncertainties: hence the Provincial Officer
was given virtual Cabinet authority (but no departmental resources). Until 1934 responsibility not assumed by that Officer was delegated almost by default
to local Children's Aid Societies. Thereafter the
divisional director in the Department of Public Welfare used advisory legal work, training courses and
conferences, supervision, and grading, to encourage
better standards. The modern casework approach, with
its regard for the interests of mother, father, and

child alike, also implied dimensions of service not
envisaged in the Act. As the societies' non-wardship
activities expanded, the anomaly of statutory provision
for wardship costs only led Ontario, in 1949, to author-
ize grants based on amounts privately raised for each
society. By now, the writer feels, a new Act is needed
to define more clearly financial and administrative
responsibility, and to bring policy into line with modern practices.

54. STEVENS, Frederick L. (1952). Parents' problems as-
    sociated with child placement.
      The Protestant Children's Homes in Toronto dur-
    ing 1948-50 interviewed 460 applicants and gave
    continued service to one-third of these: arranged
    temporary care for children and tried to help their
    parents in the interim. A parent's illness, the com-
    monest occasion for application, often coexisted with
    other stresses in the 76 cases studied (from records
    for alternate months). Some parents wanted to place
    a child during a confinement or a readjustment period
    after a death in the family; others, during such cri-
    ses as separation, or remarriage involving rejection
    of a child from an earlier marriage. Less than half
    the parents could accept either involvement in plan-
    ning and responsibility or casework to help them.
    Homes were not reconstituted for a year or more in
    one-third of these 76 cases. The records suggest
    that a cluster of services, on a scale more adequate
    to the need, might appropriately be developed —
    marital counselling, day nurseries, visiting home-
    makers.

55. THOMAS, Marion Ruth (1955). Some effects of the
    amendment to the Matrimonial Causes Act of
    Ontario, 1949.
      Ontario's divorce regulations, established in
    1930 on the basis of 1870 British law, were amended
    in response to concern about children expressed by
    Children's Aid Societies and legal authorities re-
    sponsible for custody arrangements. Of 351 divorce
    cases in 1954-55 where the Toronto Children's Aid
    made preliminary reports to the Official Guardian,
    118 came to trial. The writer analyzes data from
    these reports and from records in some fourteen so-
    cial agencies with whom 87 of the families had had
    contact. Over three-quarters of the mothers claimed

63

custody, but almost as many worked. Of 173 children there were 27 -- about double the normal ratio -- suffering to some degree the emotional disturbances that in excess characterize mental illness. Almost always schools or "outsiders" had identified these troubles. Investigating workers sometimes found parents wanting counselling -- perhaps official social machinery for screening marriages that might be saved (like that established to help judges decide custody) is now needed.

56. WASS, D. Keith (1949). A Children's Aid Society and wards over sixteen years of age.
There were 48 young people who, when they became twenty-one years of age in 1948, had been under guardianship of the Children's Aid Society of Toronto for at least seven years. This study of agency case records asks how they had fared in adolescence. Eighty per cent left school at fifteen or sixteen, and almost half lived on their own. More than half shifted from job to job without finding or giving satisfaction, and their histories showed that they had been moved through twice as many homes as the group who adjusted well at work. Almost a third received no service from the agency after sixteen; several had had a little help with board or clothes or job finding, and 6 had sought information about their parents. Since close contact is naturally irksome to adolescents, freer living arrangements for some (independent boarding residences, etc.), and earlier termination of guardianship might be advisable. The improtance of early stability in a dependable family situation is apparent in many of these histories.

57. ZIEMANN, Anna M. (1951). The changing emphasis on the use of Clause III of the Children's Protection Act at the Children's Aid Society of Toronto.
The 35 cases involving 74 children in 1930-31, and 32 cases involving 52 children in 1950, where "disease or misfortune or infirmity" occasioned a first prosecution and a first commitment to wardship, are here compared through court evidence and case records. Twenty years ago there were almost twice as many permanent wardships. "Misfortune" then was construed in terms of economic and moral factors, and agency authority perhaps influenced parental consent. Today the

focus has shifted from a child's material needs to his emotional security, kinship ties, and parents' rights. The agency, now wholly responsible for presenting the court cases, plans carefully, using temporary wardship along with family casework to strengthen family integrity wherever possible. With developing awareness of the importance of protection work, and so of casework training, comes an obligation to develop community understanding of both emotional neglect and the relevance of services like Visiting Homemakers to prevent unnecessary family disruption.

SEE ALSO Entries 121, 157, 161, 251.

Adoption

58. DAWSON, Helen P. (1953). <u>Adoption consideration for the young child.</u>
Since an agency undertakes to provide the best care possible for its wards and accepts that adoption is "closest to the normal of all types of child placement", why is it that -- of the 148 children under four years of age in the care of the Infants' Homes of Toronto who were made permanent wards of the Children's Aid Society (Toronto) in 1950 -- 63 were still not placed for adoption by December 31, 1951? The case records suggest that, although every child's situation is unique, the agency still tends to apply categorized definitions of adoptability. But even with flexible policies, ample trained staff, and enough adoptive homes suitable for retarded children, some children would remain wards: the seriously ill or retarded; children finally secure in a foster home after many placements for whom another move even for the sake of adoption might be irreparably damaging; and a few members of minority groups for whom "matching" adoptive homes are scarce, in the city and even farther afield.

59. ERWIN, Renee (1959). <u>Adoption of older children.</u>
To see why adoptions were delayed, the writer analyzed the Toronto Children's Aid Society's case records on 18 of the 39 children who, after a period as permanent wards, were over five years old on adoption

65

in 1957. In only 2 cases was age on admission to care the sole factor (almost two-thirds were less than one year old when they became wards, although a few mothers were slow to relinquish their babies finally). Two children had had potentially disabling illnesses in infancy. Of the 16 normal, healthy children, 11 had negative factors in their backgrounds, and 3 belonged to minority racial groups. Many children need time, after experiencing physical or emotional neglect, before they will be able to respond to adoptive parents. Unfortunately this interval often involved disturbing moves -- three foster homes or more for over half the children. More foster parents are needed with special capacities for helping difficult or "hard to place" children.

60. JACKSON, Eileen B. (1957). <u>Time variations in adoption placements.</u>
    How much time elapses between referral of children of various ages, from the Child Care or Protection or Unmarried Parents Divisions of Ontario's largest Children's Aid Society to the Adoption Department, and their placement in adoptive homes? In mid-June 1954 the writer examined agency records and time schedules kept by workers on 51 placements of children referred in two spring months of 1954. The full process took from 8 to 115 days, with the oldest children waiting, on average, twice as long as the youngest, and with the few parents who accepted older children the most readily served. Workers spent from 7 to 82 hours on individual cases. The most time-consuming service, casework to help older children to accept the new family situation, clearly speeded up the overall procedure. Thus, adjusting caseloads by children's ages seems realistic, as does focusing on home finding for older or "different" children. Similar study of smaller agencies is recommended.

61. KEMP, B. Diane (1957). SEE Entry 67.

62. MacLEOD, Adrienne O. (1957). <u>A study of factors involved in telling a child about his adoption.</u>
    Children legally adopted between 1946 and 1952 in homes they entered in infancy were five to twelve years old when their adoptive parents agreed to interviews for this study -- the 31 cases from the files of

66

the Catholic Children's Aid Society (Toronto) still living within range. Although all had known that they should tell the child he was adopted, 27 feared discussing it, 4 had never done so, and 2 others only after the child had learned from outsiders. Every respondent sought counsel or reassurance from the interviewer. Many dreaded mention of illegitimacy, having emphasized the "chosen child" story to evade sex questions. The children seemed to have accepted what they had been told without difficulty. Perhaps in the home-finding period agencies might clarify factors (like the natural mother's love and planning) that will matter most to the child, and pay more attention to the adopting parents' feelings in preparing them for their responsibility.

63. McCORKELL, Evelyn (1957). <u>The request for adoption placement of legitimate children.</u>
    When married parents voluntarily relinquish their own children, their "failure" has profound meanings: to a child, rejection; to a parent, self-devaluation; to the community, perhaps projected guilt. In mid-1952 a new policy of the Children's Aid and Infants' Homes (Toronto) recognized these aspects of its statutory responsibility for adoption cases. Records of the total 29 cases closed by May 1956 are examined here to see what psychological factors distinguished the 18 where parents finally kept their children from the 11 where they did not. In 80 per cent of the latter cases there was serious psychological maladjustment, traceable in most instances to the parents' own early experiences. Counselling was usually effective where positive factors predominated in the parents' relationships within marriage and with their own parents and in their attitude to children generally. Tentative comparison with protection cases, though calling for elaboration, suggests that these 29 families showed higher average intelligence and were readier to acknowledge their need for, and thus to use, agency help.

64. NICHOLS, M. Doreen (1950). <u>Adoption practices of the Children's Aid Society of Toronto in 1949.</u>
    This intensive study is based on the agency's records and interviews with staff. During 1949, 223 children were placed in adoptive homes, and fewer

than 100 were deferred; there were 602 applications
in active files from adoptive parents, 90 per cent
of them wanting babies under one year old. The agency
compares favourably with approved agencies elsewhere
in the proportion of very young children placed, partly
thanks to a special Boarding Home Adoption arrangement
for infants pending their clearance for straight adoption placement. Unduly long periods on probation,
lack of individual acquaintance with some of the children placed, and some over-reliance on ratings by psychologists and medical consultants were consequent on
staff shortages. As trained workers are available,
better service, especially for children with low-normal
intelligence, and better focusing of work loads, will
ensue. By its non-punitive, helpful attitude towards
families where doctors, acquaintances, or relatives
had placed a child privately, the agency is encouraging the community to use professional adoption services.

65. POSEN, Minda M. (1948). <u>A study of adopted children</u>.
     This study reviews 24 case records from the Chil-
dren's Aid Society of Toronto and reports on subsequent
interviews with 21 of the families concerned. From
those in the Toronto area, children placed during their
first year in their adopting homes were selected, where
adoptions were completed in 1942. The parents on the
whole seemed to be accepting the children as individuals
and helping them to use their inner resources to grow
and enjoy life. All but 3 parents had told these eight-
and nine-year-olds that they were adopted, but few had
been able truthfully to explain why worthwhile, loving
mothers had given them up. Reservations and dreads
around the idea of illegitimacy were almost universal,
although only insecure parents felt strong resentment.
It seems that caseworkers could help adopting parents
to a better understanding of unmarried mothers. Inasmuch as these interviews seemed to be welcomed as
an opportunity for decision, more counselling service
for parents -- or adopting parents -- might fill a
real need.

66. STONEMAN, Alice L. (1961). <u>Private adoptions; a study</u>
     <u>of factors influencing natural and adoptive parents</u>
     <u>to plan adoptions through agents other than an au-</u>
     <u>thorized child welfare agency</u>.
     One authorized agency's records on the pre-adoption
investigations required by provincial law are analyzed

for 33 of the 129 cases reported to it in 1959 where
child and prospective adoptive parents were unrelated.
Some theoretically unacceptable cases -- involving
overage adoptive parents, or changes from a child's
religious heritage -- were accepted as _faits accomplis_.
Natural mothers were either competent, independent
women, who usually planned through a doctor for immediate private placements, or women overwhelmed after
attempts to care for a child despite agency dissuasion,
who usually appealed directly to the adoptive parents.
Many natural and adoptive parents had tried to plan
through agencies first. Since private planners do not
always safeguard the child's interests as adoption
workers are trained to do, professional skills need
constant, convincing publicity, especially among doctors. And ideally workers should meet adult clients
with such imagination and foresight that none need
turn to a doctor or any other private resource to feel
safe and confident.

67. WARD, Bonnie M., and KEMP, B. Diane (1957). A new
    resource for the hard-to-place child.
         The Ontario Adoption Clearance Service is de-
    scribed in the context of similar American exchanges,
    through study of its files and those of the Child
    Welfare Branch (which launched the service in September
    1954 after noting that some half of Ontario's wards
    were not on adoption probation although legally avail-
    able). During the service's first two and one-half
    years, 253 children and 187 adoptive homes were listed
    in bulletins circulated among the 55 Children's Aid
    Societies. Altogether 40 per cent of the children
    achieved adoption, about one in six through their local
    agency. The homes which received children, 30 through
    the service and 71 the local agency, had predominantly
    older parents or another child already there. The
    agencies that serve small cities and environs achieved
    most results, but only after vigorous activity -- the
    three most successful referred 68 cases and handled
    74 inquiries. Through this clearing house many chil-
    dren became no longer "hard to place". However, few
    homes were found for older or minority group children
    or those of low-normal intelligence.

SEE ALSO Entry 1.

Day Nurseries

68. BOJOVIC, Novica S. (1955). Role of the social case-
    worker at the Victoria Day Nursery of Toronto.
    Following a 1950 survey of Toronto's family and
    child services, the Victoria Day Nursery was set up
    as a demonstration project in day care. In 1953, its
    first complete year on the new basis, the nursery
    handled applications from 190 families and admitted
    children between two and five years of age from 64
    families. Through 35 case records of that year the
    writer studies the caseworker's methods with applic-
    ants and, in the 15 cases where children were admitted,
    her dealings with them and their parents and teachers.
    Many applicants, whose difficulties were primarily
    with budgeting or housing, were referred to other com-
    munity services (a follow-up study of such cases was
    suggested). Most admissions indicated family situa-
    tions that imposed undue strain on the children. The
    process of using day care to locate the trouble and
    to help both parent and child is demonstrated in sev-
    eral case histories. The writer recommends that the
    long-term effects of day care on children should be
    investigated as well.

69. GOODWIN, Winifred (1955). A study of withdrawals
    from six public day nurseries.
    Do Toronto's services for children living at
    home include adequate service to the parents who need
    it, or do clients leave the day nurseries with needs
    unmet? From the hundred families who had withdrawn
    their children from six nurseries between January and
    May 1955 the writer chose alternate names, and where
    circumstances permitted (in 36 of these cases) she
    interviewed the parents. New Canadians sometimes mis-
    understood the way fees were set, and often found them
    too high during a time of unusual budgeting difficulty;
    many resorted to less satisfactory private day-care
    arrangements. In 12 of the 14 cases where fathers were
    out of work or earning too little for the family's sup-
    port, withdrawal was occasioned by illness of the
    mother or the child, and in 5 of the 9 homes without
    fathers, by the child's illness. Four emotionally dis-
    turbed children were withdrawn without referral. These
    findings point to the pressing need for social work

services to round out the contribution the day nurseries make in education and public health.

70. HUTTON, Miriam Bennett (1959). Sole-support mothers.
The 15 mothers interviewed had been using a
public day nursery for at least six months, all supporting themselves and their 22 children, each maintaining a separate household by working full time.
(No unmarried mothers were included, nor wives of men
in hospital or prison.) Only 4 had ever accepted
"welfare", 2 of them during vocational training, and
none had used Mothers' Allowances. Separation allowances supplemented income for 2 mothers, roomers for
2 more. Almost half paid 40 per cent or more of their
earnings in rent. Yet despite low incomes and limited
prospects, almost all equally accepted working and
budgeting. As mothers, all seemed responsive and responsible although overtired and lacking means for
periodic recreation by themselves. Despite transportation difficulties nursery care helped enormously,
although not with Saturday morning or night-shift
arrangements. Community resources could have been
better known and used during crises and to allay the
dread that dogged every mother -- "What will happen
if...?"

Foster Homes

71. COLEMAN, Helen E. (1957). A study of a group of successful foster homes.
What enables some wards to weather adolescence
with a feeling of belonging, a happy outlook, and
good development according to their potentialities?
The answer is sought in the records of the Children's
Aid and Infants' Homes (Toronto) on well-adjusted
children, placed in their present homes before the
age of nine and aged sixteen to twenty by 1954, and
in 28 interviews with their foster parents. Data on
the children, their backgrounds, and the foster homes
were too diverse for meaningful generalizations. Half
of the foster parents had asked at some time for the
children to be removed, and very few were well prepared
to cope with children's anxieties about their status

71

or their natural parents. Loving, child-centred homes did predominate; as one foster mother phrased it, "You have to co-operate with a child and make them feel they are human beings." The findings suggest that good foster homes are gradually created by the people involved, with agency support.

72. DUFFY, Eileen (1948). <u>The problem of foster-home replacements</u>.

No agency wants to heap new insecurity on old for a child in care, nor to waste foster parents' goodwill and agency effort. To see whether some occasions for moving children could be obviated, case records are studied of all 107 children initially placed in foster homes who became wards of the Children's Aid Society (Toronto) in 1944 and were still in care in 1947. Well over half had been moved more than once. Moves often seemed unjustified, especially those "summer holiday breaks" that undermine a foster child's confidence. The high incidence of moves for children aged five or adolescent on admission, and during the first six months of placements, suggests focal points for further study. Also recommended are: more use of periods in the Shelter for observation and treatment; and concentration of able workers in home finding and the supervising of children in foster homes.

73. DUNLOP, Jean (1952). <u>Effects of replacement on children aged three to four years</u>.

The Infants' Homes and the Children's Aid Society of Toronto grew from separate roots through sixty years of co-operation until their 1951 amalgamation. One disadvantage — the transferring of wards from one foster home to another when their cases came to the C.A.S. — was early deplored and, by 1944, 33 children stayed in the same foster homes on transfer. This study compares their cases with the records on 36 who changed foster homes when their cases were transferred. A useful technique for assessing adjustment is worked out, and the incidence of 79 per cent good adjustments in the first group as against 56 per cent in the second seems to indicate the detrimental effect of change of home on three- and four-year-olds. However, the children with more difficulties had more replacements before and after, as well as at, the time of transfer. Thus the findings are taken to indicate only that early

permanent placement is desirable — and that the provision of good foster homes is an ever-pressing need.

74. FENEMORE, Ross S. (1955). Rejected applicants for
    foster parenthood; a study to determine whether
    earlier recognition of the unsuitable applicant
    for foster parenthood is possible.
    A survey of some typical precipitating situations
    that bring children into care, and of the procedures
    in planning for them, points up the need for wise and
    expeditious foster-home selection. Thus the practice
    of the Children's Aid and Infants' Homes (Toronto) is
    examined in 50 case records on applications that were
    not accepted, selected from double that number on file
    for the year 1951-52. No correlation emerged between
    background data — age, income, size of family — and
    unsuitability. Little interviewing was needed to
    weed out homes with material disadvantages such as
    lack of reasonable privacy for a child, or health
    problems. Recognizing personality problems and in-
    auspicious attitudes took more time. No key question
    emerged that might help an interviewer to bring an
    area of difficulty more quickly into focus, unless
    further checking shows some significance to the sur-
    prising number of applicants here wanting "a companion
    for my son". The agency's criteria for foster homes
    were found to be in line with the currently accepted
    standards.

75. GORDON, David Alexander (1952). Foster care for chil-
    dren coming into care as adolescents.
    Broken marriages, the illness of an only parent,
    the breakdown of privately-arranged care away from
    home — for whatever reason, many children become
    wards at an age that can be difficult even under nor-
    mal circumstances. To assess whether one agency ar-
    rives at "the best care possible" for such children,
    Mr. Gordon undertook in 1950 a follow-up study of
    case records in the Children's Aid Society of Toronto
    on the 44 children who had been between eleven and
    fifteen years of age on admission in 1942 and had
    never been wards before. The temporary Shelter was
    used first even for the 21 children who became per-
    manent wards. Of 17 who were then moved into foster
    homes, 12 remained less than six months. Where two
    or more children in a family were wards, they were
    kept together in only one-fourth of their placements.

A shortage of suitable foster homes for this age group,
as well as of residence accommodation, was evident.
For such a group as this, with intelligence levels and
schooling records below the community averages, and
early job histories predominantly unsatisfactory, better vocational planning and counselling are particularly urgent needs.

76. HARRISON, Constance M. (1948). Foster-home finding;
a study of effective ways of increasing the number of foster homes available for children.
To assess local practices at a time when need
greatly exceeded homes available, the writer studied
case records of the foster parents who applied during
1946 to the Children's Aid Society (Toronto), interviewed representatives of the Community Chest and of
six child care agencies here, and reviewed practices
elsewhere through correspondence and reading. Of the
245 (available) case records, at least 12 per cent
showed lengthy delays between application and home
finders' visits: staffs were clearly overburdened.
Further research should investigate why, after eighteen months, only 36 per cent of the homes approved
in 1946 were recorded as still in use. In general,
Toronto agencies' practices seemed to conform to
good standards, although sometimes the foster mothers
were the only members of the prospective home whom
workers met, and some applicants likely were puzzled
and hurt by cursory refusals. Most agencies already
plan year-round publicity. For the varying homes
different children need, recruiting might be extended
particularly to minority groups, tenant families, and
substantial home-owners.

77. LINDENFIELD, Rita (1955). Changes in foster homes.
Since no human situation is static the effectiveness of accepted foster homes can be expected to
vary. To study any variations and assess factors conducive to good results, the author, using 1950-54 case
records of the Protestant Children's Homes (Toronto),
rated 22 homes at six-month intervals, each home with
two to six placements of children under sixteen years
of age with legally responsible parents. She cites
individual cases to help define the areas of performance and the elements of placement experience used in
the statistical analysis. Foster parents, it appeared,
welcome regular visits from workers. They respond most

effectively to the child who clearly needs reassurance
-- as long as he is not too disturbed to accept their
help after a reasonable interval. Releasing a child
tends to upset even the families who shared his care
understandingly. Above all, the study reaffirms that
the basic qualification in a foster home is the family's
ability to live together harmoniously.

78. McKENZIE, Joan (1961). A comparative study of child
placement practices in Jamaica.
Jamaica is a community long inured to private
placement: both history and hardships probably have
made for the loosely grouped life of lower-class
families with one child in four living apart from
either parent. The writer wondered how the community's customs compared with foster-home care under
an agency which was modelling its recently initiated
services on the best American practice. She studied
case records on 28 agency placements and, by interviews, gathered information on 25 private placements.
The fact that the agency was more systematic in home
finding, preparation, and regulating of visits made
it acceptable to the community, even though the agency
tended to set unrealistic standards on methods of
child rearing and on what parents could contribute.
The circumstances that made placement necessary were
more often long-term ones than in the U.S.A. or England. With a surprising proportion of placements
occasioned by emigrating parents, her recommendation
would be for liaison with social workers in the parent's new countries as well as for better general
social services in Jamaica and a lively concern, when
importing personnel and practices, for that country's
unique needs and experiences.

79. MANN, William Irving (1960). Closed foster homes.
Exploring the histories as reflected in Children's Aid Society (Toronto) records of the 55 homes
here studied (where 106 children were placed but where
service was withdrawn or terminated at agency request,
1953-58) may help with finding and keeping much-needed
homes. The predominant reasons given for wanting a
foster child are noted: companionship for a child already in the home; or "to give another child a break".
The fact that almost half the foster parents had positive attitudes towards the natural parents initially,
but only a handful by termination, suggests some

unreality about what they expected. Similar changes
occured in initially promising attitudes towards the
children, ultimately over one-third rejecting, over-
protective, or casual. Home finders did not report
factual data in relation to attitudes and expectations, not even noting many foster parents' preliminary feelings -- about disturbed behaviour, for example.
More focus on standards of recording and on motivation,
and more research, are recommended.

80. O'BRIEN, Michael Terence (1950). Foster parents' responsibilities.
What do foster parents see as their job, Mr.
O'Brien asks, and how realistic are social work definitions of their skills and responsibilities? He
interviewed the mothers mainly, in 41 homes selected
from those with experience of a year or more in use
in March 1950 with the Catholic Children's Aid Society
(Toronto). "To treat a foster child like your own"
defined the role as almost all respondents saw it.
Hence physical care was good, with the family doctor
preferred over clinics. School and homework were
stressed, but not, on average, the developing of tal-
ents or vocational bent. Symptoms of emotional disturbance were often "treated" by discipline, often by
corporal punishment. Giving of "extras" (treats, toys,
etc.) was common. Despite lip service to principles,
feeling towards natural parents was largely negative;
thus temporary wards whose parents may visit are hard-
est to place. Although agency expectations have not
been made clear to foster parents on some particulars,
these parents were eager to co-operate and to provide
love and stability for children in care.

81. RICH, Mabel (1962). Successful foster homes.
From foster homes currently in use which the
Children's Aid Society of Metropolitan Toronto planned
to continue using, this student selected 22 homes
opened between 1955 and 1961 for children over three
years of age where at least two unrelated children
had been boarded. She interviewed the parents, and
read agency records, both the home studies and the
evaluations made by workers at each termination of a
child's stay in a home. Among the predominant characteristics of these homes, largely of a lower socio-
economic level, were stability and flexibility;
earnings seemed to have reached a maximum; the mothers

76

had often had slightly more formal education than the
fathers, but neither was articulate about why they
wanted to board children. Most found more problems
than they had expected with their foster children but
were surprisingly unperturbed. Their greatest difficulty arose from their failure to understand, and
therefore to accept, the natural parents' behaviour
and values.

82. RUDNEY, Bernice D. (1949). The treatment of child
    behaviour problems in the foster home.
        The symptomatic aspect of behaviour problems is
    poignantly apparent in foster children. Do agencies
    understand these symptoms, and what treatments do they
    try, with what results? The answers, for 20 cases
    selected at random from records demonstrating behav-
    iour problems in the Toronto Protestant Children's
    Homes and the Jewish Family and Child Service are:
    workers did show understanding; they tried to avoid
    moving children, initiating only 6 of 68 moves; 11
    cases were treated by attempts to modify the environ-
    ment, mainly through clarifying difficulties and en-
    couraging foster mothers' attempts to help, only once
    with moderate success; 9 children were also treated
    directly by workers, consulting psychiatrists, or
    child therapists, with 2 cases of marked and 4 of mod-
    erate success. Until more extensive services for dis-
    turbed children, or specially-trained foster parents,
    are available, workers must intensively help such
    children to become receptive to the home care they
    sorely need.

83. SCHWALBE, A. Lenore (1958). Negro and partly-Negro
    wards of the Children's Aid Society of Metropol-
    itan Toronto.
        From a total of 43 such wards, those born be-
    tween 1941-45 were studied through the 21 available
    case records. These adolescents were at a stage
    calling for understanding beyond most foster parents'
    capacities. Family differentness can bother the
    young conformist. Racial differentness can intensify
    problems about identity. But especially in Toronto
    where the Negro community is small, foster homes where
    a child's negroid appearance would be inconspicuous
    are scarce. An unusually high proportion, 15 of the
    wards here, had had some institutional care. Only 6

reached the grade appropriate to their age, although
the health and mental ability of the group were above
averages for other groups of wards recently studied
here. In varying degrees 15 had suffered emotional
disturbances, 2 severely enough to need hospitalization. Portraits of individuals convey that destructive early experiences were counteracted only when
these "hard to place" children found places of acceptance. Where foster parents were able to handle the
stresses of discrimination, this seemed not serious
among the ward's difficulties.

84. SMALLMAN, Marjory Maude (1952). Foster-home finding.
        From 1920 to 1950 nurses supervised the choos-
ing of foster homes for the Infants' Homes of Toronto.
A year before this agency and the Children's Aid
Society amalgamated, social work administration introduced casework principles into the home-finding process. From agency records the writer compared the 37
homes approved during March-May 1949 with the 20 approved in the same period of 1950 which were subsequently opened for temporary care. The latter showed
25 per cent fewer withdrawing or withdrawn within a
year, and only 35 per cent wanting to change from
temporary to permanent care as against 49 per cent of
the 1949 group. To eliminate foster homes where there
is quarrelling, or where only one parent wants a child,
or where temporary care is accepted as second best or
a possible steppingstone to long-term "arrangements",
caseworkers should be better able than nurses to protect children against grudging homes and needless moves,
and to promote foster parents' and community understanding and acceptance of agency service.

85. TREEN, Harold Willis (1952). Attitudes of foster par-
        ents towards agency service.
        The author studied 40 foster homes in use with
the Children's Aid and Infants' Homes (Toronto), a
random sample of the 160 urban homes which came into
use during 1948-49. Scheduled interviews with 40
foster mothers and 8 of the foster fathers as well
conveyed their general satisfactions in working for
the children and with the agency. Special problems
were reported with most children, and special deliberation in meeting these was found necessary by most
parents. Foster parents often complained of how little
they knew about the children -- not even "whether they

are adoptable". All but a few found board rates too low. Workers apparently should visit more often in the initial period, and should discuss openly with foster mothers any difficulty these experienced women may feel in heeding counsel from a much younger worker. Many foster parents might welcome more opportunities to share with agencies instances of their successes with the children.

86. WAKABAYASHI, Akiko (1959). Long-term boarding home care for children.
Through case records of the Children's Aid Society of Metropolitan Toronto the writer examines and evaluates the experiences of the 25 children in permanent foster-home placements who were under five years of age in 1953 when their cases were decided by the Infants' Planning Committee. Over half of them had physical or mental health problems or were emotionally disturbed; a few were hard to place for legal adoption because of age or race or unknown backgrounds. After five years their situations had been gratifyingly stabilized. With foster families' co-operation, workers had been able to help many children to be emotionally and socially, if not legally, at home. Less than one-quarter were too severely handicapped to respond, or had been too damaged by the many moves and delays in permanent planning (before the above committee was established). Despite exceptional vulnerability to stress, and unusual degrees of stress, the group on the whole proved the validity of this careful professional planning and support.

Institutions

87. BOES, Lillian F. (1950). The Ontario Charitable Institutions Act and Regulations as they affected children's institutions in 1949-50.
Ontario's 1937 Act (with the post-war amendments) sets modern standards of institutional care, and the Field Supervisor's visit of 1949 to the 29 children's institutions under the Act consolidated information on actual practice in the province. The writer documents this stage of progress in child care, drawing on the Field Supervisor's report and recommendations,

follow-up reports, and official submissions from the
institutions. On the whole, the institutions were
adequate, if unimaginative, in providing physical
necessities. There were many gaps: in casework,
vocational counselling, and helping children to make
their own decisions and to develop self-reliance in
the community. Better community representation on
boards of directors, and further staff training were
recommended, and a survey of other children's institutions in Ontario -- shelters, training schools,
special care centres -- so that ultimately every one
could be brought up to standard and every child
placed where his individual need would best be met.

88. CLARK, Donna (1961). Social background and develop-
    ment of children who experienced institutional
    living in their infant years.
        Of the 48 children aged sixteen months or under
    when admitted to the Neil McNeil Infants' Home during
    the first half-year after its opening in June 1948,
    the 27 who remained in institutional care are here
    studied through agency records on their experiences
    up to June 1957. Their mothers, almost all unmarried,
    had usually themselves suffered deprivations and in-
    securities. Case histories elaborate a statistical
    picture of deprived children. When foster homes were
    in short supply and the agency was overburdened and
    undergoing reorganization, these children with question-
    able backgrounds and liable through deprivation to over-
    sensitivity, anxiety, and regressive tendencies in
    behaviour and training needed a degree of private or
    special attention not then readily available. Nation-
    wide indexing of foster homes might help, especially
    where race is a factor; close co-operation with foster
    parents undertaking care of troubled children, and
    use of institutions as treatment centres, are urged as
    basic to responsible care.

89. LATIMER, Elspeth A. (1953). Methods of child care as
    reflected in the Infants' Homes of Toronto, 1875-
    1920.
        Drawing on annual reports, minutes, and agency
    records, the writer reviews the period when this agency
    provided institutional care for infants. It pioneered
    in accepting children under two years of age -- an age
    group even hospitals excluded in the days of high

infant mortality. Unmarried mothers provided breast
feeding, and domestic work as well, in return for
refuge. Volunteer citizens helped find adopting parents and generally mobilized community support. In
time professional nurses were added to the staff and,
by 1918, a social worker was handling admissions. But
by then the dangers of contagion in an institution
were apparent. Care in foster homes was increasingly
held to be more natural for infants. A dispersed community of families thus took over the care the institution had provided. Thereafter the agency developed as
a home-finding and supervising service, and a service
for unmarried mothers.

90. SCHLESINGER, Benjamin (1953). The social worker in
    an institutional setting for pre-school-aged
    children.
         How can it be explained to a little child what
    has become of his parents and where he is, and how
    can he be reassured and prepared to move again to a
    foster or adopting home? The caseworker's part is
    studied in this description of the Receiving Centre
    of the Children's Aid and Infants' Homes of Toronto.
    The writer learned about the children, the staff, and
    the daily routines, through direct observation, ques-
    tioning workers, and reading case records on 40 pre-
    school children who had social workers and who spent
    four months or more in the centre between January
    1951 and May 1953. The 85 per cent of the children
    who had no social workers often seemed to feel left
    out, and many stayed over a year (although a limited
    time is considered best for children needing group
    experience in an "observation" institution). Case-
    work with all is set as an ideal, and for more than
    an hour a week. Meanwhile full exhange of informa-
    tion is needed between centre staff and visiting
    social workers, and as much participation as possible
    by the caseworker in looking after a child, to help
    him become trusting and communicative.

91. SHAW, Robert C. (1959). Boys needing institutional
    care.
         The 30 boys between six and eleven years of age
    admitted between 1955 and mid-1958 to the Sacred Heart
    Children's Village who were referred through the Cath-
    olic Children's Aid Society (Toronto) were accommodated
    in the new building's smaller groups under child care

staff proportionately double the 1948 ratio to residents. Case records were analyzed here in terms of individual backgrounds, and problems at admission were classified according to the Hagan categories of problems indicating need for institutional care. Some categories overlapped: emotionally disturbed boys tended to act out their feelings and to reject parent figures. Long separation from parents, mothers especially, appeared most significantly relevant to these boys' problems. One might ask why 6 cases here, all with more stable though no less negative backgrounds, had none of the characteristic problems best treated by institutional care; perhaps lack of alternative resources is implied. The modern therapeutic use of institutions is reflected on the whole in this analysis of situations and needs.

92. STANLEY, Wilma L. (1954). Frictions in a children's institution.
   To explore the implications for group work the writer spent a week in Earlscourt Children's Home studying 25 children aged six to eleven. Her self-devised form proved useful for recording friction situations, but unmanageable for noting "leadership factors". Sociometric tests supported her judgment that low status accounted for 30 of the 189 situations, here reviewed with lifelike particulars. The observer found that a mild degree of involvement helped to make her function acceptable to the children. Friction proved minimal around breakages, duties, authority, family matters, and so on. Some friction is inevitable in group living and learning: for example, here, adults' or other children's standard-setting often created trouble. Instances of quarrelling over playthings, age or sex rivalries, lack of privacy, and intrusions, and bids for attention, suggest that to support casework help, group program in institutions might be tried as a means towards protecting, encouraging, and liberating the experiences of socially inadequate children with their contemporaries.

93. SUMMERS, Georgina M. (1951). A study of the Sacred Heart Orphanage in Toronto.
   In the perspective of the century-long records kept by the Sisters of St. Joseph on their Toronto establishment, through case records, staff interviews, and frequent visits, the writer examined this

institution's service in 1948, i.e., before the new
plant was built and one year after girls were moved
to another home to make room for pre-school boys, a
move necessitated by the shortage of foster homes
and by overcrowding in the Catholic Children's Aid
Society Nursery. There were then 55 boys in residence. About half had been there less than a year,
and 23 had brothers with them. The friendly and
wholesome atmosphere would become more homelike if
a couple could join the staff, or a male group worker,
or a man to teach indoor crafts perhaps; and better
individual provision for personal belongings is desirable. Also recommended are more detailed records and
closer co-ordination between the institution and the
two associated agencies in planning for the boys' fu-
tures.

SEE ALSO Entries 317, 406.

Unmarried Parents

94. ENO, Elaine E. (1953). Decisions of unmarried mothers
concerning disposition of their children.
    Can any group characteristics be identified for
mothers who kept their babies and those who gave them
up for adoption, as a guide to caseworkers with similar clients? This student analyzed 65 records on unmarried mothers who approached the Infants' Homes of
Toronto during January-March 1949; 34 had relinquished
their children and 26 had not. Certain factors did
seem to characterize the two groups. For example,
more women who kept their babies were young and came
from the working class, where families tend to accept
this situation. Women who released children had
higher intelligence ratings on the whole, and more
often felt negative about the putative fathers. Although 58 per cent of the babies born were male, 71
per cent of those relinquished were male. Mothers
who kept their babies were often those who had come
to the agency only late in their pregnancies. The
list of group characteristics, though tentative here,
suggests a possibly useful avenue for further research.

95. FULTON, E. Claire (1952). Time used by unmarried mothers in deciding on the disposition of their children.

This study focused on single girls between ages
sixteen and forty with only one child who received
agency casework but did not live in a maternity home
before their confinements. Of 581 such clients served
by the Children's Aid and Infants' Homes (Toronto) between January 1951 and April 1952, case records on a
random sample of 50 were analyzed, with various factors grouped according to the time that elapsed between the birth and the mother's decision about the
child's future. Factors related to the mother's own
family experiences appeared most significantly associated with the length of time needed for decisions.
Many out-of-town mothers were slow to relinquish
guardianship because of reluctance to have their home
municipalities notified in accordance with the provision that home municipalities pay wardship expenses.
The incidence of evidence suggesting negative feelings
towards the agency was highest in case records of mothers who were slowest in coming to a decision.

96. GORDON, Carmina M. (1954). Wards who become unmarried
mothers -- have they atypical backgrounds?
Of the 257 children born between 1930 and 1938
who were made permanent wards of the Children's Aid
Society of Toronto, 23 became unmarried mothers while
still under the Society's legal guardianship. Their
case records are here studied beside those of 23 other
girls made permanent wards at the same ages. With
poor school and employment records despite comparable
intelligence, and more behaviour problems in childhood, the unmarried mothers had lived in 86 different
foster homes compared with the second group's 65.
They had had fewer long-term relationships with one
social worker. Their families had more disturbed
histories, with abandonment, desertion, and lack of
parental control the commonest occasions for wardship
action (as compared with family misfortunes for the
control group). The sense of human dislocation of
these unmarried mothers validates the agency's subsequent emphasis on encouraging wards to ask about
their parents and on maintaining parent-child contacts whenever possible.

97. GUNNING, Doris L. (1947). Girls in trouble again.
Would a comprehensive study support the assumption that a psychological difficulty not solved by
motherhood characterizes "repeaters" (who constitute

roughly 4 per cent of unmarried mothers in Ontario)?
This question, and concern to improve casework relationships, directed the author's study of records on
36 unmarried women not living with the fathers of their
children who had had two or more pregnancies and were
in contact with Toronto Infants' Homes between January
and June 1946. Almost two-thirds had come from broken
homes and only 4 from homes they described as happy.
But usually what they wanted from the agency was not
help with emotional problems but specific help, with
eleventh-hour difficulties about income or foster
care. Such clients might be given more effective
service if the agency were centralized so that all
contacts led to caseworkers; if every casework relationship were helpful; and if such obstacles to good
relationships as residence requirements (involving
"betrayal" to a mother's home municipality) could be
removed.

98. HICKS, P. Phyllis (1952). Institutional care in the
     Province of Ontario for the unmarried mother in
     1950-1951.
          This paper assesses, from a social worker's
     viewpoint, the homes in Ontario, all of them founded
     by and continuing to date under religious communities.
     There are 11 such homes approved under the Charitable
     Institutions Act, serving about one-quarter of the
     province's unmarried mothers. All are located in the
     southern region. The writer visited 6 of the 11, and
     studied all the government inspector's reports and
     the submissions from the institutions. She judged
     that, although the institutions seemed to serve ad-
     equately the physical and medical needs of the mothers,
     they tended to rigidity on such matters as programs
     for daily work, religious observance, free time, breast
     feeding, and discharge dates. Administrative proce-
     dures proved diverse. Only 2 staffs included a social
     worker, and staff-training projects were virtually un-
     known. Simpler procedures are urged, to keep an ap-
     licant's official interviews to a minimum. And if the
     institutions are to serve as more than places of shel-
     ter and concealment, wider application of modern group
     work techniques and modern psychological insights is
     essential.

99. HOWDEN, Gordon N. (1962). An exploratory study of
     putative fathers.

The group studied were among the putative fathers
who during a four-month period came to the Children's
Aid Society of Metropolitan Toronto for interviews
about financial support of the unmarried mother's child.
To see whether there were other aspects of their situation which they would willingly discuss if given the
opportunity, the writer talked with 11 of the 22 aged
eighteen to forty who admitted paternity, were not repeaters, were single, and were not living in common-
law union. The study found that the group interviewed
did not adhere to the stereotype of the putative father
as being irresponsible, uncaring, and easily separated
from the problem of illegitimacy. The group did express a multiplicity of problems created by the situation, and the one problem expressed by all 11 men was
that of self-image. The study concluded that if putative fathers are individuals who express social problems, perhaps they should be regarded as potential
clients who may need casework service.

100. McGUIRE, Joan (1954). The age factor in unmarried
     motherhood.
     Viewing unmarried motherhood as, in part, "an
unconscious attempt to meet needs which should have
been met at an earlier age in another way", the writer
studied cases grouped according to chronological age:
30 girls of eighteen or under, and 30 women between
twenty-eight and forty-one, a random sampling from
the records of the Children's Aid Society and Infants'
Homes (Toronto) on younger and older unmarried mothers
who had become clients between July 1952—January 1953
during a first pregnancy. Adolescents accepted continued service twice as often, and their poorer relationships with mothers (and social workers) and
rejection of adult standards often suggested rebel-
liousness. More older women managed alone, using the
agency for brief limited services only; they were more
prone to guilt. But surely these are adolescent-adult
differences, found equally where unmarried motherhood
is not a factor. Similarities appeared too. Well-
adjusted women who initially thought of "the Aid" as
"doing adoptions" predominated in both groups. In
sum, the findings do not indicate any distinctive
pattern within either group.

101. PARLEE, Mary Julia (1959). Adolescent unmarried mothers.
     What problems do these girls and their mothers

bring to an agency? Toronto Children's Aid Society records were studied on girls whose agency contact was extensive enough, all normal in intelligence and history, and from normally constituted families: 18 of the 44 who were aged sixteen years and nine months (or younger) at confinement out of a total 693 unmarried mothers' cases closed during 1958. Like unmarried mothers studied elsewhere most of the girls were apathetic or resentful under maternal domination, and 16 had no brothers or sisters and lacked friendships with contemporaries. Many needed help with planning where to stay during pregnancy and planning for continued education or future employment. The girls, though reluctantly, usually agreed with their mothers' urgings to have the babies adopted. All 18 girls had had fairly long-term relationships with the putative fathers, and, despite their parents' objections, many wanted the putative fathers to be involved in financial arrangements.

102. PRIESTMAN, Richard W. (1956). Putative fathers.
     Since casework records on unmarried motherhood deal almost exclusively with the child and the mother, and little information has been gathered in Ontario even on the cases where agreements or court orders define the putative father's responsibility, this project was made province-wide in scope and mainly statistical in form. Using records and files in the Child Welfare Branch, supplemented by records and discussions with staffs of two Children's Aid Societies, Mr. Priestman studied factors affecting the extent to which putative fathers fulfill their obligations to maintain their illegitimate children. He selected a representative 65 cases from the 523 opened in 1939 where settlements were made, 40 of them with payments completed. Completion was commonest for voluntary agreements on lump-sum or short-term payments by men without other heavy responsibilities — regardless of employment history or income level. Allowance for local variants in cultural expectations about an illegitimate child's support, and casework with some putative fathers, would make for more realistic and effective settlements.

103. ROMKEY, Lillian (1951). Disposition of children of
     unmarried mothers with limited intelligence.
     Dismay is sometimes expressed at the idea of

motherhood for women with I.Q. ratings between 45 and
89. Do the facts warrant it? This study is based on
case records of 56 such women, unmarried mothers whose
cases were opened in 1947 with the Infants' Homes of
Toronto. Almost all were native born and 32 of their
families were known to local agencies. Of the 55
surviving children, only 5 were in the "defective"
range; 30 of the 39 who were given psychometric tests
were markedly more intelligent than their mothers.
Twelve mothers kept their babies; those who felt negative about the child's father and the youngest and
oldest mothers tended to give them up. Twenty-two
of the babies relinquished were adopted and most of
the others were placed with foster parents. Thus the
outlook was good for almost all these children, despite their mothers' limitations.

104. SCOTT, Eleanor JoAnne (1960). Significant relation-
     ships in the environment of the unmarried mother.
          Two students made a joint study of eighteen- to
     twenty-four-year-old clients with the Catholic Chil-
     dren's Aid Society (Toronto) whose cases, closed dur-
     ing 1959, involved three or more prenatal interviews
     and showed no evidence of previous pregnancies or
     delinquency. The present study focuses on 15 cases
     of girls who were living at home. Their economic,
     social, and educational characteristics were not dis-
     tinctive. Many girls, as writers found with similar
     groups elsewhere, were emotionally immature or tended
     to evade reality or lacked satisfactory relationships,
     especially with their parents. The parents of only
     one girl were separated; 5 fathers had died, with 3
     mothers remarrying; 9 homes were unbroken. However,
     one parent dominated in 14 homes -- mothers in 9
     cases and fathers in 5. Her illegitimate pregnancy
     appeared to be a characteristic part of the girl's
     struggles with the conflicting feelings associated
     with pathological child-parent relationships.

105. THOMAS, F. Gwyn (1955). A study of twenty-seven
     putative fathers who came voluntarily to a social
     agency.
          The records of 441 unmarried mothers' cases
     closed in 1952 in the Children's Aid Society and In-
     fants' Homes of Toronto mention only 27 putative
     fathers as included in service. Despite this agency's
     policy -- to leave financial agreements to the province

88

-- the focus of such service was largely concrete: arrangements or social histories for the child's sake. Yet the men indicated desire for the service by initiating or extending contacts. The records on their own parental relationships, although scant and usually unelaborated, and the 17 cases abounding in terms like "indecisive", "insecure", "unhappy", suggest considerable emotional instability. Although the 41 per cent previously married seemed more concerned about the child's care, many fathers influenced the mothers' decisions. This evidence indicates that agencies should show equal concern for father, mother, and child by being approachable and responsive to whatever clients may need and by encouraging in fathers, through help about visits, and so on, what is often a positive feeling towards their children.

106. WILSON, Nora R. (1961). A study of the Victor Home for Unmarried Mothers, 1960-61.
     Although based primarily on interviews -- with 33 current Board and staff members and residents and 4 former staff members -- this study of the home's policies and procedures, especially in relation to social work theory and practice, draws as well from published reports and minutes. In 1900 the home was a "refuge" from a hostile society where girls received religious instruction and worked "to pay their keep". Today social mores seem to tolerate extra-marital sexual relations but not a consequent pregnancy; and the Church seems to be more evasive about meeting girls' guilt feelings than is psychiatry. Work and program are seen as therapeutic; and clients' contributions to this community service vary according to each individual's best interests. A staff caseworker would apparently be welcomed, especially by out-of-town girls. This study indicates a need for a clearer definition of the agency's attitudes and policies, particularly on admissions and the make-up of staff and Board.

SEE ALSO Entries 53, 399.

107. ALBERT, S. James (1958). The incorrigible juvenile
     — who is he?
        What common factors are there in the behaviour
     and life experiences of children adjudged "incorrigi-
     ble" under our present legislation? Mr. Albert exam-
     ined the records of the Psychiatric Clinic of the
     Juvenile and Family Court of Metropolitan Toronto,
     selecting the cases of 39 boys from the 120 children
     convicted of incorrigibility in 1956, to clarify the
     nature of the crisis indicated by this charge. In
     all but a few cases the boys had experienced a broken
     home at one time or another, often at a very early
     age, with frequent foster-home placements not uncommon.
     Relations with their fathers were often poor, with the
     mothers even more unsatisfactory. Their problem be-
     haviour centred at home: stealing and lying, running
     away, late hours, destructiveness. The writer urges
     further studies. A follow-up of the cases he analyzed,
     for example, would highlight present corrective prac-
     tices. And studies of case records for children placed
     in successive foster homes and institutions, or inves-
     tigations by interview of the effect on children of
     broken homes or inadequate and unstable home life,
     would point to ways of preventing situations that make
     for children "beyond control".

108. ANDERSON, Frank W. (1957). Ontario's extramural per-
     mit system.
        This historical account draws on annual reports,
     files, surveys, and very extensively on the published
     and unpublished writings of Dr. Alfred E. Lavell who,
     in October 1920, began the first systematic administer-
     ing of an experiment that was being tried then at Lang-
     staff. He worked out the official procedures: each
     permit holder was individually investigated and as-
     signed to a duly appointed voluntary costodial officer
     wherever his family or friends had found him work; he
     remained in jail or at home every night, assigned his
     pay on prearranged terms, and was liable to the same
     punishment for infractions as any other prisoner.
     Some 2,500 permits were granted altogether. Failure
     rates were very low. Moreover, custodial costs were
     reduced and many families were spared resort to public

assistance. But by 1932 with a change of personnel —
and no incumbent trained — the system became obsolete.
Perhaps the precedent could suggest new directions in
today's rehabilitation services.

109. APPLEBY, Edith E. (1948). Rehabilitation services for
the female offender in the province of Ontario.
The procedures in local institutions in 1947 are
here described and evaluated according to contemporary
standards for corrective practices. In 1947 there
were three institutions for women serving sentences in
Ontario, two of them in Toronto. Information summarized from reports of these institutions and from con-
versations with their administrators suggests that,
apart from medical and dental care, programs showed
too little concern for individuals. Initial class-
ifying was needed so that alcoholics, drug addicts,
psychopaths, and younger offenders (aged sixteen to
twenty) might be segregated. More time and a better
range of courses in the education and vocational
training program, and better interpretation of work
and recreational program, would help shift the emphasis from punishment to rehabilitation. No non-
sectarian organization then existed to help women
released from custody during the period of adaptation.
Efforts are recommended to promote more use of parole
and to develop in the community more encouraging attitudes and actions.

110. ARCHIBALD, H. David (1951). A comparison of reactions
to punishment.
Is there any difference between the punishment
for infractions in the reformatory and the punishments
a boy had experienced at home and in school which
clearly failed to "keep him out of trouble"? On the
hypothesis that punishments in the institution not
only fail to "reform" but are destructive as well,
the writer interviewed 50 of the 111 boys who had
spent about five months in Guelph Reformatory from
October 1947 on. Scoldings had been accepted oftener
at school than at home or in custody, but physical
and verbal punishments in all settings usually evoked
vengeful, hostile, or angry feelings. In most cases
attitudes towards authority, outside and inside the
reformatory, were poor. Punishment inside seemed excessive, affecting 31 boys and involving "the Machine"

91

(strapping) and solitary confinement. A more helpful
approach based on understanding of individual backgrounds would be necessary in order to change attitudes
— as three appended case histories forcibly demonstrate.

111. ATKINSON, Doris E. (1947). Sexual delinquencies in
juvenile girls.
        Sexual delinquency is, after incorrigibility,
the commonest complaint against girls in the Toronto
Juvenile Court and is usually associated with the
other major misdemeanors. To see whether any factors
distinguish these from other delinquency cases, the
writer studied probation files and the records of the
Court's Psychiatric Clinic on 58 girls with charges
confirmed in gynecological reports. Two-thirds had
contracted venereal disease and one-fifth had become
pregnant. More than two-thirds of the parents were
divorced or separated. As one girl remarked, "When
girls leave home it is because their homes are not
cheerful." Although 69 per cent had normal intelligence, 86 per cent disliked or did not care about
school. Five summarized histories portray the girls:
characteristically selfish, unhappy, quick-tempered,
constant movie-goers, and not exceptionally popular
with or interested in boys. Since sexual delinquency
appears as a symptom of emotional insecurity, could
not earlier symptoms like truancy be recognized, the
writer asks, in time for preventive action, such as
casework with the parents?

112. BARRASS, Dorothy F. (1948). A study of thirty-three
delinquent girls.
        The study includes all those committed by the
Toronto Juvenile Court to the Ontario Training School
for Girls (Galt) during 1937-1941. Court, Department
of Reform Institutions, and the training school records show stressful and deprived backgrounds for these
girls convicted usually at age fourteen or fifteen for
truancy, incorrigibility, or vagrancy. Only 7 girls
had lived consistently with both parents; over half
their families had known economic dependency, and almost three-quarters, severe mental or physical afflic-
tion. In the school 90 per cent had been isolated in
detention, 81 per cent lost "privileges" including the
right to send or receive letters, and one-third received

92

strapping. Running away was conspicuous among reasons
for punishment. Those who boarded and worked on parole
before returning home moved often and kept "switching
jobs", but there were fewer relapses than among those
discharged directly home. The fact that two-fifths
reverted to delinquency after discharge indicates a
need for a better psychiatrically-oriented program and
atmosphere, and more individually-focused vocational
help.

113. BAUMAN, Carl (1959). Drunkenness offenders.
      Although he set out to study the group "alcohol-
ics" by comparing social participation of married and
single drinkers, the writer found that his focus gradually shifted to one sub-group: non-participants in
our society. Through intensive interviews he studied
21 men in a Toronto jail in July 1956 who had been arrested for public intoxication, and who previously,
but since 1953, had taken treatment at an alcoholism
clinic operated under penal services. These men were
older than other petty offenders, with an over-all
occupational distribution below their fathers' despite
slightly better educations. Not one had managed to
stop drinking after therapy; any gains in abstinence
were negligible. All had deteriorated very gradually
but now were habituated to "Skid Row" ways. In early
life 18 of the 21 had chosen employment where shelter
and food were "found" for them (lumber camps, merchant
marine, etc.). Compulsory residential care might now
best meet both the psychological and physical needs
of confirmed alcoholics, the writer suggests.

114. BAUMGARTEL, Bernd W. (1955). A study of some aspects
      of juvenile delinquency among children of immi-
      grants.
      Full Canadian statistics are lacking, but prob-
ably here as in the United States the rate of crime
among their children far exceeds that among immigrants
themselves, although remaining below the rate for long-
established nationals. From clinic records the writer
studied 75 factors, on key-sort cards, for 418 boys
appearing before Toronto's Juvenile Court during 1950-
51 and sent to the Psychiatric Clinic for examination,
134 with foreign-born and 284 with Canadian-born parents. The latter group had proportionately more broken
homes, working mothers, and economic insecurity, less

church affiliation, and poorer school adjustment.
More boys in the first group had "satisfactory" homes,
but 46 per cent of them compared with 29 per cent of
"old Canadians" had gang affiliations, which seemed
to mean to them "belonging" in the "new world". Close-
range studies would be needed to assess the intensity
and force of influences. But where sharply different
individuals feel that their differentness must be dis-
proved before the community will accept them, group
workers and caseworkers could clearly help.

115. BLACKBURN, Walter W., and McGRATH, William T. (1948).
    One hundred graduates of B.T.S. (the Ontario
    Training School for Boys, Bowmanville).
        From records in the B.T.S., Toronto Juvenile
    Court, and the Department of Reform Institutions, the
    writers derived information on the 103 Toronto boys
    admitted to the school, April 1, 1937 to March 31,
    1939: their backgrounds and earlier experiences, their
    stay in residence, and the period of their "conditional
    release". Later adjustment of the 86 whose wardship
    had been terminated five years or more, rated simply
    in terms of subsequent criminal records, helps bring
    apparently negative factors into sharp outline. Later
    failures were predominantly boys of British-born par-
    ents from poor neighbourhoods whose families had ex-
    perienced financial dependence but not criminal
    convictions, boys young on committal who had the great-
    est number of offences recorded against them in the
    school and were kept there longest. During supervised
    placement 40 boys succeeded, more on farms than in
    their own homes, although in the period beyond super-
    vision boys at home were more successful. A more
    individually-planned, vocationally-oriented training
    program, extended preventive service, and further re-
    search, are recommended.

116. BROWN, David F. (1962). A comparison of the results
    of probation and imprisonment as methods of re-
    habilitating offenders.
        Rates of reconviction, during a 34-month period
    following discharge, of 200 offenders sentenced to
    reformatories by one court in Metropolitan Toronto in
    1958 are compared with those for 500 offenders placed
    on probation by the same court in the same year as
    determined in another thesis (the 34-month follow-up

study by William Outerbridge, Entry 134). In both
theses age, nature of offence, and previous criminal
records were analyzed. The following conclusions are
drawn: that the application of probation should be extended to include all first offenders; that present
provisions should be applied and probation used for
offenders with one previous conviction, and for those
eligible with more than one conviction; that age
should not be a criterion in selecting probationers;
that probation should be applied oftener in cases of
sexual offenders or offenders against the person.

117. COUSE, A. Keith (1960). Excessive drinking and criminal behaviour.
       The focus is on a group of offenders rather than
"drinkers", the 296 men referred in 1958 to the Toronto
Office of the John Howard Society through pre-release
services. Institutional and pre-release documentation
usefully supplemented data in the Society's and parole
authorities' files, even though it is available only
from institutions for older offenders serving longer
sentences and thus weighted the sample here. Hence a
suggestion that minor inebriate offences tend to predominate among drinkers after age thirty-five could
be supported only by inference. The excessive drinkers
-- 121 rather older men -- had committed a higher proportion of less serious crimes against the person,
fraud, and minor sexual offences; only a few excessive
drinkers were guilty of serious offences such as armed
robbery. Criminal activity had preceded excessive
drinking for all but 37, and only 4 per cent of all
offences (9 per cent of excessive drinkers' offences)
were committed during intoxication. Thus, caution is
counselled in attributing offences to drinking and
thereby occasioning treatment that may be unrealistic.

118. DINGMAN, Frank S. (1948). The story of the Wellington County Family Court.
       Reports, records, and interviews with five in-
terested citizens provided facts on the 1941-46
campaign to bring this court into being and on its
first two years' history; Children's Aid Society
files documented the earlier phase -- four decades
of crusading, interrupted by the 1914-18 war and then
the depression. Family stresses during the Second
World War, the growing interest of some twenty-five

agencies, and their readier co-operation after the
Council of Social Agencies was formed in 1941, built
up the pressure for action. Apportioning of Guelph
and County responsibilities for this joint project
was time-consuming, and only a last-minute direct
approach forestalled a provincial-local deadlock on
choice of personnel. The Family Court in Guelph
works closely with social work and psychiatric services in the community. Since Guelph has no detention home and no family agency, the court employs
probation whenever possible, and provides some counselling service for adults.

119. ELLIS, Barbara L. (1953). A comparative study of
        delinquent girls.
        Two decades after the opening of the Ontario
Training School for Girls (Galt) this study examines
a five-year total (from 1948 when the school introduced casework services) of girls transferred to the
Mercer Reformatory, in the hope that factors in these
25 cases might suggest new methods of therapy. Their
case histories are compared with files on 25 of the
225 girls in that period not sent to the maximum security institution. In intelligence the reformatory
group rated equal or superior to the control group.
Nor could abnormal home structures explain their continuing difficulties, for the control group contained
the only three illegitimate children and twice as
many wards. But the transferred girls had almost all
known rejection or abuse at home, significantly often
with a substitute parent involved. The school found
all but three "unable to relate to anyone", and all
beyond reach of the school's services.

120. FELSTINER, James P. (1961). Admissions by application
        to Ontario Training Schools.
        Section 10 of Ontario's Training School Act,
passed in 1939 and still in force, empowers the Minister
of Reform Institutions to determine "as he may think
fit" the admission to a training school of any wards
of a Children's Aid Society or any child whose parents
or guardians consent. The writer collected official
figures on all such admissions, and read the 258 case
records for 1956-61 in the Departmental Office of the
Training School. Training schools assume guardianship
in those cases admitted without court hearings, without

96

legal review; this applies even to temporary wards. Records on which the Minister's Advisory Board bases its decisions vary widely, but no request for fuller information was noted and only one of 107 applications in 1959-60, for example, was refused. All but 3 of the 258 cases could have been taken before a juvenile court judge for commitment. Local variations in the over-all 7 per cent proportion of admission to committal cases reflect disagreements on policies between court and agency. Development of more diverse resources and scrupulous administration are urged, pending the repeal of Section 10.

121. GIBSON, Barbara (1955). Twenty-nine delinquent children.

The subjects of this study were the 29 permanent wards of the Toronto Children's Aid Society and Infants' Homes who had appeared in the Juvenile Court and had been sentenced to institutions, 1947-51. By examining court records and agency case records the writer hoped to increase understanding of the delinquent. Although many of the complex factors cited by authorities as conducive to delinquency apply to many wards, the 29 represent a minute proportion of the agency caseload over a five-year period. Yet insecurity and lack of clear parental standards and control predictably increase the difficulties at adolescence. The court psychiatrists portray this group's deprivations when they list the most frequent problems: stealing, then lying, then disobeying, then running away. The 29 children had had a total of 273 moves while under wardship. Hence the writer suggests a treatment centre for disturbed children when foster homes seem ineffective, and continued emphasis on work to protect families against breakdown.

122. GLASSCO, Leon H. (1956). Meeting the needs of dull normal delinquent boys.

To assess this community function, records are analyzed for 48 boys identified as delinquents in the Toronto Juvenile Court and enrolled in 1948-52 at the Church Street School for children with low-range intelligence ratings. Such children, often further limited by poor health, know much about deprivation and little about warm human relationships or meaningful learning and play. Although the court's clinic

assesses each boy's background, comparable care in
treatment is not evident; e.g., periodic re-assessment
was often recommended but not once carried out; medical
or psychiatric services were not secured when the clinic
noted such symptoms as eneuresis, stuttering, or tic.
Training school and supervision by a probation officer
were mainly used, and sometimes recreational organizations, but never where a group worker was available.
The high incidence of alcoholism or separation in the
homes of these children indicated the need for more
casework services. Judged by this sample, the community is not yet functioning coherently in the interests
of these boys.

123. GROSS, Dora Pishker (1955). A study of the Ontario
Training School for Girls.
    As a resident visitor for two weeks in 1952 the
writer gathered information from staff and records for
an evaluation of the school in the context of its history and the established criteria for such corrective
institutions. Most of the 129 girls, committed through
the Juvenile Court after other resources had failed,
were fourteen or fifteen years old, of normal or superior intelligence, and progressing with their age group
in school. Of 43 judged in need of psychiatric treatment only 17 were receiving it. However, other facilities — for sports, medical care, counselling, education
and vocational training — seemed adequate and well
staffed. Admission and placement procedures were perhaps in need of review. Research is particularly recommended on the connection between disturbed girls'
hostile feelings and the pressure for "good behaviour"
imposed by the percentage system of discipline, the
proportion of runaways, and the effect of isolation on
those who offend against disciplinary regulations.

124. JACKSON, J. David (1957). Rehabilitation after prison.
    The writer studied case histories of 71 men who
served full terms in two penitentiaries, were released
in 1954 from September on, and had contact with the
John Howard Society. He compared the 24 men "rehabilitated" with the 47 convicted again within eighteen
months. Most were Canadian-born, in their thirties.
Differences were negligible in post-release employment,
financial help, housing. The "rehabilitated" men had
been slightly more co-operative in prison and markedly

more realistic in planning how to resume responsible
life afterwards. A significantly larger proportion
were married, and had strong relationships with relatives at the time of release. The findings suggest
that social workers' pre-release interviews should
occur well before the stress of the last few days,
and that the first six months outside are the crucial
ones. Indecisiveness rather than hostility or apathy
marked the recidivists. To help them, social workers
may have to accept limited goals, or work with consulting doctors, or perhaps through group counselling.

125. JUDD, Fernand (1961). The sentencing policy of the
    Juvenile Court of Hamilton.
    The court's range and flexibility in using
available resources are studied here from data in the
court and probation officers' records on the 28 boys
committed to training schools and the 115 placed on
probation out of the total of 461 boys who appeared
before the Hamilton Juvenile Court in 1960. Of the
group committed to training schools (characteristically a solitary offender, unsatisfactory in school,
charged with incorrigibility or theft, whose family
was known to a social agency and to the courts), pre-
sentence reports were provided on 27 of the 28, and
mental health reports on 16. For the probationers
there were proportionately fewer reports. The judges'
reliance on these reports, and the extensive use of
social workers in preliminary investigations, indicate
need for more court probation officers. But although
present facilities permit careful planning for only a
small proportion of young offenders, the court's readiness to use these facilities reflects its respect and
concern for the boys it treats.

126. KLEIN, Isobel M. (1949). Recidivism among juvenile
    delinquents.
    This statistical analysis of factors in the
background of offenders is based on the Toronto Court
Clinic's records. All 257 male juvenile cases examined
there for the first time in 1940 are included, the 117
who appeared only once before the court as well as the
140 subsequently charged at least a second time. Hypotheses based upon studies elsewhere are tested, and
most of the expected correlations recur here: between
parental alcoholism or broken marriages, for example,

99

and a child's stealing or truancy. Many children
became recurrent offenders in spite of having participated in organized group activities and having experienced school treatment in special classes for
those troubled and troublesome. The writer calls
for early efforts to reach and work with parents
where homes are emotionally unstable, and a steady
communal concern about the economic insecurity which
is found in close association with high delinquency
rates.

127. LACEY, W. Robert (1952). Factors in the background
of the imprisoned chronic inebriate.
     This study investigates one group of problem
drinkers in an attempt at better understanding and
insight into treatment possibilities. Records of
the Ontario Department of Reform Institutions were
consulted: on a control group of 88 committed in
1948-49 to the Burwash Industrial Farm for various
indictable offences; and on 240 "inebriates" (defined for this project as those serving at least a
second sentence for drunkenness under the Ontario
Liquor Control Act) selected monthly over the same
fiscal year from committals to the Mimico Reformatory; 10 per cent of the subjects were also interviewed. The chronic inebriates were older on average
than the other offenders, more rootless, and with
poor school, job, and marital records. Those previously indicted for other offences, perhaps turning
from anti-social to asocial behaviour, should be
studied fruther as a distinct group. Since the reformatory seemed to offer respite but no remedy, it
is recommended that special clinical or custodial
care and therapy for alcoholics be developed.

128. LUCAS, Jane I. (1958). A study of girls charged
under the Female Refuges Act.
     Through the records in the Psychiatric Clinic,
Juvenile and Family Court of Metropolitan Toronto,
all 27 girls aged sixteen to eighteen when so charged
in 1952-57 are here studied. Although almost two-
thirds were of average or superior intelligence and
all the families were self-supporting, none had stayed
in school past sixteen, 14 having truancy and 5 expul-
sion in their records. Yet only 8 were employed when
charged. Few had enjoyed satisfactory friendships or

recreation. Many girls' mothers were neurotic or hap-
less, fathers were present in only 10 homes, and only
4 homes were without unmistakeable discord. Drinking
and criminality appeared in half the backgrounds, and
repressive, unrealistic attitudes in one-quarter.
Sexual misconduct was the commonest complaint. Two-
thirds of the records noted girls "profoundly disturbed and overcome with a resentful hostility
against all authority". The others seemed, through
more inherent strengths or some chance association
that had been positive, able to co-operate. The community needs more preventive alertness, and adequate
institutional resources.

129. McFARLANE, George Gordon (1956). Where do they turn?
To what extent do families of men incarcerated in
penal institutions seek help in the community?
Toronto Magistrate's Court lists showed that 79
local residents, committed during 1954 to over three
months' imprisonment for indictable offences, had dependent families, including some 160 young children.
Their cases were compared with those of 52 childless
married male prisoners, and investigated by questionnaires to 52 agency units and by study of agency records as the 41 responses directed. Families turned
oftenest to the City for public assistance and to the
Salvation Army for supplementary help. Only 3 applied
for Mothers' Allowances, which are available only in
specified circumstances, although provincially-
administered allowances could best allow families mobility and self-respect. Both prisoner groups were
80 per cent recidivists, using community services 23
per cent more than had their parental families. Courts
did not regularly consider personal grounds in sentencing or granting supervised early release. To co-
ordinate services, prevent relapses, and more justly
distribute the burden crime imposes, centralized statistics are needed, more use of pre-sentence investigation, and more accessible recourse for families until
the offender is again employed.

130. McGRATH, William T. (1948). See Entry 115.

131. MAIN, Stanley (1950). A study of thirty-six adult
male recidivists.
Who are these perennially unreformed in provincial

reform institutions and what do they think of their situation? Choosing local residents (whose provincial and institutional records the Social Service Index could supplement), men under thirty-five, not addicted to drugs or alcohol, and with histories of three or more convictions, the writer interviewed 36 who in June and July 1949 were serving sentences in the Ontario Reformatory (Guelph). Almost all had grown up during the depression and war, in overcrowded homes in deteriorating neighbourhoods. Alternatives to imprisonment -- probation, fines, suspended sentences -- had initially been tried for two-thirds of the men. Almost all resisted training or recreation. Over half had been strapped in prison. Workers', teachers', and parents' groups should explore the evident inadequacy of schools for such boys. Where anti-social behaviour problems are deep-rooted, more staff, including a psychiatrist and several social workers to provide therapy, may be able to help both individuals and, in the long run, the public purse.

132. MELICHERCIK, John (1954). Employment problems of former offenders.
     Economic concern is only one factor in the total dislocation a man experiences when he leaves prison with one new suit and cash enough for a day or two, at best. To find out how employers receive him, and why, Mr. Melichercik interviewed 50 of them (6 in the civil service and public utilities and 44 in private business and industry chosen in proportion to the occupations of prisoners released in 1952) and 5 men in bonding companies or trade unions. Apparently the greatest obstacles to economic rehabilitation are a man's high expectations, society's prejudices, and a poor labour market. Only one employer in three -- and then always hiring unskilled labour -- would disregard a "record". Thus vocational training in reform institutions will only increase later frustration unless combined with concentrated efforts in job finding; and suitable employment for former offenders, mechanics and businessmen especially, will depend largely on public attitudes.

133. NAGEL, Harry N. (1957). Employment problems of male offenders on parole.
     The writer interviewed 27 of the 34 Toronto parolees under John Howard Society supervision who

were out of penitentiaries for at least a month and
agreed to co-operate in this study. His Time Projec-
tion Chart, identifying as significant the immediate
post-release days, the first payday, and the "doldrums
period" ending with self-sufficiency, provided a useful opening topic. Although they were, by definition,
the best rehabilitation risks, these men had all experienced occupational downgrading. After an average
of twenty months almost half, including those highly
skilled in needed occupations, had not been able to
get into their own line of work. Telling about their
"record", most agreed, meant joblessness; "living a
lie", though nerve-racking, at least gave them a chance.
After being a robot "down below", the parolee needs
trained counselling during his decompression period.
The men's psychological condition, employers' preju-
dices, and financial pressures, all endanger their
rehabilitation. Further studies might follow up this
group, analyze the post-release "fog" experience, and
examine the relationship between recidivism and inadequate gratutiies and periods of joblessness.

134. OUTERBRIDGE, William R. (1962). An empirical study
of the restrictions on eligibility for probation.
        This study was designed to provide some answers
to the following questions: To what extent are legal
restrictions on eligibility for probation employed in
the granting of probation? Do the restrictions, when
followed, achieve their purpose, namely, differentiating between offenders who have a good rehabilitative
potential and those who have not? Is the purpose of
these restrictions a legitimate one in terms of the
broad social issues inherent in corrections? A sample
of 500 probationers placed under supervision in Metropolitan Toronto in 1958 was grouped according to the
extent of previous criminal record. These groups were
further sub-divided according to whether or not they
were legally eligible for probation according to the
restrictions on eligibility found in the Criminal Code.
The rates of success or failure on probation were then
established for each group of eligible and ineligible
offenders. Cross-references were made with other possible determinants of success or failure, such as age
at the time of conviction, and the type of offence
for which members of the sample were convicted. Results indicate that legal restrictions are employed

only to a limited degree, partly because they are regarded by some members of the Bench as suggestions rather than mandatory bars to eligibility, partly because of lack of clarity of certain phrases found in the law, and partly because criminal records are not always submitted at the time of disposition. When applied, the legal restrictions tend to serve their purpose, but whether this purpose is a legitimate one is open to question.

135. REID, D.C.S. (1962). Factors affecting application for after-care service.
    The purpose of the study was to provide information on the factors fostering or inhibiting applications for after-care service. Indirectly the study aimed at permitting more effective use to be made of the services of after-care agencies, and at better planning of pre-release procedures. It was conducted at the John Howard Society in Toronto. Data on 179 ex-prisoners were examined and the results tested for statistical significance where appropriate. It was hypothesized that economic need, and willingness to work and to improve one's occupational status, would foster application for after-care service; lack of understanding due to foreign nationality or poor educational standing would inhibit it; criminal sophistication might affect it either way. None of the hypotheses was supported, but some specific results were statistically significant or nearly significant. They implied that lack of accommodation, alcoholism and drug addiction, and disturbed family relationships foster after-care applications. They also provided suggestions for future research.

136. ROBINSON, Ruth B. (1948). Truant-delinquents.
    The Toronto Juvenile Court Clinic has been amassing medical and social information on delinquents for over twenty-eight years. Coded facts are here analyzed on 225 patients of a total 596 examined in 1946-47 whose truancy had been stressed, and records are examined on 115 such cases in 1947. The prominence of English-born parents, the English school-leaving at age fourteen, and the high incidence among patients of mid-teenagers, may be correlated. Almost 80 per cent of the parents compared with 58 per cent in the general population had passed no more than eight grades in

school; 53 per cent of the truants studied were academically retarded, over half of these of normal or superior intelligence but almost all of them from broken or unsatisfactory homes. Only 15 per cent of parent-child relationships were adjudged "sound": such phrases as "struck her and broke her nose", "alcoholic", "constantly nagging", etc., appeared in the first ten case records examined. Truancy is a danger signal; these findings can guide preventive work through schools and family agencies.

137. SCOTT, J.A. (1957). Twenty-one problem boys in the training school setting.
Do factors in home and community experience predetermine behaviour of "difficult" boys? Out of the group transferred as unmanageable from one of Ontario's open training schools to the closed school in Guelph between 1950 and 1957, Mr. Scott selected cases where background records were available (18 from Toronto and Hamilton Juvenile Courts and 3 from a Children's Aid Society). He rated behaviour in the training school by combining questionnaire returns from three staff members for each boy. Although no single factor, such as poor father-son relationship, emerged as decisive, boys with most negative social histories tended to have lowest behaviour ratings. Surprisingly, faulty work habits appeared in vocational as much as in academic courses. In view of the importance of understanding every factor in terms of its meaning to a particular boy, further study of this group through interviews is recommended. A comparative study is also proposed of behaviour in an open and a closed training school setting.

138. STRATHY, Peter Arthur (1961). The expectations of the parole and parole supervision experience held by penitentiary inmates prior to their release on parole.
The applicant's approach to the new parole system (established since the 1956 Fauteux Report) may condition both his success and therefore the community's support of rehabilitative efforts. In three months of early 1961 the writer interviewed 30 of the 35 applicants for parole in three penitentiaries who had never been paroled and had experienced the pre-release program. They had absorbed less than officials

expected, partly through tension during interviews, partly because of misinformation from parole violators within the inmates' social system, and partly because suspicion and resistances had not been worked through. John Howard Society representatives had communicated more effectively than had government spokesmen, but still only 40 per cent struck the writer as "ready to make a productive use of the professional relationship" offered by the parole system. Separate pre-release communities may best enable workers and supervisors to counteract distortions, and to support and prepare men for the transition through parole to responsible freedom.

139. TAYLOR, Dickson E. (1952). A study of adult probation in Ontario.
England and the States have used probation for over a half-century with ever-increasing confidence and flexibility. Ontario, according to documents and spokesmen interviewed, was slow to develop arrangements for provincially-supported probation officers, and municipalities were even slower to avail themselves. Statistics for ten years' work of the Toronto Adult Probation Department and analysis of a random 8.6 per cent sample (75 cases) from 1951 records, convey the limited and uneven development of the service here. Only magistrates' courts use probation to any extent, and then only for some 3 per cent of offenders. In Toronto 3 female probation officers prepare pre-sentence reports as requested (959 in 1950-51); 6 male officers supervise 76 to 111 probationers each (870 in the same year, not necessarily those on whom reports had been prepared). The present facilities are poor and inadequate to give uniform service if courts were to use probation fully, which they will do only as persons concerned explain the program to the public.

140. TESSARO, Angelo Fortunato (1956). The juvenile male sex offender.
Mr. Tessaro studied comparative statistics and analyzed data from records in the Psychiatric Clinic of the Toronto Juvenile Court on boys aged twelve to sixteen who were examined there during 1948-52 -- 60 who had been involved in sexual misbehaviour and 60 general offenders chosen at random. The sex offenders' fathers were often of higher occupational status; fewer

of their families were known to agencies or had histories of criminality or alcoholism; more claimed church affiliation. However, in many instances births had been abnormal and parents were rejecting or overprotective. The number outside regular schools despite average or superior intelligence points to inadequate preventive and diagnostic service. The relevance of birth trauma to later sex offences is suggested for further study: perhaps postnatal service should be emphasized when births are abnormal. A surprising proportion of these boys were sent to training school. Perhaps concurrent parent-child counselling could make probation more workable.

141. VINE, William George (1962). <u>The child, the court, and the training school.</u>
     This is a study of the 65 boys committed by juvenile courts to the Ontario Training School, Bowmanville, and subsequently transferred to Cobourg January to May 1960. The original objective of the study, i.e., to assess the boys' needs as a basis for judging the adequacy of the treatment program, proved unworkable. The records in the Department of Reform Institution's files were often sketchy, in only three cases designed for assessment of a child's need. Presentence reports were nonexistent for over half the 65 boys. Statistical analysis did reveal a disproportionate number of convicted "delinquents" (including almost all the mental defectives in the group) coming from small cities with inadequate community resources. Study and observation showed the school to be overcrowded, pressed to keep releases in balance with court-controlled admissions, and limited in facilities for serving any but overt needs. Some centralizing of information and of preventive and treatment services is desirable: one case now may involve three disconnected administrative authorities, thus permitting the perpetuation of an outmodedorientation to the offence rather than the young offender's behaviour as indicative of his needs.

142. WILSON, H.L. (1954). <u>The use of the prerogative of mercy in Canada.</u>
     The criticism of the Canadian Remissions Branch by the Archambault Commission, 1938, suggested the focus of this study. The basic data from Dominion

Bureau of Statistics' reports, 1899-1948, supplemented
by other official documents such as Dominion Parole
Officers' reports, until 1931, show that although population and indictable offences increased steadily,
the proportion of pardons and paroles levelled off
around 1914. In war years and during the depression
of the 1930's the prerogative was exercised oftener --
1933 marked the fifty-year peak for conditional re-
leases on tickets-of-leave. By 1938 the ticket-of-
leave system seemed too informal and unregulated in
the selection of men, without affording requisite
supervision in social and work adjustments. The
higher incidence of severe sentences (to sidestep
wretched local jails?) -- and so of clemency -- in
Eastern Canada suggested the need for centralized
planning. Further explorations are suggested of the
history of pardons, paroles, Ontario's Parole Board,
the old Extramural Employment plan, and a follow-up
of men released after tickets-of-leave.

GROUP PROJECT. Social and emotional needs of the
    chronic petty offender.
    This project, closely related to social action,
was undertaken by a group of social work students,
supported by two doctoral candidates in psychology.
It was assumed that repeated short-term sentences imposed on chronic petty offenders are serving no deterrent purpose and might even satisfy some social and
emotional needs of the repeaters. The project aimed
at determining more precisely the nature of these
needs so that more humane and more economical action
could be planned in order to meet them, possibly outside the penal system; 79 male and 30 female offenders
in two Toronto reformatories were interviewed and
tested. The social work students developed and used
an interviewing schedule dealing with the social background, the present situation, the desires and fears,
and the attitudes of the offenders towards their confinement, their mode of life, and possible social
action aiming at solving their problems. The psychologists used intelligence and personality tests to determine some of the handicaps and emotional needs not
easily tapped by interviews.

143. ALLEN, Dexter R. (1961). Employment and the chronic
     petty offender.
          Work histories, qualifications and skills, and
     expectations of future employment of male and female
     offenders are examined by the author. He analyzes
     reasons for their liking or disliking the occupations
     they have had, and reports their attitudes towards
     work, to find that quite a number left their best job
     because they did not like it, and most others left
     their best job -- and other jobs -- through drunkenness.
     Some of the subjects interviewed stated that, if the
     release program helped them more effectively to make a
     proper start and to get accommodation and a suitable
     job, they would not return to drink and would not re-
     turn to the reformatory. It was found, however, that
     the very same subjects did, at some time or another,
     have relatively suitable jobs -- relative to their own
     qualifications -- but they did return to drink and sub-
     sequently to the reformatory. Their pattern of employ-
     ment shows clearly deterioration, until they are unable
     to work outside the prison walls. The author concludes
     that it is unrealistic to expect the chronic petty of-
     fenders, who have so many inadequacies, to compete with
     the more energetic workmen for employment in the open
     labour market. They need help to be as productive as
     their ability permits, and it seems that this can be
     done only through a sheltered workshop.

144. LICHTENSTEIN, Doreen H. (1963). The chronic petty
     offender and his attitude towards institutional
     experiences, authority, and the law.
          The author describes in some detail the institu-
     tional setting in w ich the enquiry was conducted, and
     then analyzes the attitudes of her subjects as revealed
     in interviews and in personality tests. She deals with
     features of the institutional life which the inmates
     like, and those which they dislike. Their reactions
     to the first and subsequent incarcerations, and to the
     agencies of law enforcement and the administration of
     justice, are reported. It appears that the main dis-
     satisfaction of the chronic petty offenders in the
     institutions springs from their humiliation, from the
     fact of forceable detention. Being arrested is what
     they hate, rather than being in prison. Their attitude
     to reformatory staff is generally positive, while that
     to the police, the courts, and the law is negative.
     The reformatories satisfy most of their social and

emotional needs: for steady work and shelter, for companionship provided by other inmates, and for understanding which, the inmates claim, the reformatory staff possess to a greater degree than does society at large.

145. WALSH, Norma M. (1961). Chronic petty offenders and their patterns of life: a study of 109 inmates at Mimico and Mercer Reformatories.
    Background data for other studies in the same group project are provided in this study, which contains a detailed description of the setting and method of the total project. It describes the sample in terms of birthplace, race, age, religious affiliation, marital status, intelligence, education, health, employment, criminal history, and use of alcohol. Personal relationships of the subjects are examined -- especially contact with family and friends, shared activities, and mutual support -- as well as participation in organized activities, patterns of sexual behaviour, church attendance, activities immediately after the last release from confinement, and plans for the future. The author concludes that heavy drinking and repeated imprisonment are integral parts of her subjects' pattern of life and reflect their social and personal inadequacies. They seem to live in isolation and to have no friends outside their own peculiar society. Three typical case histories are appended.

GROUP PROJECT. Social status, personality, and behaviour of juvenile delinquents in Ontario Training Schools.
    This project aimed at examining a number of loosely interrelated topics within the framework of a common methodology, which included: behaviour ratings by Training School staff, a sociometric questionnaire, a personality test (Grygier's Likes and Interests Test), and a schedule aimed at concise recording of material extracted from the files and amenable to statistical analysis. The project aimed at developing a method of measurement capable of showing the extent to which a Training School can be a "therapeutic community" or, conversely, is split by a cleavage between the children and their relationship to the nature of their offences, the tendency of some children to escape from the School, recidivism, institutionalization, and family

history, with special reference to separation from the father, the mother, or both, and to inadequate parental image. Data on 185 boys and 108 girls in 4 Training Schools were collected and analyzed.

146. AARON, Joan S. (1962). A study of escapees: their sociometric status and personality.
    Data on the social background, the sociometric status, the personality profile, and behaviour at the Training School were collected on each child involved in this study, and the differences between 70 children who had attempted an escape from any institutional placement and 220 other children were analyzed. No statistically significant differences were found, except for behaviour ratings; it was impossible to determine whether escape can be treated as a cause or the effect of rejection of the child by the staff. Data on personality structure, although not statistically reliable, suggest that, in contrast with a normal school, these children are not necessarily socially or mentally maladjusted; most of them merely react to a temporary maladjustment due to an abnormal social situation.

147. EWALD, F.E.A. (1962). A study of values in Ontario Training Schools.
    The author hypothesized that a cleavage in values between the children and the staff of the Training Schools would reflect conflict and disharmony, characteristic of a "prison community". Conversely, agreement on values would be typical of a "therapeutic community". Agreement on values was measured by correlating the sociometric status of the children with their behaviour ratings by the School staff; it was assumed that if the children chosen as friends by their peers tend to be chosen as well behaved by the School personnel, there is agreement on the desirable pattern of behaviour and a value system consistent with it. The data suggest that in Training Schools for boys there is a statistically significant agreement on values; this is particularly true of a school for younger children and a small school for very difficult and disturbed children which has an active treatment program. There is a greater acceptance of staff values if these are clearly expressed in rules of conduct and if definite limits of freedom are set; conversely, units which follow a principle of minimal restrictions, and which avoid

a clear statement of policy, are less successful in influencing children's behaviour. The girls studied showed no agreement on values with the School staff, and a special research is suggested to elucidate this.

148. WILSON, Elizabeth A. (1962). The effect of father separation and faulty father image on juvenile delinquent behaviour in girls.
      Data on family background, early history, and later adjustment on 105 delinquent girls in a Training School were examined. In each case data concerning the father were compared with those on the mother. It was found that where there was evidence of paternal pathology (especially permanent separation of the father from the child other than by his death, or a faulty paternal image) there was almost invariably evidence of maternal pathology. The converse was also true. It was difficult to isolate paternal and maternal pathology and, consequently, the effect of each; but paternal pathology was more frequent to a statistically significant degree. The study questions the present emphasis on the supposed detrimental effect of the early separation of the child from his mother; separation due to death or illness was extremely rare in the sample studied; the role of the father appeared to be even more important than that of the mother for subsequent social and sexual adjustment of the girls.

SEE ALSO Entries 18, 294, 304, 400, 409.

149. CRANE, Elizabeth L. (1951). <u>Factors affecting the
     employability of twenty-nine widows ineligible
     for war veterans' allowances under the Depart-
     ment of Veterans' Affairs.</u>
        The veterans' widows under fifty-five who, from
     January 1950 to April 1951, were refused allowances
     after medical examiners found them employable, were
     studied through DVA files and by interviews. The hus-
     bands of many had died suddenly leaving no savings; 13
     widows had school-aged children when they applied; all
     had worked before marriage but few were vocationally
     trained. Only 12 of these women had found and kept
     jobs, 10 through friends or on their own, 2 through
     the National Employment Service. None of the 17 who
     were not working had tried placement services. Some
     received Mothers' Allowances or help from working
     children, or kept boarders. These histories showed
     much general misunderstanding about resources and
     eligibility. Although the widows felt they had a
     right to Veterans' Allowances, they either did not
     know about, or did not feel confident about claiming
     help from, those other facilities in the community
     which offer widows some protection.

150. GILES, Harvey A. (1948). <u>Counselling services for
     young people.</u>
        Through their records and through staff inter-
     views, three Toronto services -- Vocational Guidance
     divisions within the Y.M.C.A. and Y.W.C.A. and the
     Youth Employment Centre subdivision of the Unemploy-
     ment Service Commission, established in 1945, 1940,
     and 1946, respectively -- are here studied in detail
     as instances of newly developing needs and techniques
     in a postwar industrial city. The public service of-
     fers actual placement as well as counselling. The
     two private agencies are free to extend counselling
     from vocational to personal problems, as full histories
     of two individual cases illustrate. All three services
     have facilities for psychometric testing, with two tend-
     ing to overemphasize this facet of guidance work. All
     three give interviews, but only one provides adequate
     intervals between sessions. Casework training among
     counsellors is still a rarity. Ideally one central

clinic could provide Toronto's young people with the
fullest range of vocational, personal, educational,
and medical and psychiatric counselling, psychometric
testing, and information and placement services.

151. GRAHAM, Lloyd B. (1950). Factors in repeated applications for employment at the Youth Employment
Centre of the National Employment Service, Toronto.
The undertaking here was to search through 19,771
Youth Centre registrations, extract the 548 records of
people under twenty-two years of age who had been placed
since January 1948 in three full-time jobs within one
year, and note and tabulate the recorded data on these
"repeaters". Weight abnormalities appeared with 59 per
cent of the girls and 37 per cent of the boys. About
half the "repeaters" had left school before age sixteen,
and over three-quarters had worked full time before applying at the Youth Centre. Only one-third of the boys
and one-quarter of the girls had had any vocational or
commercial training; 65 per cent had not gone beyond
Grade VIII and 86 per cent not past Grade IX. Most of
those with Grade X standing or better were in more
skilled, but not better paid, jobs; family stress was
commonly noted as occasioning early employment. The
physical and social disabilities of which "repeating"
is a symptom merit further investigation, perhaps
through interviewing.

152. MacQUARRIE, Lachlan B. (1953). Some social consequences
of continuous unemployment.
Intending to study the effect on families, the
writer in May-June 1950 selected 46 registration cards
from the files of the Toronto Local Office of the Unemployment Insurance Commission -- every fifth man unemployed for 120 days or more. But many of these had
no dependents. Further, in interviews many men proved
unable to convey family feelings or to give precise information on budget items. Almost half were entirely
dependent on unemployment insurance benefits, 80 per
cent were worried about mounting obligations and the
insecure future, and many reported serious curtail-
ments of budget, especially for clothing. The employment problem of older workers was unexpectedly brought
into focus, as was the problem for children: in 29
cases here children were helping to supplement incomes,
2 had stopped school and 4 more were unlikely to resume

in the autumn. A study of unemployed men with dependent children is recommended, especially of those exposed,by ineligibility for unemployment insurance benefits, to the most drastic social consequences.

153. REGIER, Otto (1952). Older men looking for work.
From the 213 complete records on one year's applicants to the National Employment Service's Counselling Service for Older Workers in a recently developed one-industry centre, the predominance is established of men with wives and/or other dependents, in good health, with stable work histories but, latterly, the succession of short-term jobs typical of older workers' experience. After counselling, 133 found or were placed in jobs. Since 65 of the 125 in the fifty-five-or-older group were employed, chronological age alone is clearly not the deciding factor. Family responsibilities, veteran's status, and placement according to realistic work preferences marked the employed group. Almost half the applicants mentioned additional difficulties which nonetheless affected employment: family illness disrupting schedules, or financial need precipitating unrealistic choice of jobs. Community leaders interviewed by the writer acknowledged the discouragingly stubborn problems which older workers faced. Policies and practices that exclude them need separate study. This survey demonstrates that fuller community services could help hearten and re-qualify such workers.

154. TIESSEN, Leo H. (1954). Factors in the re-employment of older workers.
Community attitudes have not caught up with rising life expectancy, and thus unemployment is increasingly a problem with older workers (those of forty-five years and up who experience employers' discrimination). Under the National Employment Service of Canada a Counselling Service for Older Workers was tried in Toronto in 1947 and confirmed on a permanent basis in 1949. Mr. Tiessen's study is based on every third record in the Counselling Service of the 750 cases for 1950, with facts about years of schooling, special training, health, work histories, etc., and employment situation after counselling, coded on key-sort cards for analysis. War, depression, lack of vocational planning during school years, technological changes, inflation: such factors rather than

115

health or adaptability seemed behind employment difficulties. Of the 250 studied, 58 were placed and 108
found work themselves after counselling. Retraining
and morale-building groups for older citizens are recommended, as well as increased counselling staffs with
skills, sympathy, and the requisite knowledge of community resources.

SEE ALSO Entries 132, 133, 212, 213, 214, 215, 216,
   217, 221, 250, 296.

155. COOPER, Vera E. (1959). <u>An examination of twenty-two</u>
<u>case conferences involving the Neighborhood Workers</u>
<u>Association and two or more agencies.</u>
Toronto's present-day family service agency originated, in 1912-14, as a district association to trans-
late varied private and group "philanthropies" into
community obligations. As the city and the times grew
more complex, and as governments and organizations
provided for specific categories (the disabled, or
neglected children), social work became increasingly
specialized. Today the Neighborhood Workers Association too specializes -- in family counselling and
allied services -- but its historical concern with
integrated services is expressed in terms of modern
procedure (case conferences), as here studied from
1955-56 case records. Nine agencies in all participated, and sixty-four different social problems were
involved, predominantly child care and mental hygiene.
Surprisingly, conferences seemed to be called rather
infrequently, too late sometimes for efficiency. Often
a new agency's involvement with a case precipitated a
conference, or a new referral occurred as a consequence.
This procedure will best serve families with many
chronic problems when agencies can use it flexibly and
with full mutual understanding.

156. FIELDS, Betty Penn (1952). <u>The Resident Homemakers</u>
<u>Service offered by the Visiting Homemakers Assoc-</u>
<u>iation of Toronto.</u>
A family threatened with disintegration by the
mother's protracted absence usually needs both casework and homemaking services. Since the Visiting
Homemakers' short-term service had been directed by
nursing and later home economics specialists, long-
term care, with its social work emphasis, was exceptional, and policies and administrative structures
remained uncertain even after the setting up of a
separate Resident Department in 1940. Salaries and
working conditions for its staff were slow to come
up to Day Service standards. Although referrals by
other agencies did not decrease, by 1949-50, 34 of
the 64 families served were self-referred. After
documenting this history from records and staff

interviews, the writer notes the unifying and educational potential of a service to all parts of the community from three collaborating professions, and recommends the development both of the existing Toronto agency and of a new nation-wide organization similar to the home care programs in the United States and Great Britain.

157. FOSTER, Ann E. (1957). Common-law unions and child welfare.
Records of 80 cases active during January–March 1952 in the Children's Aid Society and Infants' Homes (Toronto) are here analyzed for comparative adequacy of family functioning -- half (in the over-all ratio of three cases closed by June 1954 to one still active) selected from the 93 cases involving common-law unions, the other half a similar selection of legal union cases. All Protection cases have much in common. In financial circumstances, drinking, dependency, incidence of desertion, the two groups were indistinguishable. The common-law families had better records for employment and physical care, but the mothers were on the whole less reliable, and more prolonged and intensive agency work was involved here than with the control group. Five case histories illustrate that a satisfactory stable common-law union can be less damaging to children than an unhappy marriage. Further studies might focus on fewer factors, it is suggested, and on certain categories of common-law unions.

158. GALLEAZI, Mario J. (1956). A study of referrals to the family agency.
This study examines the integration of community services as revealed by referral and intake records on the 54 cases which other agencies in 1955 referred to one west-central district office of the Neighbourhood Workers Association (Toronto) -- only 15 per cent of the total applications to that office. Well over half of the cases studied received only brief service, i.e., needed little help, or a kind of service outside the agency's function. No cases were referred from any group work agency and none from the large veterans' hospital or the city's mental health clinic; very few elderly clients were referred, and no adolescents. Only one request for family counselling originated in the Family Court, and problems related to income and

unemployment predominated among referrals from public welfare agencies. Too little information was either given or recorded in many inter-agency telephoned referrals. More widespread knowledge about various agencies' distinctive functions would make for more appropriate referrals.

159. GILLEN, Doreen M. (1955). Effects of unemployment on family life.
     Between January and March 1955 the Neighbourhood Workers Association recorded applications from 113 unemployed persons. Excluding those without unemployment insurance coverage or in exceptional circumstances and those who had moved away, the writer selected and interviewed 26 families. Among them they had 77 school-aged and 3 older children. Almost all the breadwinners had good employment records, all but 5 in year-round occupations. Since they were employable, they were ineligible for public assistance, even though unemployment insurance benefits were far below former earnings and well below their families' subsistence needs. During an average of four to five months out of work, family care was characteristically substandard in food and sometimes in clothing and shelter too. Debts, and often medical bills, further depressed morale. Another such winter would be destructive to family solidarity, many felt. Adequate provision for emergency needs is essential, but nothing short of work will ease the dislocations, worry, and wretchedness that haunt such households.

160. HEADRICK, Margaret E. (1961). The results of a planned program of financial assistance given to thirty needy families, studied through eighteen months of service.
     The generous and fearless handling of "relief giving" where service is based clearly on casework principles, invoked in an epigraph, is assessed through a scheduled reading of case records in the Neighbourhood Workers Association on a random one-in-three sample of the families mainly supported by the breadwinners' earnings who applied for financial assistance in an emergency January–June 1957 and had received at least $100 by June 1958. In 10 cases one marital partner showed reluctance to become involved, 3 because of suspected, but untreated, mental disturbance. Since

119

half the families, with more than half of the 104 children, were trying to live on earnings between $41-$60 weekly when basic weekly food costs alone were $30 for a family of six, the high proportion carrying heavy debts was predictable. Most improvement was noted in external problems -- debt-payment plans, child care, medical help, housing. Yet the severely beset can be seen, in a few instances here, responding to slow re-education.

161. HOLMES, Louise (1955). Child care plans made by families during a mother's hospitalization with a psychiatric illness.
    To see how families managed, and what part community services played, the writer interviewed the 29 families still accessible where mothers of children under twelve years of age had been admitted voluntarily or by certificate to the Toronto Psychiatric Hospital between October 1950 and March 1952. A friend or relative, in the child's or her own home, provided care most frequently, with housekeepers or homemakers the next commonest solution. One to five changes of plan took place for 18 of the 44 children involved. Fathers tended to consider changes and care away from home less acceptable for school-aged children. Five- and six-year-olds, those whose care varied and those whose mothers were longest in hospital, showed most effects of stress. One gap in community resources -- round-the-clock homemaker service -- was noted; and city day-care nurseries were used little. Hospital social workers apparently must encourage fathers to discuss arrangements, as well as explain what resources exist in the community.

162. KATZ, Barry (1957). Clients not completing service at the Jewish Family and Child Service.
    Of various factors that might contribute to high rates of turnover, certain factors related to clients are here studied through agency records on 215 who applied for service January through March 1956, particularly on 33 who continued beyond three months' service and the 33 who remained for at least one casework interview out of the 76 who terminated service within three months. No factor seemed significantly to discriminate the group who continued from those who did not. Both groups had similar proportions of immigrant and

120

Canadian clients and similar ranges of waiting time between reception and intake interviews; in both groups economic problems predominated and in both most of the clients had brought the same problems to the agency a year or more earlier. The writer concludes that, since the factors studied seemed not relevant, others involving clients' personalties and client-worker relationships must affect duration of service.

163. LAW, H. Bernice (1956). The value of family casework service.
     While employed by the Neighbourhood Workers Association of Toronto, the writer often wondered what families thought of the service rendered and how they got along after contact with the agency had ended. Here she seeks the answers, through interviews with 30 whose cases, representing various districts and durations of service, were closed during four typical months of 1954-55. While over-all improvement since the first assessment recorded in case histories was apparent, many problems had persisted. Yet 25 families felt they had been helped, and the 5 who reported no change had had brief contacts. Even those who had received casework service tended to see the agency as, mainly or exclusively, a source of material assistance. This project suggests that regular follow-up interviews might both complement agency service and extend the community's understanding of agency function, and would certainly be welcomed by most clients.

164. McRAE, Mary A. (1962). A study of cases referred to a family service agency from social agencies.
     The nature of the referral is studied here through records of the 36 cases referred, by social agencies and the Department of Public Health to one branch of the Neighbourhood Wo kers Association, which were opened after June 30, 1959, closed before July 1, 1961, and involved at least one in-person interview. The lack of consistency in the referral process placed heavy responsibilities on workers in the agencies involved. The degree of motivation for help varied widely, some clients having needed only direction to the family agency and others not having set out for such service and now unwilling to accept it. However, the referrals did seem appropriate insofar as the

clients' problems were appropriate to a family agency's service. In fact most people did get some kind of help, but it was not always the kind they had expected or as much as had been expected.

165. PALMER, Sally (1960). Conflict in the economic aspects of marriage.
    Are economic problems central or peripheral in marital conflict? the writer asked, studying histories on 42 cases closed with the Neighbourhood Workers Association in 1959 where both economic and marital problems had been noted and where no acute economic distress existed -- i.e., where no financial assistance had been given. The interviews were predominantly with wives. A child had been born during the first year of marriage to 20 wives, 17 of whom felt they were carrying a disproportionate share of household responsibilities. Where husbands felt inadequate as providers their self-confidence was affected, and yet it was the wives rather than the husbands who seemed resentful in the 18 homes where women had to go out to work. Although many women complained about frustrations over planned savings, debts were usually due to spending on unessentials rather than to emergency needs. On the whole economic problems here were adjudged salient enough to justify a caseworker's focusing on them.

166. PEEBLES, Jane M. (1957). A descriptive study of sixty-four cases accepted for marriage counselling by the Neighbourhood Workers Association of Toronto during 1956.
    In the records here studied, a couple's relationship had emerged as the primary focus during the initial interview. Contact was rarely sustained long enough to permit intensive casework. The 64 clients were mainly within their first two years of marriage, which suggests that this preventive service might be amplified by premarital counselling. Backgrounds, size of family, and circumstances seemed typical of residential (suburban) Toronto as far as could be judged by the case records, which tended to stress psychiatric rather than environmental data. Most clients initially blamed a partner's "bossiness" or "stinginess" or spoke in terms of "saving their marriage" or of drinking or unfaithfulness. Workers saw "personality difficulties" and "immaturity"

122

as the commonest problems. Husbands initiated contact
in 29 per cent of cases and became involved in 50 per
cent. The 4 clients referred by lawyers were men.
Further study would be needed to see why so few
professionally-referred clients, and relatively few
self-referred men, use the service.

167. ROSEMAN, Renee (1960). Two hard-core families.
     To further document an anomaly first highlighted
in 1948 in a study in St. Paul, Minnesota, the writer
read 30 case records and visited 15 social agencies,
all concerned with two Toronto families chosen, from
a group known to a Settlement House staff, for the
large number of their registrations and contacts with
social agencies and their varied difficulties. Through
an aggregate period of 42 years, 64 caseworkers and
many other unrecorded community representatives were
working with the 19 members of these two families,
both of them into a third generation of dependence in
1958. Both families had inadequate, overcrowded housing, many children, sporadic or insufficient income.
With one family, undisciplined children often occasioned action: truancy, theft, unmarried parenthood;
the parents, never themselves individual clients any-
where, often sought agency help. In the other, neglected children of a moronic mother and an evil-tempered
father forced agencies to intervene; 16 foster homes
were involved during 1941-58. Further analysis is
recommended of attitudes and techniques that will enable agencies to collaborate better in meeting such
disheartening needs.

168. SINGER, Carolyn B. (1954). Intake at the Jewish Fam-
     ily and Child Service.
     From case records and monthly summaries on all
217 applications during March, June, and September
1953, the writer studied agency-community relationships. Recent immigrants, although constituting only
about 8 per cent of the area's Jewish population, made
46 per cent of these applications, often for services
inappropriate but offered here to preclude threats of
deportation. Such interlinked difficulties as financial need, unemployment, sickness, problems about care
and custody, were common. Under pressure of requests
the agency tried to maintain emergency services and to
meet as many needs as possible with the time and staff

available. Inevitably, backlogs developed -- a waiting
list for counselling services, for example. Over half
the applicants here came on their own. Since only 2
per cent were given no service, the appropriateness of
their requests, and the agency's responsiveness, can
be inferred. However, work in public relations is
needed to encourage schools and other local services
to refer more clients.

169. WOODSWORTH, Jean E. (1962). A study of the needs of
mothers of Grade IV children, in a public school
in Toronto, for community Child Care services.
Through an interested Principal in West Toronto
the homes of all 55 children in one grade were con-
tacted and 36 mothers agreed to interviews. All 36
had worked at some time since marriage; 19 were employed, 7 of these the sole support of broken homes;
3 were seeking employment and 7 more planned to do so
as soon as younger children were all in school. The
nearest Child Care centre, used by only one mother,
was one hour and three streetcar transfers away.
Various arrangements within the family and neighbourhood, shiftwork, part-time work: all these devices
worried and wearied the mothers, whose earnings and
services at home were both needed. They all said
children needed milk or soup, and supervision, at the
noon-hour, and supervised recreation after school.
Their own circumstances reflected working women's
needs for vocational counselling, retraining, sound
placement, fair wage structures, and more adequate
and more flexible assistance from Mothers' Allowances.

———————

GROUP PROJECT. An exploratory study of two-generation
cases serviced by two Children's Aid Societies in
Metropolitan Toronto.
A group of students investigated the social,
psychological, and environmental factors related to
25 two-generation families, i.e., families who had
been on the active caseloads of the Catholic Children's Aid Society and the Children's Aid Society of
Metropolitan Toronto, in the city of Toronto. Through
a close and careful examination of 50 voluminous case
records, an attempt was made to trace generational
patterns of dependency, deviance, multi-agency contacts, health and welfare needs, mobility patterns,

124

and family-life relationships. Characteristics of the one- and two-generation family were compared with the characteristics of the multi-problem family, as portrayed in other social work studies.

170. CAMERON, Elizabeth H. (1962). Disposition of Children of two-generation families.
    The setting of the study provided the background for data-gathering on the disposition of the children of two-generation families. The author examined private and institutional placements, as well as placements with the two agencies under study. There appeared a great amount of work involved in the manifold court actions required in relation to these children. Fifty per cent of all first-generation children, and 69 per cent of second-generation children were placed in various settings; 38 per cent became permanent wards in the first generation, and 32 per cent in the second generation. Adoption was successful for only 8 per cent of the permanent wards in the first generation and 10 per cent in the second generation. It appears that the cycle of child placement among two-generation families is not broken, but continues into subsequent generations.

171. CHATTERJEE, P.K. (1962). Alcoholism and the two-generation family.
    Forty-eight per cent of the families under study presented a problem related to alcoholism in one way or another. Twenty-four records were examined in detail and compared with those of other families in the sample. It was found that the "alcoholic" families had a higher mobility, had more problems, had more children placed, and had more contacts with social agencies. When problems were ranked in order of frequency among the "alcoholic" families, delinquency and crime stood at the top, followed closely by marital discord, and with desertion as the most frequent factor associated with child neglect. The "alcoholic" families had more frequent contacts with private social agencies than with public social services. Yet none of these families had contact with any service where they might obtain information, help, or treatment for the problem of alcoholism. On the average, the first-generation "alcoholic" family had been on the active caseloads of agencies for eight years, the

second-generation family for four to five years, although some second-generation families were still active cases at the time of the study.

172. EDMISON, Elizabeth A. (1962). Housing and the two-generation family.

The geographic location of the two-generation families under study was principally the central core of the city of Toronto, an area characterized primarily by heavy industry, business offices, and small shops, with a predominance of sub-standard residential housing scattered over the area. The author mapped out the location of the families according to last-known address. Nearly 50 per cent of the families found that housing was a major problem in their day-by-day existence and a very high mobility was characteristic of these families. The main factors contributing to the problem of housing were: non-payment of rent, neglect of the premises, and disturbing behaviour on the part of the families in the neighbourhood. The author reviews studies of public housing done in Britain, Holland, the United States, and Canada to suggest ameliorative methods of dealing with the problem of decent housing and two-generation families.

173. ROBINSON, Jean A. (1962). Unmarried mothers and the two-generation family.

The families in the second generation presented as their most frequent problem the area of illegitimacy. The rise of illegitimate births is examined, using statistics from England, Ontario, and Toronto, and all the figures seem to support a rise in unmarried motherhood, especially among the teen-age members of today's families. These statistics are borne out by examination of the age groups in the second generation families who bear children out of wedlock. The author examines previous studies in the area of illegitimacy, to look at causes, and attempts to relate some of the findings of these studies to the present sample. Case illustrations give the social history of the unmarried mothers in the sample. The first-generation families did not indicate such a high incidence of illegitimate births as the second-generation families.

174. SHARPE, Mary Jane (1962). Mental disability and the two-generation family.

126

Earlier British studies of similar families had indicated a high incidence of mental disability, or immaturity, among members of two-generation families. The present sample showed that 17 out of 25 families in the first generation, and 13 out of 25 families in the second generation had problems relating to mental disability. The author focused the investigation on 11 families in which mental disability was evident in both the first and second generation. Among the families, illegitimacy was very high, marital discord was frequent, and problems of physical illness were constantly evident. Lack of parental control was the highest form of child neglect. These families used a large number of health and welfare agencies, among which the Department of Public Welfare and the Public Health Department were used most frequently.

———————

GROUP PROJECT. An examination of multi-problem families in London, Ontario.
Through the case records of the Children's Aid Society of London and Middlesex County, 60 multi-problem families were examined in this group project. The definition used to denote multi-problem families included the criterion that these families would have children who are in clear and present danger, such that the community has a right to intervene. Additional data about the families were obtained from the files of the City Welfare Department. The investigators also interviewed 11 families in the sample, using as the basis the St. Paul Project schedule.

175. GENDRON, Peter V. (1962). Agency collaboration in working with the multi-problem family.
Service to the multi-problem families by health and welfare agencies in the community tended to be fragmentary and crisis-oriented. Duplication was evident, in that no single agency serviced the whole family unit, but concentrated on a piecemeal approach to a specific problem or a specific individual within the family unit. For the last 12 years, 58 per cent of the families were known by the agencies in London, Ontario. Most of the inter-agency contact was between workers at the Children's Aid Society and other agencies. The author anlayzed in detail 11 families, which were interviewed on a personal basis. Among this group, an

average of 6 agencies had been involved over an average
period of 14 years; 58 different organizations had
served the 11 families. This included welfare assistance from public, private, religious, and service
organizations. In most cases one agency was unaware
of the help given to the same families by other agencies in the same community. The author feels that
collaboration is an essential part in rehabilitating
the multi-problem families.

176. VEITCH, Beverley A. (1962). <u>The values of the multi-
   problem family</u>.
     Values were examined by the selection of six
areas of family functioning: housing, neighbourhood,
kinship patterns, social activities, economic practices,
and child rearing practices. Most men in the sample
were between 21 and 45 years of age, while the ages of
the women ranged from 21 to 35 years: the average number of children per family was 4 - 5. Marital discord
was evident in most of the husband-wife pairs. Most
were native-born, white, of Protestant faith, with low-
income jobs. The employment situation seemed to be an
intermittent one. The families in the sample were
known on an average of 12 years by the social agencies
in London. Other characteristics included little emotional support from neighbours, absence of meaningful
relationships with relatives, restricted social life,
physical punishment in child rearing, and large families. It was found that contrary to popular belief,
these families do not form a lower-class sub-culture;
most of their values are middle-class values, which
they see as desirable but which they have been frus-
trated in achieving.

GROUP PROJECT. <u>Family and neighbourhood network of
   relationships in relation to need and use of
   services</u>.
     Family living in new suburban communities differs
in many ways from the patterns prevailing in longer
established and more central parts of Metropolitan
Toronto. This group project was designed to examine
variations in living patterns in two quite different
communities -- Midland Park, a new suburban development in Scarborough Township; and the town of Leaside,
an older and well established area which is much
closer to the centre of the city. A representative
sample of 30 families was chosen from each community.

128

These families were interviewed following the preparation and testing of a detailed schedule of questions.
Based on the data collected by the group as a whole
each student selected an individual topic for detailed
analysis and report.

177. NAUNDORF, Ronald (1962). The middle-class family and
     illness.
     Despite the relative security of the middle-class
family, illness inevitably creates stress and, if serious, requires significant modification in daily routines
and living patterns. This study compares the range and
incidence of illnesses in two groups of 30 families
each in the two quite different types of communities.
It gives detailed attention to the way in which friends,
neighbours, relatives, and services within the community helped and influenced these families in meeting
their health needs. Particular attention is directed
to symptoms commonly related to emotional stress.
Comparisons are drawn between the two communities
studied and explanations are presented for significant
differences in the incidence of illness and in the use
of treatment services. Both groups had ready access
to medical services. Only when the mother of small
children was ill was any extensive use made of outside
help, usually from relatives and only rarely from
neighbours, friends, or social agencies. Evidence, on
the whole, supported the view that suburban families
are more mobile and more isolated than more central
urban families and that a relationship exists between
these factors and emotional stress.

178. OKE, Janet K. (1962). The use and need of leisure
     services in two areas of Toronto.
     Modern technology has greatly extended the
amount of time available for leisure-time pursuits.
In order to provide opportunities for creative use
of leisure, most urban communities have developed a
wide range of facilities and organized programs.
This study explored how middle-class families looked
upon their recreational needs and the extent to which
they used the organized facilities provided by the
community. In carrying out the study two samples of
30 families each were drawn from the two communities.
Some interesting differences were discovered. The
Leaside families had more contacts with relatives,
while Midland Park families visited and did more

things with neighbours. Midland Park families expressed a desire for more recreational facilities, while Leaside families were generally satisfied with existing services. In both areas much of the leisure-time activities of both husbands and wives were carried on within the house, despite the presence of extensive organized resources on a community basis. The study points out the need for detailed attention to the social structure of communities in planning new recreational facilities.

SEE ALSO Entries 40, 129, 294, 295, 296, 401, 408.

179. ALDERWOOD, Jean Avon (1953). <u>Motivations of volunteer group leaders</u>.
In the hope of contributing insights to help agencies to use volunteers to mutual advantage, the writer studied records on the 88 volunteers at the University Settlement during the program year 1952-53, collected answers to a questionnaire from 50, and then interviewed 14, half of those who gave priority to a service motive in answering questionnaires. In the questionnaire responses, reasons given for volunteering corresponded closely with alleged bases of satisfaction. There were further depths, however, that only interviews elicited; for example, the need to be needed, to compensate in leisure time for the frustrations of repetitive work, or to explore a new vocational field, or in one case to win approval. Those who enjoyed the human contacts and recognized the members' needs, or leaders who grew from membership ranks, tended to serve most satisfactorily. The high degree of turnover is predictable when many single young people undecided about their vocations are accepted as volunteers.

180. BYLES, A. Jack (1948). <u>A survey concerning the employment of volunteer leaders in program by recreative agencies in the Greater Toronto area</u>.
The eight representative agencies here examined for the program year 1947-48 reported a total of 1,124 volunteers, 65 per cent of them leading club groups, 19 per cent directing physical activities, and 16 per cent teaching arts and crafts. Staff attitudes towards and experience with these volunteers were explored through questionnaires (53 returned), supplemented by interviews where agencies had significant training programs. Although almost all said volunteers were indispensable -- because they represented community involvement, contributed enthusiasm, or made possible existing or expanded programs -- 22 per cent would prefer professionally-trained leaders if budgets permitted, and 12 per cent would prefer to pay all leaders. Respondents found 72 per cent of the volunteers reliable, and reported only 14 per cent discontinuing their assignments. Perhaps the Community Chest's Volunteer Bureau could help with recruiting, since age

limits were low despite the 10 per cent rejected for immaturity, and with some centralized training to supplement individual supervision, since better-trained leaders are essential to higher standards and expanded services.

181. CHANDLER, Robert G. (1961). Motivations and expectations of volunteer leaders in Scouting.
A concern with the quality and effectiveness of the Boy Scout movement, and thus of its leaders, animates this study. The reasons why men take volunteer positions as Scout leaders, and what they hope to give and receive in this role, are elicited through an interview schedule that covers as well the background of the leaders and their views on the movement's significance for members. Interviews were conducted with 28 Scoutmasters, one from each District in the Greater Toronto Region, chosen at random. Their answers suggest that Scouting is middle class in orientation. "Trouble makers and gang types" are often mentioned as undesirable to the movement. "Perhaps many Scout leaders are those who feel a need for a traditionally-laid-down code and structure which they themselves can use as a moral guide in life while they are teaching such a code to their boys," the writer observes. Focus on the individual boy's development and on group relationships appeared to be increasing. Comparable studies were recommended on rural Scout leaders, female leaders in the Cub section, and volunteer leaders in other organizations.

182. DORRICOTT, William M. (1950). The Music School in the Settlement.
Toronto's experience since 1921 is described in the context of English and American institutions designed to develop, within Settlement Houses or through independent schools, the musical ability of interested individuals and the musical awareness and pleasure of communities. Various schools provided information on written request; in Toronto the teachers, executive officers concerned, and University Settlement personnel and records were consulted. Clearly, professional musicians supplied the impetus here, maintained standards, and often subsidized the school. The Settlement House now pays administrative expenses, but not for instruments or their maintenance, or books or, of

course, teaching. Fees are minimal. The 149 pupils
registered in 1949-50 were mainly children coming for
the first year for individual lessons in piano or vio-
lin. More instruments are urgently needed; and more
group projects, adult participation, and informal musical collaboration in the Settlement's entertainment,
dramatic, and craft programs, are recommended.

183. HADDAD, John N. (1948). Teen-aged canteen in Toronto.
        To assess the movement that within four years
of its wartime beginnings involved some 50,000 young
people in the Toronto area, the writer sent questionnaires to 219 organizations and, through the returns
from 135 active canteens, analyzed their 1948 programs
in relation to youth needs. The clubs stated that
their objectives were "wholesome recreation", "self-
improvement and fellowship", "citizenship", and "crime
prevention". Social dancing and sports predominated
in their programs. In all but ten classes planning
was done by democratic committees, but only half of
these had an adult member who could guide youthful
members towards activities that would reflect their
interests in vocations and skills, home life and human relationships. Unaffiliated clubs, all those
sponsored by local governments and service clubs, and
many under churches and social agencies need to broaden
program. Training for leaders should be provided.
Above all a co-ordinating central committee is recommended to stimulate and nourish individual clubs and
link them with the whole community.

184. McCONNEY, Douglas M. (1957). The eleven-year-old boy:
        a study of drop-outs from the Boy Scouts Associa-
        tion.
        From a one-tenth random selection of the Toronto
Cub Packs the drop-outs among eleven-year-olds (about
one-third) were investigated through interviews with
28 boys who left between January 1, 1954 and April 30,
1955. Almost half of the reasons given for leaving,
mentioned by 22 boys, reflected preferences for athletic or other activities atypical of the Wolf Cub
program. Since many more preferred "earning badges"
than "working for badges", and activities were often
more valued in anticipation than in experience, dissatisfaction evidently derived also from having
friends who were not interested in Cubs, feeling out

133

of place among "little ones", or having delegated
leadership resented. Many of the 15 Cubmasters interviewed had recognized neither the boys' need for more
share in choosing leaders and programs nor their readiness for transfer to Scout Troops. Leaders' training,
pack size, etc. seemed relatively unrelated to drop-
outs. Comparative study (with continuing members)
might clarify whether drop-outs indicate particular un-
met needs or simply that an optimum interest-span has
been exceeded.

185. OKAM, Mercy O. (1957). <u>A study of the day program for
young mothers in the Y.W.C.A.</u>
Since the wartime influx of servicemen's wives
into cities led the "Y" to adapt and expand morning
"gym and swim" classes, this type of program has become well established. To see why members join, what
they gain, and whether agency intentions are thereby
satisfied, the writer analyzed 68 questionnaire responses from members in one Ottawa and two Toronto
branches and conducted 20 follow-up interviews with
Toronto members and 10 with workers. Both workers
and members recognized the need for recreation, a
"break in the routine". Almost universally mothers
welcomed gym, swimming and sports activities (although
in one group badminton skills were seen as determining
a members' acceptance or relative isolation). Almost
all sought and welcomed adult associations. While
they enjoyed crafts, many wanted to learn things related to homemaking. Members expressed more willing-
ness to participate in planning than workers reportedly
noticed. A minority felt they had learned about the
agency and none mentioned spiritual development, although both were explicit parts of agency objectives.

186. SMITH, M. Rowena (1952). <u>After Councils -- what?</u>
The implications for citizenship of representing a Y.W.C.A. Branch on a Members' Council are sought
through questioning the 17 traceable of 27 Central
Branch (Toronto) representatives during 1943-47. About
one-third had been prewar "Y" members. Through postwar
changes, few maintained active contact, although most
kept in touch with "Y" friends. All but one had held
many different executive positions in varied groups,
and almost all had attended conferences. Yet many dep-
recated their knowledge of the Association when

approached for interviews. Their memories were often hazy -- for example, of the use for the World Service Funds they had helped to raise. Despite the common disparity between Branch and Association interests, many had learned procedural skills or gained confidence and adaptability. Their later participation in community activities demonstrated, in quality rather than quantity, a benefit of Council experience. This outcome, in turn, seemed to reflect the skills of staff leaders in enabling members to learn in the Council experience.

SEE ALSO Entries 22, 27, 28, 308, 309, 310, 311, 314, 319, 322, 323, 324, 344, 410.

187. BELLAMY, Donald F. (1953). <u>A study of the impact of
a public housing project on unemployment relief
in Regent Park (North)</u>.
    This comparative study for 1945-47 and 1950-52
analyzes records of the Housing Authority which ad-
ministers Canada's first slum clearance project,
launched in 1947, and Department of Public Welfare
files on the 277 households receiving relief within
the six years -- about 8 per cent of all the households in the area. Although the number of relief
cases per year remained fairly constant, the cost for
the whole group rose one-third more than city-wide
relief costs in that period. The cost increase was
concentrated among people still in the area's condemned dwellings: those deferred as "problem cases"
or recently attracted into the area by hope of re-
housing (including many handicapped householders and
deserted wives receiving public assistance); and those
with needs not provided for by the project who were
attracted by the low rents in the condemned buildings
(largely single persons or aged couples). Further
study of such groups is urged, and of the same area
after another comparable interval.

188. HOPWOOD, Alison Lindsay (1947). <u>Subsidized rents in
public housing, with a proposed rental scheme for
the Regent Park (North) Housing Project</u>.
    The Toronto Housing Authority wanted to set in-
dividual rents in the Regent Park (North) Project so
that tenants would be paying about one-fifth of their
incomes but the per-unit average rentals would be
about $25 a month. Mrs. Hopwood reviews British and
American precedents for fixing rents according to
the unit (space and amenities) or the tenant (means
tests or other eligibility scales) and, on the basis
of the City's 1957 survey of the project area, suggests for Toronto's Authority a rental scale in terms
of family size and income in relation to prevailing
price and wage levels. A basic rent, at one-fifth of
a basic or subsistence income, is worked out for families of every size. Rents would increase at the rate

of $1 monthly for every $5 income in excess of the
subsistence income, up to a maximum (economic) rental.
They would decrease at the same rate when incomes fell
below subsistence, to whatever minimum rental and sub-
sidy funds permit.

189. SCHREIBER, Marvin S. (1958).   Beech-Hall Housing Pro-
     ject.
          To explore attitudes, the writer interviewed
     half the tenants in each of the eight buildings hous-
     ing 64 elderly couples altogether and the eight hous-
     ing in all 64 elderly individuals, during this project's
     third year of occupancy. Unexpectedly, almost all
     stated preference for the "peace and quiet" or "common
     interests" of segregated housing for the aged, although
     over half would have liked "a few children around" and
     the writer felt that their views often meant they felt
     rejected by, rather than rejecting of, the general com-
     munity. The damp valley site was almost universally
     criticized. Three-quarters said they had to take a
     bus to their supermarket, and many noted penny-pinching
     details like out-of-reach, unenclosed kitchen shelving.
     However, the project clearly satisfied needs for inde-
     pendence, privacy, security, and self-esteem. A trained
     intake worker, a defined policy on eligibility, and a
     recreational worker to encourage group-planned improve-
     ments, would help counteract the loneliness in Canada's
     largest apartment project for the aged.

190. TOEWS, Helena (1953).   The relationship of public
     health and public housing in the Regent Park
     Housing Project.
          To see whether this relationship can be traced,
     the writer studied interview data: from 21 public
     health, school, and social service employees in the
     area where Toronto's pioneer, publicly-financed, low-
     rental housing project was opened to occupants in 1949;
     and from 62 tenants, a representative sample by age and
     family constitution of the 547 families rehoused at the
     time of the study. Outsiders stressed evidence of im-
     proved morale, better receptivity to health education,
     and greater social confidence. Tenants were positive
     about specific benefits -- space, air, warmth, hot
     water, refrigeration. Apparently infants were markedly
     healthier, whereas more schools than parents noted im-
     provements among older children. Statistical evidence

137

is not available on the apparently reduced incidence
of illnesses, as overcrowding, cold, and infestation
were remedied by rehousing. Self-contained and anti-
social families outbalanced consciously neighbourly
ones; a tactful group organizer might gradually encourage the community to develop the self-determination
and resourcefulness that are conducive to psychological
health.

GROUP PROJECT. Significant differences in the social
and economic histories of a group of families admitted to public housing.
Public housing offers many opportunities for research. This group project was undertaken with the
co-operation of the Metropolitan Toronto Housing Authority. The research was undertaken at Regent Park
(South), a federal-provincial housing project involving slum clearance and the rehousing of eligible persons who lived on the site prior to clearance. Students
sought answers to the following question: what significant differences are there in the social and economic
histories of a group of families admitted to public
housing while in receipt of public assistance as compared with a group of families admitted while self-
supporting but of relatively low income? Following
the preparation and testing of an interviewing schedule the group interviewed all families in receipt of
municipal welfare assistance and a matched group of
families who were self-supporting upon admission.
Students interviewed a total of 152 families, about
one in five tenant families. After an initial analysis of the data by the group, each student chose an
individual focus and carried out his own detailed
analysis.

191. BOESCHENSTEIN, Gertrude Maud (1959). Families referred to Regent Park (South) by a social agency.
Do families admitted to a public housing project
on referral by a social agency differ significantly
from other families admitted to such a project? No
outstanding differences are revealed in Regent Park
(South) through a study of 32 families whose presence
in this subsidized housing project arose from the
intervention of social agencies. Low economic status

is not the sole determining factor for admission. The
age-old distinction between the deserving and undeserv-
ing poor continues to exert an influence. Most of the
families admitted, regardless of the source of referral,
were intact and independent; they were not on public
assistance and were not problem families. Social agencies, in referring families to Regent Park (South),
appear to have followed the above pattern; there is an
underlying preference for the low-income, independent
family. The study, however, provides evidence that
many families economically independent on admission
have to rely on public assistance in emergencies for
precisely the same reasons that brought about economic
dependency for certain families prior to admission.

192. BURGESS, Barbara (1959). Public assistance and public
housing.
Regent Park (South), as a public housing project,
admits only low-income families. The sole income
available for some of these families is through public
assistance. This study compares a group of 40 such
families with a group of families whose incomes, though
limited, came from earnings. Both groups included a
predominance of separated or widowed mothers with dependent children. The evidence points out the special
problems facing such mothers in assuming a dual parental
role and in contending with the fact of separation from
the marriage partner. Important differences are identified between the two groups. The loss of the marriage
partner in the group on public assistance appeared to
be a more traumatic experience related in many instances
to prolonged illness and to serious social and family
problems of long standing. The economically independent group had less pronounced feelings of bitterness
and frustration. This group had fewer children and
fewer still of pre-school age. The economically dependent women experienced a greater sense of inadequacy
and a greater need for help with personal problems.
The study concludes that, helpful as public housing is
for all tenants, there is a continuing need for close
co-operation between the housing authority and community agencies providing counsel and guidance on family
and child welfare problems.

193. KULYS, Regina (1959). A study of twenty-five priority
families rehoused in Regent Park (South).

Housing authorities have been skeptical concerning the admission of "welfare cases" to public housing projects. A number, however, were admitted to Regent Park, primarily because they were living on the site before the project was started and consequently acquired a high priority for re-housing. This study examines the background of 25 on-site families, the majority of whom were welfare cases. These 25 families, because of limited education and occupational skills, experienced great difficulty in meeting changes in the labour market; all but 4 required public assistance for at least temporary periods while in Regent Park. While their social and economic background was similar to other low-income families, they differed in some respects from off-site families. They were critical of the inconveniences encountered during the time their old homes were torn down and the new ones built. Their attitudes revealed a close identification with their old neighbourhood and some feelings of discontent about administrative arrangements in their new housing. At the same time they expressed satisfaction with the housing itself. The study concludes that many on-site tenants face special difficulties in adapting to a new environment.

194. LAUDER, Eleanor G. (1959). The relationship of health and housing in Regent Park (South).
Illness is a particularly serious threat to the economic stability of low-income families. In this study the health problems of 22 tenant families in Regent Park are examined in detail. All of these families gave ill health as their major reason for application to public housing. A high incidence of chronic, disabling conditions is revealed. These conditions were much more prevalent among those families whose financial support came from public assistance. The self-supporting families among the 22 studied, for the most part, experienced acute but not prolonged illnesses. While their earning power was low they could carry, nevertheless, full-time jobs. The study draws attention to the lack of knowledge of tenants concerning rehabilitative health services and community social agencies in general. This is especially significant because the evidence reveals clearly the impact of severe illness on family life, both financially and emotionally. The need is stressed for more follow-up on health conditions.

195. LUTES, Jack R. (1959). <u>Social and economic differences between public assistance families and self-supporting families in Regent Park (South)</u>.
  Families in receipt of public assistance usually have a background of irregular employment, ill health, or serious problems in interpersonal relationships. A comparative study between these families in a public housing project and a group of low-income self-supporting families in the same project was designed to test similarities as well as differences. The evidence strongly supports the proposition that there are few basic differences. The majority of the group who were self-supporting at the time of admission had been on public assistance at some previous time or were receiving financial aid at the time of the study. When given the opportunity all family heads became self-supporting although some could not retain this status continuously. The conclusion is drawn that many low-income families in times of crisis may have to rely on public assistance. While certain families may have to be refused admission to public housing, such refusals should be based on more objective grounds than being in receipt of financial aid from the municipalities. The study concludes that any refusals based solely on the fact that families are on public assistance are unjustified.

196. THURINGER, Harold P. (1959). <u>Low-income families and public housing</u>.
  Every low-income family experiences sooner or later one or more of the risks inherent in our industrial society and may well become a consumer of our social services. Public housing is designed to assure low-income families of a better opportunity to make more effective use of their limited resources. This study, in providing a detailed description of 46 such families, emphasized the feelings of anxiety and inadequacy which so frequently dominate the outlook of heads of families who barely earn enough to maintain fully their economic independence. These families can rarely accumulate a reserve of any kind for emergencies and frequently face the necessity of seeking financial aid. Public housing is seen as a definite help, but it provides no solution to their continuing problems. The conclusion is drawn that much more needs to be done to help these families with their emotional, employment, and health problems. Attention

141

is drawn to the strengths of the tenants, the ability
of some to benefit from further training and the will-
ingness of others to work together to advance the
neighbourliness of the project. Help and encouragement
in these areas require close liaison between public
housing and other community services.

197. TONOGAI, S. Larry (1959). <u>Low-income families in
Regent Park (South) public housing project.</u>
Our society places great emphasis on production
of goods and services. Skill in production is rewarded
through increased earnings. But a substantial number
of our people have limited capacity or limited opportunity. Consequently, their earnings are low and are often
insufficient to meet the daily needs of their families.
Incomes in this study ranged from $1,500 to $3,500 per
year. Evidence indicates that these low-income workers
want more and hope to get more. There are, however,
serious handicaps in their way. Their education rarely
goes beyond Grade IX. They are not able to compete
with a younger generation with somewhat better education.
It is extremely difficult for them to take time to learn
new skills when they have families to support. The
study stresses the importance of assuring better opportunities for their children. Attention is drawn to
precarious family finances which so frequently cause
many of their children to leave school early and thus
run the risk of taking jobs with little security or
chance for advancement. An examination of the background and outlook of tenants who were earning with
those on public assistance revealed no significant
differences.

SEE ALSO Entry 21.

198. ABRAMS, Percy (1955). <u>A study of the Jewish immigrants in Hamilton and their relationship with the Jewish Community Centre.</u>
    This study was made in 1952, only four years after Hamilton organized its services for 50 of the immigrant orphans sponsored by the Canadian Jewish Congress, only three years after the first caseworker (part-time) joined the centre's staff, and within a year of the arrival date of many of the 37 families interviewed. From the 34 families immigrating in 1947 or later on the centre's casework records, 18 were still available, and through them another 19 were introduced and also interviewed. Three had joined a synagogue for every one who belonged to a group in the Jewish Community Centre, several had no contact with Jewish groups, and very few participated in general community affairs. The centre's services were used most extensively by children. Among adults, practical help (employment, health services, loans) predominated. Language difficulties, vocational downgrading, feeling "left out", still kept many newcomers isolated. An epilogue shows adult participation increasing by 1955, and integration with the general community progressing.

199. ALEXIADE, Helen (1962). <u>A comparative study of the behaviour of children of Greek immigrant parents and those of Canadian-born parents.</u>
    The writer gave scheduled interviews to 24 boys, half from Greek and half from Canadian homes, selected from a group of children similar in intelligence ratings, socio-economic levels, grade, and age in three Toronto public schools. Unlike their counterparts the Greek boys felt they were heavily burdened with chores. They reported their parents as more authoritarian, often using physical punishment as well as the deprivation of privileges which Canadian-born parents usually resorted to for discipline. The Greek boys had fewer club memberships and hobbies, and were oftener alone in their recreational activities. They were noticeably more willing to express their feelings than the Canadian boys, who tended to respond with passive acquiescence. No differences were evident regarding clothing, money, friends, church, and vocational and educational aspirations. Both groups showed a tendency to conform

to parental standards. Among their contemporaries
the Greek boys tended to be individualistic, the
Canadians to conform more to group pressures.

200. BEAR, Myrna L. (1955). A study of the program for
new Canadians at St. Christopher House.
The needs of adults in downtown Toronto in relation to their club program in 1954-55 are here
studied, primarily through interviews with the 20
Italian and 13 Portuguese members in attendance during a June-July fortnight. All had been at least
five months in Canada, and almost all were single
young men. They came initially to meet other persons from their homelands. Some moved on from re-
laxing -- as onlookers at movies, for example -- to
working on committees or taking part in special
events or recommending such future activities as a
choir or woodworking. But most members, after they
learn the essential minimum of English, seem to need
encouragement through special programs -- learning
to play Bingo or dance, for example -- to begin confident participation. Under agency guidance the
electing of committee members, and such projects as
the group discussion of vocations requested by many
members, can be used to make Canadian ways familiar.

201. DAVISON, Anne M. (1952). An analysis of the significant factors in the patterns of Chinese family
life as a result of the recent changes in immigration laws which permitted the wives of Canadian
citizens to enter Canada.
Forty families reunited after 1948, following
separations often of sixteen to thirty years, are here
studied through interviews in their Toronto homes.
They were introduced to the interviewer by a church
agency. Wives and Chinese-born sons were usually employed in home-based businesses. Despite the cost of
bringing in relatives, most husbands had provided adequate accommodation. Family evenings now replaced
the club night-life previously characteristic in
Toronto. A few had established homes with Canadian
wives and now had two families here. Limited educational opportunities in China, and the resistance
to learning English engendered here by traditionally
unfriendly immigration policies, made language a general problem. Literacy in the women's own language

144

should be encouraged first, perhaps through daytime classes. A Cantonese-speaking nurse to explain our medical procedures, and a social worker to counsel on specific problems and explain woman's position in Canada, would help these newly arrived wives.

202. FELDBRILL, Zelda (1952). The adjustment of European youth in the Toronto Jewish Community.
    The 24 Jewish Family and Child Service case records on European youths aged sixteen to eighteen where recording was up to date after ten months' service illustrate the experiences here since October 1947 of the thousand immigrants sponsored by the Canadian Jewish Congress under the Canadian government plan. The difficulties of foreigners, adolescents, family-less children, were compounded by wartime experiences (concentration camps for 16, life in hiding among Aryans for 6, partisan warfare for 2), by their unrealistic expectations, and by the intensely emotional basis of the community's reception of them here. Most wanted employment and early independence — but preferred living arrangements involving some dependency. In every case an apparently positive initial adjustment was followed by a struggle; the sooner it erupted, the better the hope of ensuing integration. At least one move was usually necessary, from jobs and foster homes alike. By accepting this invariable growth process, caseworkers could offer secure footing enabling clients to discover and use their own strengths.

203. GRANT, Charity L. (1955). Occupational adjustment of immigrants.
    As part of a larger project carried out for the Canadian Department of Citizenship and Immigration at Toronto and Laval, this subject, together with housing and health and welfare considerations, was explored in 300 scheduled interviews by a sociology student and the writer. Respondents -- reached through places where they worked, did business, or met socially -- were chosen as far as possible according to the distribution by ethnic groups of Canadian immigrants from January 1951 through September 1952. Their occupational adjustments were rated and tabulations made to see whether correlations appeared significant between ratings and certain background facts. The 57 per cent satisfactorily adjusted in employment included a preponderance of English-speaking immigrants, the

young, and skilled or semi-skilled workers. Refugees
and displaced persons apparently had increasing occupational difficulty here. The highly trained immigrants in the group may improve in occupational
adjustment after a longer period, or they may need
improved placement services if they are to make their
maximum contribution in Canada.

204. KOHN, Ruby Garbath (1950). <u>Jewish Vocational Service</u>
     <u>of Toronto.</u>
          The survey made prior to the inception of this
     agency in 1947 established that Toronto's vocational
     services were inadequate, especially for Jews. The
     agency's history, gathered from records and conversa-
     tions with persons involved, is here studied in the
     context of other Canadian and American member services
     in the Jewish Occupational Council. The Toronto serv-
     ice, a member of the Community Chest since 1949, planned
     to offer counselling, testing, and placement, undertake
     research, and work against discriminatory employment
     practices. However, placement was stressed in those
     emergency years -- the Toronto agency's émigré regis-
     tration by 1948 was second only to New York's, although
     8 other agencies had more registrants over-all, and 9
     others placed more clients in employment. Under such
     pressures, staff was too small to serve many of the
     functions initially envisaged, and even after immigra-
     tion subsided more money was required, for salaries
     and facilities, to meet the needs of clients referred
     from other community agencies, and to extend service
     to the high-school-age group and older workers.

205. LAFLAMME, Katharyn Jefferies (1957). <u>The role of the</u>
     <u>family during the beginning adjustment process of</u>
     <u>a group of Greek nationals immigrating to Canada</u>
     <u>from Iron Curtain countries.</u>
          In 1954 the first of 180 Greek nationals, re-
     patriated after negotiations through the Canadian Red
     Cross, were reunited with their families. The writer,
     a Greek-speaking caseworker then in the Neighbourhood
     Workers Association, was appointed by the supervising
     authorities to help the newcomers in Toronto. From
     her records on 51 adolescents, sponsored by 33 families
     who were often themselves recent immigrants, she docu-
     ments the problems: personal relationships, divergence
     between immigrants' high aspirations and sponsors'

plans, the formidable competition for jobs outside
the ethnic community (the National Employment Service
placed only one of twelve boys who applied), and the
difficulty of working towards independence and learning English too. Yet, thanks to closely-knit families,
all made encouraging adjustments here. Judging by this
group, immigrants would welcome year-round, daily English classes stressing occupational vocabulary, and
need introduction to unfamiliar community resources.

206. LATHAM, Carl R. (1958). Indian placement program administered by the Indian Affairs Branch of the
Department of Citizenship and Immigration.
        Since all the traditional occupations on reserve
lands are increasingly vulnerable to market conditions,
and the population on Canadian reserves is growing,
Indian young people must seek work, either on northern
development projects or in towns near reserves, or by
moving to populous areas. The Indian Placement Programme was launched in 1957 to encourage their integration in the national labour force. In 1958 the
writer interviewed all 11 who had been located in an
urban area four months or more under this program for
the Southern Ontario region. Through the National
Employment Service, jobs had been found for 7, and
work-and-training situations for 4. Modern industrial
work rhythms, goals, and co-operating groups are not
scaled to individual human measure. For Indians there
are additional stresses; many city ways make them feel
disoriented and lonely. Education in the general community (among social workers too) and on reserves
could ease the necessary mutual adjustments. Meanwhile,
by widening the Indian's scope of experience, this program better equips him to make his own plans.

207. MARGULIES, Lillian (1951). An analysis of some techniques employed by a voluntary vocational service
agency in assisting new Canadians.
        Besides the familiar challenges of work with
immigrants and with people seeking work, Toronto's
Jewish Vocational Service had the added hazards of
discriminating employers, the limited opportunities
implied by occupational concentration, and the postwar émigré's special needs. In four formative years
the agency served about 4,000 clients, some 60 per
cent of them New Canadians. Records for 1947-50 show

147

how the agency at first met urgent pressures by mass
placements and (wherever possible and increasingly)
by stressing intensive service: knowing the person,
his background, the local possibilities; meeting fears
with simple, direct information; recognizing and working through real feelings -- difficult for the Canadians
involved as well as the émigrés; and thus finding a basis for mutual responsiveness and respect. The searching and constant evaluation necessary in such a process
is glimpsed in specific cases cited.

208. NEWTON, Margaret J. (1948). A study of the information
and opportunities available to single displaced
women in the city of Toronto.
By June 1, 1948, 284 women had come here on
government-sponsored one-year contracts as domestic
servants and 74 through a private firm as garment
workers, under 1947 Orders-in-Council regulating immigration of persons uprooted by the war. The National
Employment Service introduced them to employers, Education Department language and citizenship classes were
made available to them, and three private agencies made
individual visits and offered services. However, interviews with a random sample of 63 after they had been
here at least three months revealed that many thought
their contracts involved compulsion; that less than
half had been able to use language, and fewer still
civics, classes (all 40 "domestics" worked at least
ten hours daily); and that almost all were concerned
about relatives in Europe. Many had no idea that
tracing services or agencies' counselling services
existed. Clearly, more responsive arrangements are
needed if the newcomers and Canada -- as well as employers -- are to be adequately served.

209. SIBBALD, Patricia A. (1962). A study of a multi-ethnic
transient area of Toronto.
Respondents from five professions (clergymen,
social workers, policemen, nurses, and English-language
teachers) were interviewed on the needs and services in
the area they serve, two centrally-located census tracts.
The population was found to be fairly heterogeneous and
mobile, although a new pattern was emerging of a stable
Italian nucleus surrounded by a transient fringe of
other immigrants. Five main problems appeared to face
area residents: lack of education, lack of English,

unemployment, inadequate income (these four inter-
related), and insufficient recreational facilities.
There were educational and English-teaching resources
to meet the need had they been used to capacity.
Since the Italians seemed most to need and least to
use the services available, further study of their
reticence and of the possibility of gearing the services to the Italian community is recommended. But it
is urged, as well, that all community resources be
kept flexible enough to adapt continuously to a changing community.

210. THURLEW, Setsuko (1960). Cultural influence upon
decision-making in two Japanese-Canadian groups.
Prewar political and economic exclusion, and
wartime forced removal from British Columbia, both
isolated from Occidental influence the Issei, most
of whom had immigrated as young adults, and compli-
cated the Canadian-schooled Nisei's attitude to Japanese traditions. The two generations are represented
here by two small groups, studied through four successive monthly meetings each. Observations (tabulated according to Bales's set of categories) showed
more spontaneity and initiative among Nisei members.
However some Issei members seemed only half-heartedly
submissive to traditional, hierarchical concepts,
e.g., that the good chairman is one who through
haragei ('belly art") knows the group's wishes intui-
tively, without asking. (The Chairman here ignored
a contribution by "F", who "accepted the situation
passively with a slight smile", and, in arbitrarily
naming a new officer, overruled "O", who, although
his nomination had been ignored, "joined in replying
Sansei ('agreement')".) Despite parliamentary forms,
Nisei practice often reflected traditional concepts
too. To ease culturally-imposed restrictions without
imposing another culture needs well-informed group
workers.

211. WASTENEYS, Hortense (1950). The adequacy of the social
services made available to displaced families in
Toronto.
The writer interviewed 90 such families chosen
from lists of names compiled with the help of several
groups: the National Employment Service which supervised those who came on contract as domestic workers;

the garment trades and furrier employer-sponsors; and
the newcomers' personal friends, priests, and so on.
Most newcomers commented favourably about their reception, especially those served by Jewish groups
here. Some had little contact beyond their own ethnic group, with housewives often reluctant to avail
themselves of Board of Education classes in language
and citizenship. Either told too little in Europe,
or too agitated there to absorb information, many
seemed unprepared for certain economic and social
difficulties they were now encountering. A minority
were unsure about employment services, the school
system, or emergency help available. Clearly a central counselling service would usefully complement
the existing services of public and private organizations.

————————

GROUP PROJECT. Application of Fair Employment Prac-
    tices Act in Ontario.
    To assess the effect on employment practices of
the 1951 provincial legislation (against discrimination on the basis of "race, creed, colour, nationality,
ancestry, or place of origin" applying to any employer
of more than five persons excepting those employing
domestic workers in private homes or certain non-profit
organizations as defined in the act), a group of students began their research by a study of the files at
the Department of Labour. The Director of the Fair
Employment Practices Branch in 1951 ruled that complainants should present their cases: on Form I, if they
claimed that an employer had discriminated in relation
to hiring, firing, promotion, or conditions of employment, or that an employer or trade union, by excluding
from membership or expelling, suspending or otherwise
had manifested discrimination; or on Form II, if they
complained of job advertisements, application forms,
or other written or oral evidence indicating that an
employer had sought facts which could be used as a basis for discrimination against applicants or employees.
The students read all the files, noting facts on complainants, complaints, and subsequent settlements under
the act including the Conciliation Officer's judgment
on the validity of the complaints. Then they interviewed employers or someone representing them in 87

firms, 30 of whom had been involved in Form I and 57
in Form II complaints, 77 in Toronto and 10 in other
Ontario centres. Interviews were also held in 68
firms never named in a complaint, matching the first
group as far as possible in nature of businesses and
size of staffs. Each student then analyzed the data
from case records and interview reports in terms of
an individual focus of concern.

212. JAMES, Alice (1961). Attitudes of employers towards
the employment of New Canadians.
Comparing 52 employers charged and 52 never
charged under the act, the author noted that there
was no difference between the groups in the proportion of postwar immigrants hired. Employers in the
first group made slightly more comments unfavourable
to New Canadians (for example, "We spread them thin,"
implying a quota system). Only 25 employers in all
seemed to hire without regard to nationality. Employment agencies accepted fewest New Canadians proportionately, hotels, restaurants and community agencies most,
and manufacturers the widest range of nationalities.
Technically-trained immigrants appear to be counteract-
ing the notion that there is an "immigrant's kind of
work" — and that it is menial. The under-trained are
still exposed to unemployment and exploitation.

213. KROEKER, Bernhard J. (1961). A study of the effects
of the F.E.P. Act upon employers, and their attitudes towards the regulation.
Attitudes were compared in 44 firms with under
100 employees and 40 employing 500 or more. Large
firms usually knew the act and expressed theoretical
approbation. Several had revised application forms
to comply with the regulation, but regretted their
inability to check educational records now that they
could not ask which school the applicants had attended.
More small employers mentioned specific interpretations
of the act and spoke of "the encroachment". Each group
felt the act applied mainly to the other. Each criti-
cized "loopholes" in the legislation. Appointment of
field officers is recommended to help enforce and explain the act to employers and improve the meeting between them, the well-established representatives of
local culture, and persons not yet well-established
who represent other cultures.

214. NORMAN, Anne C. (1961). Attitudes of employers towards the employment of Negroes.
Over half of all the Toronto employers interviewed had hired Negroes. Their comments were predominantly negative, however, and staff policies in
20 cases were plainly discriminatory. Among the 7
Windsor employers interviewed 5 asserted segregation-
ist policies. Complaints had not altered Windsor views.
In Toronto complaints had meant limited advance in the
2 cases of 6 filed under Form I where the Conciliation
Officer found evidence of discrimination; in 3 others
the student found such evidence. People may think
twice, she feels, if some action they know is wrong is
labelled illegal as well. The records show that ster-
eotypes about what Canadians look like and what kind
of jobs Negroes do are still widespread. Employers
often cited, but rarely tested, customers' or staff
objections to Negro employees.

215. SOHN, Herbert A. (1961). Knowledge of and attitudes
towards the F.E.P. Act expressed by employers
charged under the act.
Of 30 Form I complaints against the employers
interviewed, 28 involved hiring and firing and 2, job
status. Only 4 of the companies admitted the charges.
Conciliation Officers found 4 complaints valid, and in
one case a settlement was reached satisfactory to both
complainant and company. The student noted indirect
or explicit disavowals of fair employment principles
in interviews with all but 9 of the 25 companies where
complaints had been found invalid. Of the 57 employers
interviewed who had been charged under Form II, 20 were
governmental agencies or departments. Charges often a-
rose when newspapers were careless about screening want-
ad wordings. Most employers remarked that circumventing
this law was easy. Strengthening of both support and
enforcement is urged. And investigation is recommended
of the employment experiences and opinions of the act
of highly skilled, professional, and executive persons
from minority groups none of whom were represented a-
mong the complainants here.

216. WHALEY, Barbara (1961). Hiring policies in relation to
the proximity of the employment to the public.
Employers in 36 firms "near" the public, such as
hairdressers or clothiers, frequently mentioned appear-
ance, status, and personality among qualifications

152

desired in employees. The 36 selected as "far" from public contact, mainly manufacturers, chiefly stressed capacity for the job. Hiring was based on an interviewer's impression alone for over 28 per cent of both groups. The groups' stated policies differed little. However, employees from minority groups were mainly in background positions, and most employers assumed that the public would have difficulty in accepting New Canadians (even when English-speaking), Jews (especially in senior positions), and Negroes (the likeliest to rouse irrational fears). Experienced firms, i.e., those where these assumptions had been tested, were found least inclined to antagonistic pre-judging.

217. WING, Dorothy M. (1961). A comparison of the practices of employers charged with discrimination in employment with employers matched as a control group.
   Material on two groups is compared: 25 firms which had never been named in complaints; and 30 charged under the act. Only one of the 30 plaintiffs had been reinstated with full protection at the time of interview. Respondents in 7 of the 30 firms denied even knowledge of the legislation (one of these having experienced six complaints), and 10 disclaimed implication in it. Stereotyped judgments, unabashed hostility, and token-hiring abounded in both groups. Prejudice -- against Jews and, to a lesser extent, Negroes and Orientals -- was apparent even in "positive" comments ("I like to take a very liberal approach...and fit them in when I can."). Whether "caught" by the act or not, employers appeared confident that the government, having declared itself theoretically against discrimination, was willing to permit it in practice.

SEE ALSO Entries 36, 83, 114, 249, 345, 373.

MEDICALLY AND PHYSICALLY HANDICAPPED

218. AMOS, Jack Loyal (1942). Vocational rehabilitation:
     a comparison of programs for the physically hand-
     icapped.
          Noting the failure of rehabilitation programs
     after the First World War to maintain their initial
     impetus and to reach out and include all who could
     profit whatever the occasion of the disability, Mr.
     Amos surveyed existing programs, considering them as
     a basis for a more effective, all-inclusive service
     in Canada. He drew on general, governmental, and
     institutional publications, on his field work experi-
     ence with disabled men and employers, and on case
     records and interviews in various provincial, federal,
     and private agencies. Although the individual's need
     and right to work is increasingly acknowledged, even
     veterans whose problems are particularly challenging
     have been "paid off", i.e., maintained in dependence
     rather than helped towards self-reliance. Ontario's
     Workmen's Compensation Board has showed how various
     rehabilitation services can be integrated within one
     program. American experience shows how a central
     authority can subsidize and encourage local programs.
     Both systems may help shape plans for an all-inclusive
     co-ordinated rehabilitation service for all Canada.

219. BOYCE, Wilfred A. (1954). The rehabilitation of long-
     term public relief recipients.
          In spite of Workmen's Compensation, veterans'
     programs, and associations for particular disabilities,
     there are now more than 142,000 handicapped persons in
     Canada needing additional services. This project,
     through case records and interviews with clients, their
     doctors, and Welfare Visitors, studies one such group:
     30 male heads of families who are medically unemploy-
     able and receiving relief, selected from Toronto's Pub-
     lic Welfare files according to over-all proportions
     under various handicaps, age groups, and periods of
     agency contact. Almost half this group had been dis-
     abled for more than ten years, and more than half were
     assessed as capable of light work although almost all
     of these were unskilled with limited education. Medical
     treatment was inadequate for more than half, largely be-
     cause of their own discouragement or apathy or dread of
     suggested procedures. More intensive casework,

therapeutic administration of payments, and efforts
to involve clients in a total rehabilitation plan,
might make for more effective use of existing resources pending their extension.

220. BROCK, Margaret (1959). The effect of illness and
hospitalization on the marriage relationship.
The group studied through case records and
medical charts were the 28 male inpatients who received continuing social service while in the New
Mount Sinai Hospital during 1956-57, all resident
in Canada for over five years and currently maintaining domicile as married men. Middle-aged and
older couples predominated. Although medical insurance or City Orders covered hospital bills for
all but one, two-thirds were referred -- primarily
by doctors or internes -- for help with financial
problems. The real problem often turned out to be
social or emotional. Marital problems were acknowledged by 5 directly and by 6 more ultimately, and
8 others found the physical separation disturbing.
Only 4 marriages showed interdependence and were
free from marital problems. In 5 cases wives reluctantly accepted the decision-making role during
husbands' illnesses. Sexual maladjustment was recognized once, and perhaps existed oftener. Illness,
which frequently precipitates or reveals marital
problems, can also make casework help more accessible,
and acceptable.

221. BROWN, Ruth I. (1951). The function of the Special
Placements Section of the Women's Division of the
Toronto Office of the National Employment Service.
Employability was redefined after the manpower
shortage in wartime showed how the handicapped could
be fitted in where needed and the wounded could be
rehabilitated. Since women's work history is often
interrupted by marriage and children and traditionally
limited in range, a disabled woman is usually ill
qualified as well. The writer analyzed facts -- disabilities, age, education, and marital status -- from
477 available records on applicants during 1949, noting, for example, the predominance of older women a-
mong those with hearing defects and of the better
educated among those who had experienced mental illness, and the high incidence in all groups of separated

and divorced women. Studying services in Britain and
the United States, observing workaday procedures here,
and interviewing officers in two private agencies concerned with rehabilitation, convinced the writer that,
even with the fullest use of community resources, special placement affords limited help in the absence of
more preventive and supportive health services, vocational training facilities, and allowance of time and
skilled staff for counselling.

222. BROWNE, Helen (1950). Emotional problems arising from
the presence of a cerebral palsied child in the
home.
The writer interviewed 25 families whose children
were accepted by the Hospital for Sick Children for a
Nursery Clinic operated since 1949 by the Junior League
of Toronto. All the parents expressed hostility towards the medical profession, sometimes having miscon-
strued information or having pursued unrealistic
"cures" or having been hurt by too abrupt disclosures,
but almost always seeking to shift the burden of guilt
and anxiety by blaming others. Although 70 per cent
of the cerebral palsied show normal intellectual ability, physical restrictions and "staring strangers" and
over-protective families can delay learning. Those
specialist practitioners who themselves surmounted
such odds in childhood emphasize how much the home
atmosphere can help a child to develop self-acceptance
and self-reliance. Believing that psychiatric and
social services could assure the children of the necessary support and encouragement and provide for the
emotional and practical needs of the parents, the
writer recommends group counselling under skilled
leadership within the Parents Council, and a staff
caseworker within the clinic.

223. COWAN, Louise D. (1948). Home teaching in Canada: a
rehabilitation service for blind persons.
The writer, the first Canadian teacher qualified
by the standards of the American Association of Workers
for the Blind, reviews the theory and practice of home
teaching of the blind in the United States and Britain
and, throughout thirty years, in Canada. Current Canadian experience is documented by the 28 responses to
questionnaires sent in May 1948 to the other 37 home
teachers in Canada. Early courses for teachers stressed

Braille- or Moon-type reading, typewriting, and re-
munerative crafts and hobbies. Training in psychology
and basic casework was gradually added, until in 1947
a new course included gardening, diseases of the eye,
and social work according to certification standards.
By 1951, it is hoped, Canada will have 20 certified
home teachers and a correspondingly high level of in-
service training and supervision for experienced and
newly recruited workers. Fully qualified social
workers are needed in some homes, the writer notes,
and one occupational therapist could ensure abundant
craft resources, as supplementary services within
the home teaching system.

224. DAVID, Renee (1953). Emotional problems of children
     with poliomyelitis, during the period of readjust-
     ment to home and community after prolonged hospi-
     talization.
         The readjustment is studied, primarily through
     interviews with their mothers, of the children still
     in the Toronto area in July 1951 who were victims in
     the 1949-50 epidemic and spent at least four months
     in the Hospital for Sick Children (Thistletown Branch).
     All but 2 were happy children before illness, but 13
     suffered afterwards from frustration (nervousness,
     irritability, hypersensitivity) or withdrawal (depres-
     sion and self-pity). Severity of handicap was not
     correlated with degree of adjustment. The child com-
     fortable in school life and with friends usually had
     a good home. Some mothers worried about having to
     accept needed transportation and appliances. Since
     every parent had found the initial diagnosis crushing,
     and two-thirds had had unanswered questions through-
     out the child's hospitalization, with many admittedly
     fearful about resuming care -- "We went home with two
     pieces of paper, one for his exercises, the other for
     follow-up clinic!" -- hospital social work is clearly
     desirable.

225. FELTY, Isabel K. (1961). Parental assessment of ap-
     parent values of a camp experience for diabetic
     children.
         At Camp Illahee the Neighbourhood Workers Asso-
     ciation, with the help of the Kinsmen's Club, operate
     three camp periods every summer for some 150 ambula-
     tory handicapped children between the ages of six and

sixteen. This study, based on interviews with 26 families, includes all the diabetic campers of 1960 whose parents lived in Greater Toronto and spoke enough English to communicate (excepting one unwilling to participate). Ten homes rejected or overprotected the diabetic child to some extent -- but since 8 of the 9 one-parent homes were in this group, apparently the child's illness was not the decisive factor in the disequilibrium. The 15 families enthusiastic about the camp seemed a miscellaneous group. Opinions varied about the medical and social benefits, but overwhelmingly parents reported emotional benefits: children learned to accept their disability and developed self-reliance in the controls it necessitates. Unquestionably the camp is promoting the hoped-for balance between care and protection, and the carefreeness proper to childhood. This study includes a history and bibliography of camping for handicapped children.

226. FRIESEN, David H. (1954). Job adjustment of disabled employees.
Ontario's provision of prompt and automatic benefits for workmen injured on the job has been celebrated widely and justly. Emphasis is increasingly on vocational, medical, and psychosocial rehabilitation. The writer used the files in the Rehabilitation Department of the Workmen's Compensation Board and then scheduled interviews to study the 35 more seriously injured men employed in Toronto of the 255 cases "closed as rehabilitated" in 1950. Were they satisfied with their jobs five to seven years after their accidents? Youth, moderately good schooling, skills, satisfactory housing, family life without too many dependents: such factors predominated among the 66 per cent who were content with their jobs. Better adjustments were correlated with better salaries, but not with degree of injury. Poor adjustments were related to emotional impairment -- usually prior to, even if aggravated by, the accident -- and to vocational downgrading. Thus intensive casework in such instances seems as essential to successful rehabilitation service as good selective placement.

227. GAMBLE, J.E. (1951). The emotional and social rehabilitation of the tuberculous patient.
A 1947 provincial survey of thirteen Ontario

sanatoria concluded with recommendations that emphasized physical, vocational, and economic rehabilitation.
The present study, drawing on first-hand experience and
observation as well as on published materials, points
out that in this long-term serious illness there are
other relevant factors. Enforced rest can magnify a
patient's fears and worries. His emotional conflicts
can make him troublesome, prone to malingering or re-
bellion. After discharge he may want to prolong dependence or he may overwork and relapse. Supersti-
tious dread of the disease still poisons the social
atmosphere for some families and convalescents. Despite the obvious need for skilled casework and for
help with family and employment problems, only one
Ontario sanatorium at the time of writing had a full-
time medical social worker on the staff. Better co-
ordination is urged of medical and non-medical staff,
of sanatoria and local rehabilitation centres and
provincial consultants and supervisors, and of the
general community services.

228. HETHERINGTON, Ewart Sim (1947). Rehabilitation in
     tuberculosis control; current services for the
     tuberculous in Toronto.
          Diagnostic services in Ontario and the treat-
     ment in thirteen sanatoria here met a high standard
     by 1947. But a patient who "signs himself out" be-
     cause of concern about his dependents swiftly counter-
     acts the "prevention" which clinics strive for, and
     pressures on a worker who is recently convalescent
     can quickly undo what prolonged care accomplished.
     In 1938 the province assumed indigent patients' main-
     tenance costs, but post-discharge care is a municipal
     responsibility, with the Samaritan Club, for example,
     or employment officers, providing some supplementary
     services. A survey of rehabilitation practices else-
     where points up the needs evident from 14 interviews
     (with former patients designated by the Samaritan
     Club and the city's TB Nursing Division) for help
     with family separations, sense of stigma, and above
     all economic worry. "Finances run all the way through,"
     as one man put it. Two major needs are defined: com-
     plete rehabilitation teams in every sanatorium, and a
     sheltered workshop for ex-patients.

229. HUNTER, T. James (1956). The social and economic ef-
     fects of a visual disability on the adult male.

159

The 32 men chosen for interview from the Toronto files of the Canadian National Institute for the Blind had all enjoyed sight during school years, and were under no other handicap — from age or health or language, for example. Neither age at onset of blindness nor its suddenness appeared significantly related to later employment or leisure time adjustment. However, those with a little sight earned more on the average and were more successful in finding work on their own; and all 19 learned to travel on foot independently, whereas 5 of the 13 able to perceive only light or less made little attempt at independent travel. Almost all had suffered from over-protectiveness or rejection, and many had lost contact with friends and group associates. Initial training in travel and everyday skills, and counselling, and then vocational training and placement, especially for the least-sighted group, are urgently needed.

230. KINZIE, David M. (1958). Parental assessment of change in handicapped children resulting from a camping experience.
   At the camps of the Ontario Society for Crippled Children boys and girls are free from social segregation and ostracism and from excessive demands or the commoner over-protectiveness at home. To explore the effect, Mr. Kinzie interviewed the parents and children in 28 homes of campers of two or three consecutive summers, aged eight to twelve. Many children had made gains in physical development and self-care according to their varying potentialities. Many parents reported them as more relaxed and accommodating at home after camp. Although 75 per cent had never had particular interests, all responded enthusiastically to campcraft, swimming and crafts, and 26 later continued with new interests. Several recalled cabin roughhousing with delight, and had more friends now — perhaps children coping with slighter handicaps need camping more than those (excluded from this study) receiving clinical help. With casework support parents might better consolidate gains made at camp, especially if they knew and used more community resources.

231. McCOOL, Maureen E. (1954). The psychosocial problems arising from rheumatic fever.
   To explore the impact of a child's isolation in

hospital and of subsequently restricted activity on
his development and his parents' attitudes, and their
interrelationship, the writer interviewed all 26
available families of children aged ten to fifteen
who were outpatients in the Hospital for Sick Children's Cardiac Clinic, having had rheumatic fever
within five years of the interview date. Medical
expenses had often intensified the stress; welfare
agency help was needed in 7 cases, 4 involving foster children, one a widowed mother, one an unemployed
father. Only half the children had adjusted well or
fairly well at home after the illness, fewer than in
hospital. Well over half the parents showed understanding and firmness. On the whole preventive medi-
cation, the doctors' alleviating of parents' anxieties,
and the children's functioning up to capacity (which
is now encouraged), have minimized the damaging effects of the illness. For some of these parents casework service would have been helpful.

232. McEACHERN, W.D. Colin (1950). <u>Vocational rehabilitation of the visually handicapped in Canada.</u>
Prior to wartime developments, Americans pio-
neered in staff training, the British in occupational
research, and the Canadian National Institute for the
Blind in actual placement of the blind in general employment. Records from the Ontario section of the
Institute's Industrial Employment Services Department
on the 124 adults placed and working in May 1949 are
examined alongside data on the 230 then unemployed
who had asked for and needed work and were not disqualified by age or a further disability (some 85 per
cent of whom the department at some previous date had
placed in jobs). Trained counsellors concerned with
individual problems of personality and adjustment are
needed to help the disqualified. The department also
needs facilities for preliminary medical and psychological tests, and fuller, more uniform recording.
The usefulness of sheltered workshops for pre-placement
training is limited by separate, sometimes un-co-ordinated,
administration. However, considering the department's
limited funds and the caution path breakers must use,
it has served well-qualified clients effectively.

233. McLEAN, Edith (1954). <u>Diabetic patients; a study identifying the psychosocial-economic difficulties of
fifty patients attending the diabetic clinic of a
general hospital.</u>

The study group was selected proportionately by
age, sex, and marital status (i.e., with the same pre-
ponderance of middle-aged and older women and married
persons) from a random sample twice as large of some
one thousand diabetics' case records in the hospital's
active social service files. Data recorded had been
gathered in the interviews given to all new clinic
patients and in any subsequent crises when doctors
had referred patients or workers had made emergency
visits to their homes. Medical, economic, and/or
emotional problems were found interconnected: overwork interacting with insulin reaction, or worry or
grief coexisting with disrupted regimes of diet and
exercise. The illness was under poorest control for
younger men with family responsibilities and patients
in economic need (5 here needed help with basic maintenance and 22, help with medical expenses, diabetic
scales, dentures, etc.). But despite problems the
majority managed fair or good control. Another study
-- of patients' personalities and attitudes -- is recommended.

234. MACMILLAN, Elizabeth J. (1955). Adjustment of blind
persons through the rehabilitation services of
the Canadian National Institute for the Blind.
This project emphasizes quality of service and
its meaning for clients. It is based on interviews
-- with all 35 C.N.I.B. registrants between twenty-
one and sixty-five years of age in Greater Toronto
in 1949 and 1950 who were accessible and willing (excepting invalids or those with an additional disability) -- and on supplementary interviews and case
records. Although such factors as prompt registration
and the family's attitude were decisive and the predominance of older persons and of recent blindness
meant relatively slow adjustment, progress seemed encouraging to most and agency services well explained
and helpful. Many wanted more counselling. Almost
all the homemakers, for example, felt inhibited in
their work, but none had received agency help in retraining for it. Perhaps speakers from the agency's
departments could explain, at C.N.I.B. club meetings,
such difficulties as job finding and staff shortages,
and then hear clients' suggestions. Client participation, agency concern for individual requirements,
and informed, imaginative community attitudes are
emphasized as keys to rehabilitation.

235. MAIER, A. (1957). A study of a group of patients
        with digestive disturbances to examine the kinds
        of problems which they experienced.
        Case records in the Social Service Department,
New Mount Sinai Hospital (Toronto), on patients referred between June 1954 and June 1956, 32 from the
Gastrointestinal Clinic and 9 from other clinics or
from wards, noted that 28 had diagnosed ulcers and
13 had similar symptoms although no ulcers. These
41 patients showed no unusual deviation from census
distribution in age, sex, or marital status. They
were grouped according to the four main ("social")
problem areas; and their response to treatment was
assessed from medical records. Though no significant
over-all correlation appeared between problem areas
and medical progress, particular correlations did
emerge: more patients improved when specific problems
with medical bills or housing were involved than when
marital conflict, for example, was the problem. Group
work agencies might help some cases. When digestive
disturbances express reaction to traumatic wartime experiences or to multiple illnesses and difficulties,
the medical social worker's concern may convey help
even though psychogenic complaints are not deep-seated
and chronic.

236. MONSON, Irma A. (1950). Social problems of general
        hospital patients.
        Case records were studied of 60 patients referred
between January 1949 and June 1950 to the Social Service
Department of Toronto General Hospital for help in rehabilitation. One-third were inpatients, mainly surgi-
cal cases, the rest outpatients with diagnoses indicating
a fairly high incidence of psychogenic illness. A majority saw a connection between their trouble and relationships at home (one woman, for example, expressing her
guilt about an impending separation by psychogenic symptoms). About one-fifth, younger patients especially,
saw adjustments at school or work as their central difficulty. Although some economic problem was usually
present, it was often as much related to the emotional
disturbance that had occasioned referral as to such objective factors as medical expenses or earning capacity.
In these records the patient's own versions of their
troubles illustrate the way clients can direct the social worker to the emphasis they need to enable them
to use help constructively, even in short-term contacts.

163

237. MOORBY, Kathleen Vetter (1958). The psychosocial ex-
     perience of parents admitting children to hospital.
         When she had worked in the Hospital for Sick
     Children (Toronto), the writer had witnessed the dif-
     ficulties of parents, expecially when fear or guilt
     was strong in them, in turning their children over to
     someone else's care. Her study considers the hospital's
     admissions procedures through interviews before the
     child's discharge with 30 parents who had recently
     brought in a "pre-schooler". Of the 18 parents who
     had told the child ahead of time something of what
     would happen, 13 had been well prepared themselves,
     usually by staff doctors. Yet only a minority brought
     "something from home" to leave as reassurance to the
     child, few anticipated the economic arrangements, and
     almost all left feeling "just sick", to be torn be-
     tween longing to visit and fear of "upsetting him".
     An informative booklet beforehand, and a medical so-
     cial worker on staff, might enable parents to accept
     the hospital even more fully, and so help the child-
     ren to feel safe there.

238. NEWBURY, Mary Alice (1951). A study of the reopened
     cases in the Social Service Department of a vet-
     erans' general hospital for the year 1950.
         Cases reopened in 1950 were relatively few, 198
     compared with 7,513 hospital admissions or 1,016 first
     referrals to the Social Service Department. But the
     hospital records and departmental condensed factual re-
     ports were investigated to isolate any factors that
     might appear characteristic in these reopened cases.
     The patients involved were predominantly the chronic-
     ally ill with families, receiving disability pensions
     or allowances at an age normally associated with peak
     earnings. When Casualty Welfare Officers had referred
     cases, they had usually stressed financial and domestic
     problems; medical staff had requested mainly social
     histories, discharge plans, and reports on home
     conditions and behaviour problems. More patients came
     on their own than through these two major referral
     sources put together. But this acceptance does not
     imply understanding of the services offered — only
     14 requests were specifically for casework. In the
     setting studied effective social work is inhibited by
     lack of provision for continuous prolonged post-
     discharge contacts whenever needed with patients and
     their families.

239. NOELL, Marilyn A. (1956). A study of the vocational
     adjustment of sixty-five rehabilitated paraplegics.
     Data on the 65 with complete lesion paraplegia
who had had two or more years to re-establish themselves since leaving Lyndhurst Lodge were derived from
385 responses to the Canadian Paraplegic Association
questionnaires sent to over 500 who had been patients
from 1945 to 1953. The 35 who were working had all
had adjustments to make, 26 of these drastic ones involving occupational shifts. The proportion with full-
time, year-round, well-paid work was below what should
be possible, judging from reliability records for similarly disabled American workers, or from English experience with graduated work and retraining. Health-
scoring did not establish whether non-workers had more
ailments or less capacity for coping with such difficulties. Most of the rehabilitated women, and the
men in "white-collar occupations", found employment.
Records were poorest for labourers with little education, and perhaps little inclination, for "light
work". Their "right work", after technical schooling
if need be, will involve improved employer and community acceptance.

240. OLDHAM, Heather Patricia (1958). Social services for
     female veteran patients.
     In Shaughnessy Hospital (Vancouver) the proportion
of requests for social service to women veterans was
almost five times higher than to men in 1955: of the
50 in a random 50 per cent sampling of all the females
admitted that year, 29 were known to the Social Service
Department. Data from hospital and departmental records showed that married women, and those acutely ill
choosing this hospital despite ineligibility for free
treatment, needed social workers least. Casework was
required for most of the 21 with histories of psychogenic disorders and for almost all the older, long-
term patients. Since the small section for women
lacks such differentiated facilities as for convales-
cent veterans, or for permanent residents, the wide
range of social problems there necessitates service
on a highly individual basis. The writer recommends
staff conferences, group work with long-term ambulatory patients, and the encouragement of supplementary service by volunteers, especially to elderly
women living alone after discharge.

241. ROUSELL, Carmon T. (1953). Multiple sclerosis: some
     social implications.
     The effects of this illness on patients and
their families were investigated through interviews
in 25 homes chosen from among the 212 registered
with the local chapter of the Multiple Sclerosis
Society of Canada. The bedridden, those in hospitals, and outpatients participating in experimental
programs of physiotherapy or hydrotherapy were excluded. The rest, and the random sample of 25,
showed a ratio of four ambulatory to one wheel chair
case. Although patients' attitudes varied with their
personalities, good attitudes appeared decisively affected by social circumstances: doctors who stress
the remissions and longevity when explaining the diagnosis and who continue to support the patient with
genuine concern; considerate and loyal families; and
understanding employers and neighbours. The interviewed patients were almost unanimous in stating that
"the community does not understand", and in reluctance
to be associated with a multiple sclerosis group. Renewed efforts are needed both to provide realistic information for the public and to hearten patients and
their families.

242. THOMAS, Mary-Claire (1959). The social needs of
     rheumatics.
     To see what these needs are and how they are
met, the writer read records on 100 cases closed in
1957 in the Toronto Branch, Canadian Arthritis and
Rheumatism Society, where non-hospital social service
was reported. Simply help with medical planning or
housing or information about services they might one
day need were required for 61 patients, half of them
past working age and almost all women. The 39 given
intensive service usually needed help to accept their
illnesses and to work out realistic plans. Only 19
were eligible for disability maintenance grants, but
65 needed assistance with financial stresses arising
from illness. Shortages of jobs, of retraining and
sheltered workshop facilities, and of services to the
aged sometimes impeded service, and medical problems
coexistent with marital or personality problems meant
some overlapping with other appropriate services. It
is recommended that social workers and doctors confer
on ways of easing referrals, since many whom doctors
sent were resisting help.

SEE ALSO Entries 190, 296.

243. ALDRIDGE, Gordon J. (1949). <u>The changing use of
     Toronto Psychiatric Hospital Outpatient Department
     by social agencies.</u>
     Trends are sought by a study of the clinic's
records in five representative years between 1927 and
1948. A 15 per cent sample of the total of 1,150 new
cases in these five years, stratified by age and sex,
shows that referrals by agencies declined steadily
from 60 per cent in 1933 to 16 per cent in 1948.
Needless referrals diminish as knowledge increases of,
for example, the mentally defective person's capabil-
ities. As other community resources develop, fewer
children or unemployed persons are referred and the
clinic's specialists are used less for psychometric
testing and consultation, and more for treatment. A
gap in community resources is suggested by the increasing referral of young people. More detailed studies
from agency records are recommended. Since over half
the agencies participating in the Community Chest were
not represented in these 1,150 referrals, a widely
distributed statement of clinic policy is proposed,
to stimulate use of this communal, multi-discipline
service.

244. BLEZARD, Ruth J. (1956). <u>Referrals of emotionally
     disturbed children to the Child Guidance Clinic,
     Kingston.</u>
     To assess the clinic's relationships with other
professional agencies and persons and with the community, this project reviews the case records of 80 children referred from varied sources and coming on their
own initiative between December 1953 and May 1956.
Chronic cases and those where mental or physical defects
might have contributed to disturbance were excluded.
Then a proportionate selection was made from each group:
the self-referred (a few); medical referrals (more numerous but all involving the same few doctors); agencies' referrals (usually in crises only, perhaps
because agencies tended themselves to cope with the
mildly disturbed); and school referrals (the most
consistently satisfactory referrals). Families generally see "problem conduct" rather than illness. If
the clinic is to reach children before disturbances
become severe, and if the attitudes of parents (or

adolescent patients) is to be conducive to successful treatment, the clinic must find ways of extending the good relations it has developed and maintained with the schools.

245. BRIAULT, Margaret A. (Non-degree Candidate, 1954).
    History of the Toronto Mental Health Clinic,
    1946-1954.
        This history since the service began in 1946 demonstrates the gradual clarification of function and administrative authority that occurs as a community's needs become more precisely defined and its range of services develops accordingly. Records of the clinic, the Canadian Mental Health Association, Toronto's Welfare Council, and the School of Social Work, supplemented by recollections of some who took part during the formative years, show the agency gradually shifting from casework consultation to diagnosis and treatment of children and adults. Facing overwhelming needs and without defined policies, unified direction, or staff continuity, the service nonetheless persisted, providing a self-appraisal to complement the community survey that led, in 1952, to reorganization. By then local educational facilities were beginning to supply the consultants and leaders whom the casework agencies had needed, in a context of national planning for mental health services. The clinic thus emerged as an autonomous agency with feasible realistic objectives defined by both community and the professional staff concerned.

246. BROWN, Julia (1956). The schizophrenic child in the school system.
        Records were studied for 29 children, all who were diagnosed as schizophrenics between May 1954 and September 1955 in the Child Adjustment Services, Board of Education (Toronto). Nine months to two years after diagnosis 15 of the children were in regular school grades; 11 others were in special classes where more individual attention and less pressure were possible. Almost 75 per cent of the 53 teachers who had had the 29 children in their classes prior to diagnosis, and virtually all the 26 teachers currently in charge of them, were fully accepting — although 33 per cent of the latter were unaware that the Child Adjustment Services had ever seen the pupil concerned.

169

Better clinic-teacher communication has since developed.
The clinic's records suggest that service had focused
on helping parents of schizophrenic children, but not
on the special difficulties their teachers face. However, the effect of the service, combined with the as-
signing of especially gifted teachers, had helped even
classroom adjustment in many cases.

247. BUTKEVICIUS, Sefije (1962). Post-hospital adjustment
of schizophrenic ex-patients.
    The writer compared information from interviews
with, and pre-hospital histories in case records on,
20 patients who had been in the community at least a
year, selected from the former inpatient schizophrenic
group who had been referred to the After-Care Service,
Ontario Hospital, Toronto, after July 1, 1959 but discharged by December 31, 1960. Nine aspects of social
behaviour (involving habits, attitudes, relationships)
were found to be relevant to improved social adjustment, and among these the most noticeable change was
in performance at work, a factor closely associated
by ex-patients with improvement in self-concept.
Least evidently related to improvement or noticeable
change were vocation, duration of employment, earned
income, other income, living arrangements, living ac-
comodation, living stability, living location, social
activity, and heterosexual relationships. Clinical
records showed that psychiatrists' "ratings" and the
social worker's assessments were in striking agreement in 18 of the 20 cases.

248. CAMPBELL, Catherine (1950). The value of social work
    interviews preceding outpatient treatment at the
    Toronto Psychiatric Hospital.
    In September and October 1949, of 146 recorded
new cases, 76 were accepted for outpatient treatment
— 47 patients coming through their doctors directly
to a psychiatrist, and 29 otherwise referred coming
through intake where their initial interview was with
a social worker. Comparative study of their case records shows that 40 per cent of the doctor referrals
and 52 per cent of the intake referrals had been able
to participate in effective treatment. Uneven distribution of severe cases apparently did not explain
the disparity, for the advantage was even more markedly with the intake group when diagnosed psychotics
were left out of account. Well over twice as many

170

doctor referrals broke treatment. Families were involved in treatment for almost twice as many intake
referrals. The use of the "hospital team" -- with
13 per cent of doctor referrals and 41 per cent of
intake referrals -- was plainly conducive to improvement. These findings justify further research into
the relation between intake interviews and effective
treatment.

249. CASTELLANO, Vincent G. (1959). Mental illness among
        Italian immigrants.
        The effect of a number of psychosocial stresses
is explored through case records from the Ontario Hospital (Toronto) on the 55 Italian immigrants with no
background of mental illness who were inpatients between 1952 and 1958. They were predominantly under
age forty, from rural areas, having Italian elementary
schooling -- men with families still in Italy or single men. Despite residence of up to five years, only
3 could communicate in English. This language barrier
compounded difficulties of isolation and economic insecurity. Anxiety and guilt over separation from families or parents goaded many to overwork and excessive
saving. Many physically in Canada were "home" psycho-
logically, and even after hospital stays averaging
eight months had little or no insight into their illnesses. Further studies should explore whether fear
of deportation dangerously postpones treatment, whether
preparation of and for immigrants might minimize
stresses, and what factors delay language learning
and explain the drive for early house ownership.

250. CLARK, Doris C. (1957). Attitudes of employers to-
        wards mental illness.
        To study one factor that conditions the adjust-
ment of ex-patients from mental hospitals, the writer
interviewed 34 officials in Toronto, representing
large and small production and service industries,
retailing, and the civil service. Only one would reject anyone who had been mentally ill. Few could
distinguish types of illness. Former employees and
older applicants with good work records would usually
be considered, but for the simpler jobs only. Suitable placements are least readily offered the young
and those with good education and skills. Although
the most enlightened were personnel managers in large

171

firms, the most willing to see an ex-patient through
a period of rehabilitation were supervisors in smaller
organizations. All would welcome a psychiatrist's or
social worker's guidance. Education has still to overcome much generalizing from slight experience and much
evasion of realistic knowledge about mental illness.
Further studies might establish whether any basis exists in the work experiences of ex-patients for certain
categorical assumptions still widespread among employers.

251. De MARSH, Helen R. (1950). Services of the Outpatient
Department, Toronto Psychiatric Hospital, to the
Toronto Children's Aid Society.
     The abnormal stresses to which every child who
becomes a ward is exposed makes the community's psychiatric services a concern of the agency responsible for
such children's well-being. This study, through Children's Aid Society case records of 40 wards referred
to the clinic during 1944-49, and through interviews
with their caseworkers of the 15 subsequently treated,
undertakes an evaluation of the help given. Excluding
11 cases of subnormal intelligence -- a category no
longer routed through the clinic after 1947 -- the
commonest disorders were temper outburst, running a-
way, enuresis, and masturbation. Of the 15 who received psychotherapy 60 per cent showed improvement,
compared with 20 per cent from the group given only
diagnostic service. Sometimes clinic recommendations
were unrealistic, e.g., foster-home care for a child
whom the agency's best foster parents had already
found beyond them. Sometimes better preparation by
the agency might have precluded a child's refusing
treatment. A similar evaluation of the new psychiatric
consultation services within the Children's Aid Society
is recommended.

252. FINLAY, Donald Gordon (1956). The mother-child
relationship after treatment at a Child Guidance
clinic.
     From records of the Toronto Mental Health Clinic
the writer assessed significant changes between the
initial contact and the termination of treatment of
all 20 families served between March 1954 and May 1955.
Then he interviewed the 14 mothers still in the area,
at the clinic by the mother's choice in every case of

172

marked improvement. Individual case histories reveal changes effected, and illustrate various difficulties and responses to treatment. Some mothers had been able to accept and apply what the clinic found and explained only long after contact had terminated. Other mothers continued to feel negative about the child's condition, and thus inhibited recovery in children too young for independent psychological development. Unless parents seemed unable to involve themselves in treatment, or the social situation was untenable, casework with the adult and play therapy with the child seemed to promote effective self-help.

253. GRANT, Jean (1957). The change in parents of mentally subnormal children.
      To elaborate one aspect of the family problem involved in any case of mental retardation, the writer analyzed parents' attitudes at both first and last contact from records in the Toronto Psychiatric Hospital Outpatient Department on the 35 closed cases between May 1951 and May 1956 of children up to age twenty-one with I.Q.'s of 80 or less. Parents' attitudes were initially satisfactory in 2 cases, and showed improvement in 20 more. Parents of the older children tended to have more long-standing defensiveness. In 27 cases parents were puzzled about the child's condition and its irreversibility, pinning hopes on later growth or therapy or employment. Many consulted the hospital because of community pressures rather than conviction, and only longer, closer contact would have enabled them to co-operate until a satisfactory plan was concluded. Group experience with other parents also tormented by similar guilt, denial, or rejection might prove helpful.

254. HERTZMAN, Phyllis (1955). A community study of Census Tract 39 in Toronto.
      A joint study of 1951 and 1953 admissions to the Toronto Psychiatric Hospital showed a slight clustering of patients' homes in certain scattered areas. One such area is studied from census data, and interviews with public health nurses, probation officers, a school principal, a local dairy proprietor, etc., and with 14 of the 20 residents admitted to the Toronto Psychiatric Hospital between 1950 and 1954. The area showed few notable differences from city averages. Commerce and industry were not replacing

173

residences, and although increasingly foreign-born
owners used homes as rent-producing investments, there
were also many long-term home-owners still there. The
city as a whole had, proportionately, eight times as
many subscribers to the Community Chest. Patients'
attitudes also reflected this loss of community feeling: few had contact with neighbours or used the available better-than-average facilities for outdoor
recreation. Further study is invited of the stresses
in ethnically mixed neighbourhoods, and the effectiveness for community feeling of community programs.

255. HINDLEY, Joyce D. (1954). Treatment methods and
      philosophy of Sunnyside Children's Centre.
        From records (in this centre in Kingston for
disturbed children aged three to twelve and in referring agencies), and through first-hand observation,
the writer studied 16 residents between 1947 and 1950
who were placed for adoption at discharge. Half
needed preparation for adoption rather than the intensive therapy the centre increasingly stresses.
Plant, intake policies, admission procedures, and administration were found well up to "standards" derived
from fourteen other well-known treatment centres. The
institution, which had no psychotherapist among the
professionals on its staff, has developed a strong
residential program. Warm, spontaneous response from
staff, group feeling, light duties assigned to build
confidence, and bonds with neighbourhood children in
playground and nursery school and through community
programs, had helped all this group, judging by the
successful adoption of 14 by 1950, and all 16 by 1954.
Other centres' policies differ mainly in psychiatric
and casework orientation. Only long-term follow-up
would establish the ultimate effectiveness of this
therapy: teaching socially accepted behaviour mainly
through a gratifying day-to-day experience of communal
living.

256. HOLMES, Rosalie F. (1957). Factors related to outcome
      of treatment in Child Guidance.
        The group studied are 30 children who, between
1952 and 1954, were accepted by the Toronto Mental
Health Clinic for psychiatric treatment, whose cases
were currently inactive, and both of whose parents
had accompanied them at some time during treatment

174

(usually only one parent attends, meeting the clinic's
stipulation that the parent concerned must see the
social worker while a child is seeing the psychiatrist).
Children of ages six to twelve from Jewish homes predominated, but the relevance of background data to
prognosis could not be established. However, the analysis of records kept by social workers, psychologists,
and psychiatrists shows that in all 8 cases where treatment was effective, the marriages were stable and both
parents had warm, accepting, and firm attitudes towards
the child concerned. A father's close involvement in
the process, too, appeared conducive to his child's
progress. Effective treatment tended to have been
long-term and well supported by the patient's home.

257. IWASAKI, Elsie M. (1957). The emotional problems in
a sibling relationship when one child is mentally
subnormal.
In 1957 a Toronto school for retarded children
included 44 children aged five to eleven with one or
more brothers or sisters under thirteen; the 34 of
their families located, able, and willing, were interviewed. Mothers talked mainly about the subnormal
child, usually reporting "nice quiet" behaviour and
almost always touching on "the cause" but not mention-
ing genetic factors. They reported that younger children tended to let the slow one play with them "but
kind of ignore him" (or her), older ones to exclude
him "but you couldn't blame them"; and that "they have
to learn to humour him" although "quarrelling is no
problem". Although many acknowledged difficulties,
only 5 mothers showed extensive insight. With one
child needing much practical care and often overprotected, the others tended to suppress their own claims
or to feel unloved. Casework help for parents, if possible when the subnormalcy is diagnosed, will best help
others in families to meet these particular stresses.

258. JAFFEY, A. Diana (1955). Social characteristics and
circumstances of patients admitted to the Toronto
Psychiatric Hospital.
The writer, in a joint project investigating
the socio-economic context of mental breakdowns in
Toronto and York Township, analyzes case histories
of 545 patients, a random sample from 1,100 outpatients and the 259 inpatients admitted in 1953.

Facts about patients' neighbourhoods are drawn from
1951 Census reports. Young adults were over-represented
because of the hospital's admissions policy, and Roman
Catholics and Jews perhaps because of the over-
representation of recent immigrants. More North Americans at both extremes than at the middle income levels
fell ill; however, among immigrants illness and low incomes were correlated. A disproportionate number of
patients were unmarried. Rooming-house neighbourhoods
predominated, but instances of overcrowded dwellings
were few among patients' backgrounds. A more intensive
and representative study is recommended to test the impression from these findings that social isolation is
a significant environmental factor in mental illness.

259. JARVIS, Donald L. (1960). Common psychosocial patterns
    presented by a group of young boys in a special ed-
    ucational setting.
        Impressed by the response of a lad on probation
to the Frank Oke School's special program, the writer
studied through records, staff comments, and interviews
43 among the 70 boys admitted to the school in September
1959. Selected geographically all were retarded, about
80 per cent by two or three years. An even higher proportion had trouble with reading (but not arithmetic),
and showed emotionally disturbed behaviour. All but 3
had physical defects. In all 19 cases of conflict at
home, economic need was also evident, as in this comment: "We always move if the rent is too much money."
One-quarter of the boys had part-time jobs and the
mothers in 19 homes went out to work. Television absorbed over 20 hours weekly, on average, and "playing
on the street" overwhelmingly outbalanced any organized activities. Better vocational focus is needed
to help these boys, and clearer admissions policies
and extended facilities to help more like them.

260. KAY, Marion (1958). Parental problems in the home
    care of a schizophrenic child.
        One consequence of a study made by a Toronto
hospital in 1953-56 was the organization by parents
of the Association for Emotionally Disturbed Children. The writer interviewed 20 members of the association, each giving home care to a child under
thirteen who had been diagnosed as schizophrenic.
Although all 20 children were reportedly well developed,

their resistance to conventional routines meant that
sleeping, eating, toilet training, washing and dress-
ing were all more or less severe problems for the parents. Gropingly these discovered what could be expected
of their sick child and how to discipline him within
his limits. Relatives, neighbours, and passersby seldom understood; consequent "unpleasantnesses" led to
increasing parental isolation. Households tended to
revolve around the patient, often at other children's
expense, but to most parents an institution seemed un-
thinkable, just yet at least. For the parents casework
help, and for the children experimental educational and
recreational groups, are recommended.

261. KAYE, Elaine (1956). A follow-up study of children
     dischared as improved from the Clinic for Psycho-
     logical Medicine, Hospital for Sick Children, be-
     tween January 1951 and July 1952.
     On the basis of clinic records on long-term
treatment where some improvement was noted at discharge and of subsequent interviews with the 30 (of
a total 37 families) still in Toronto and willing to
participate, the writer applied the Witmer Rating
Scale to assess patients' conditions a year or more
after termination of clinic contact. All the children had showed problems in symptomatic behaviour,
29 in family and 27 in social relationships, 24 at
school, and 13 in psychosomatic symptoms. Some family relationships were still troubled at discharge.
By the interview date, 8 ex-patients had regressed
and 7 others had not continued the progress begun
during therapy. In general the children who had been
able to consolidate and build on gains made during
therapy were those with harmonious, accepting homes
whose parents had learned from and appreciated the
clinic experience.

262. KILEEG, John (1950). The family life and home envi-
     ronment of disturbed children.
     The "disturbed children" of this study are those
who were referred to Toronto's Protestant youth counselling services because of behaviour or personality
problems. Information about their backgrounds and
the reasons for referral are drawn from 188 case records supplemented by discussion with some of the social
workers concerned. All 88 of the teen-aged boys whose

177

cases were active with the Big Brother Movement in
March 1950 were included, and about half the caseload
of the Big Sister Association. Educational standards
and levels of income for the families of these clients
were slightly below Canadian averages. About two-
thirds of the children had experienced broken homes,
and unhappy relationships within the family were recorded in most of the histories. The parents' disciplinary practices were generally assessed as poor.
The writer concludes that it is not possible, on this
recorded evidence, to establish with any precision
the effects on disturbed children of their home life.
But he makes it clear that effective marriage counselling and family guidance clinics are part of the
program of preventive action.

263. LAVENDER, Joan (1961). Wards admitted to a psychiatric
     hospital.
        Case records are studied on the 20 wards of the
     Children's Aid Society (Toronto) who, not referred
     through the courts, were admitted before age seven-
     teen to the Toronto Psychiatric Hospital in the period
     1947 - 1957. Circumstances that had occasioned ward-
     ship in the 1930's — parental misfortune for 8, il-
     legitimacy for 9, neglect for only 3 — suggest that
     a child's right to his own home was not as well pro-
     tected then, when resources were inadequate to the
     widespread need. Only one mother appeared to have
     been normal in health and behaviour. The group's
     average intelligence level was emphatically higher
     than would be inferred from performance levels in
     school or adjustment in foster homes or community.
     Compared with the hospital's averages, these children
     remained inpatients longer than most, although only
     6 were sent to another treatment hospital on discharge.
     Only comparative study with wards who were never in
     hospital would establish the relevance to their mental
     illness of the factors noted in these cases.

264. LAWSON, Clifford A. (1955). Social characteristics
     of patients admitted to Toronto Psychiatric Hos-
     pital with a diagnosis of schizophrenia and manic-
     depressive psychosis.
        Hospital records on admissions from Toronto and
     York Township for 1951 and 1953, compared with popu-
     lation figures, established a .36 per thousand annual

admissions rate; 28 per cent of the patients admitted (156) were diagnosed as schizophrenics and 8 per cent (43) as manic-depressives. These proportions proved constant when concentrations of admissions and population were studied in different metropolitan areas. However, the proportion of patients aged fifteen to thirty-four was higher among schizophrenics, and aged thirty-five to sixty-nine higher among manic-depressives, than in the general population. A disproportionate number of patients were males. Single persons predominated in the total group but not in the predominantly older manic-depressive group. Proportions of Jews, Roman Catholics, and European immigrants were higher among admissions than in the metropolitan population, though perhaps many patients were counted both as immigrants and as Jews or Catholics. Any coincidences of social characteristics and these two diseases herein noted might suggest avenues for future research.

265. LEPPANEN, Airi E. (1952). The vocational rehabilitation of patients discharged from Toronto Psychiatric Hospital.
All 20 of the ex-patients studied had had a vocational problem on discharge and had been in the community one to two years at the time the writer interviewed them (June 1952). Hospital records, on their earlier work history especially, provided a background for assessing how readily and firmly each had been able to decide on a course of action, to follow through, accepting whatever help proved necessary, and to carry out the responsibilities of work unimpeded by effects of mental illness. Apparently counselling patients' relatives contributes to rehabilitation, since all 7 here who made a good vocational adjustment had worked out good relationships with their families. The 5 poorly adjusted had trouble with general social contacts too. Few seemed perturbed if their work did not employ their full potentialities, but almost all felt steadied and rewarded by recognition and understanding supervision. For easier contact with patients and consultation with staff during vocational planning, the placing of an employment officer inside the hospital is recommended.

266. LESSER, Sara Martin (1960). The schizophrenic patient in the home.

Since recent therapeutic methods permit an increasing number of discharges from mental hospitals, new questions arise about the patients' adjustments at home. The writer as a social worker at Ste. Anne's Hospital, Ste. Anne de Bellevue, Quebec, worked with patients after discharge. She studied records on 18 who had been referred by a psychiatrist, all the schizophrenic ex-servicemen discharged to their families in 1958, and then interviewed the families. Some form of negative change occurred in almost 90 per cent of the homes. Where pensions improved finances, overcrowding might outbalance the gain, for instance. Changes in patterns of living (e.g., adults' reluctance to entertain or to go out and children's nervousness) seemed least tolerable. More patients who tended to be withdrawn met acceptance from families than patients showing aggressive traits. Further study is urged: of the adjustment of patients without all the services available to veterans; and of characteristics in patients or relatives that militate against good home adjustment.

267. LUGSDIN, Mary I. (1950). Rehabilitation achieved by patients discharged from the Toronto Psychiatric Hospital, June 1951.

In September 1949 a three-month period of aftercare was introduced as part of the social service available from workers on the Toronto Psychiatric Hospital's staff. As an initial exploration of that service's functioning, the writer studied hospital and social service records on the 38 cases of patients discharged as improved, to note their progress after the three-month interval. Although 7 were supervised from other agencies or maintained medical contact only, and 7 would not or could not continue accepting service, 16 were supported for three months and 8 stayed longer under supervision. In the many cases where a home situation had been a precipitating factor in the illness, every improved home was reflected in an improved patient. This preliminary survey suggests that, since environmental strains are slow to appear, three months is a minimal period, and that the service should be carefully explained beforehand or patients and relatives may suspect that the hospital's continued observation endorses the dread of recurrence they themselves feel.

268. LUSTGARTEN, Peter (1955). Breaking treatment in a
      psychiatric outpatient clinic.
          Of 335 outpatients applying in 1951 and treated
      at the Toronto Psychiatric Hospital Clinic, 113 saw
      their psychiatrists at least once but failed to keep
      another appointment. Of these, 33, selected chiefly
      according to intake procedure, were interviewed in
      mid-1952. The response to preliminary letters and
      the degree of co-operative participation astonished
      the interviewer. Most of those who had accepted pro-
      cedures like student clinics had been prepared for
      them at intake interviews. Change of therapist had
      disturbed the few who mentioned this procedure. How-
      ever, no single factor emerged as correlated with, or
      commonly contributing to, break-off from treatment.
      About two-thirds were worse now than during clinic
      contact, according to both the respondents' and the
      interviewer's judgment. And very few said they wanted
      to resume therapy. Yet the interview was fairly gen-
      erally interpreted as "evidence that someone still
      cares about me" and almost all said, in varied ways,
      "If you would have phoned or sent a letter I would
      have come back." To help such patients sustain treat-
      ment or end their clinic contact more comfortably, a
      follow-up program is recommended.

269. McCLELLAND, P. Ross (1956). Families caring for an
      adult mentally subnormal offspring at home.
          Through a local agency providing day care, sub-
      jects aged eighteen or more but functioning at a two-
      to eight-year-old level were selected, 25 of their
      families were located, and 22 were interviewed. Re-
      spondents' attitudes were sometimes defensive, and
      post-interview comments that came to notice often
      appeared sharply at variance with responses during
      the interview. Only 6 parents said they had been
      told exactly how their child's case had been diag-
      nosed. Many had long cherished unrealistic hopes
      of a "medical cure". The majority, seeing reading
      and writing as symbols of adequacy, felt that "with
      proper teaching" their child might have learned once,
      but was "too old" now. The school system had excluded
      him, they felt, strangers stared at him, and author-
      ities "heartlessly" proposed an institution (i.e.,
      "rejection"). Almost all the families experienced
      stresses: social isolation, disagreement on plans,

181

anxiety, or an unequally divided burden of care. Casework services for such families, and clinical, training,
and recreational facilities for the subnormal children
should be extended.

270. MACFARLANE, Phyllis Osborne (1961). Factors affecting
the capacity of adolescents to utilize psychiatric
outpatient treatment.
This exploratory study uses what information
case records supply on the 30 patients between fifteen
and nineteen years of age who registered for the first
time, or after at least a six-month interval, with the
Outpatient Department, Toronto Psychiatric Hospital,
and for whom treatment was recommended. Over half the
group accepted very little treatment (less than six
interviews), and a few who stayed longer failed to respond positively; but these groups showed few marked
differences from the patients who benefited. (The
hospital's admissions policy had already sifted out
some categories of patient, of course.) Where the
patients had been referred by a community agency, or
where a social worker interviewed the patients first
at the clinic, the proportion who stayed and accepted
treatment was surprisingly high. Thus preparation
for diagnostic and therapeutic procedures might be
considered conducive to good response, especially in
view of the correlation, in this group, between improvement from treatment and "good attitude" on admission.

271. MARSHALL, Helen (1954). The effect of relative's involvement with social service on the treatment of
the patient.
The writer compared cases of 22 outpatients in
the Toronto Psychiatric Hospital who had relatives
also receiving service from social workers during
March 1954 with those of another 22 adult patients
then with no relatives involved but referred from
comparable sources and treated by the same doctors.
Comparisons were based on doctors' and social workers'
records and on specific evaluations. The first group
had three times as many patients with psychotic or
organic illnesses, none of whom was assessed as improved after treatment. The inference from this study
suggests that doctors tend to refer cases to social
service when prognoses are unfavourable, rather than

that relatives' participation influences outcome. However, over half the relatives involved did develop better acceptance and understanding of the illness and in most of these cases the patients' attitudes improved correspondingly.

272. MENDEL, Anita (1956). <u>Social situation and hospital readmission.</u>
Readmission to mental hospital means renewed stress for all concerned. Yet the numbers readmitted increase, more rapidly in England since 1948 (when the National Health Services Act became applicable) than in Canada. The implications of readmission to Banstead Hospital (England) during the winter of 1954-55 for 35 women patients and 30 of their relatives are here explored through interviews. Some relatives genuinely glad to have patients home can encourage them and defer relapses, but others help little, often because they themselves are discouraged by recurrent homecomings and exhausted because while at work they worry and in rest times they need to be watchful during the intervals when the patient is living at home. By securing discharge against doctors' advice, 16 respondents had expressed negative attitudes towards the hospital or misapprehensions about the illnesses. More social workers are needed to interpret the hospital's concern to individuals. Relatives might be helped by regular group therapy; homeless patients by a "halfway house"; and aged ex-patients and patients resuming responsibilities for aged parents on discharge, by day-care services.

273. NICHOLS, Lyla N.M. (1958). <u>The ecology of mental health in Toronto.</u>
A joint project at the University of Toronto School of Social Work in 1954 in which 1951 and 1953 admissions to the Toronto Psychiatric Hospital (totalling 552) were analyzed for geographic distribution did not reveal the patterns of concentration expected on the basis of findings in other cities. The present study — of geographic distribution for all 601 local area admissions in 1953 to the Ontario Hospital (Toronto) — similarly does not show the expected patterns, either by itself or when findings are considered together with those of the earlier study. Such differences as appeared to demarcate the clienteles of the

two hospitals could be accounted for by the hospitals'
different admissions policies. In other cities, studies
showed significant differences between patients and general population in distribution by sex and marital status. Not so here. Other studies showed fewer native-
born, proportionately, among patients. Here there were
proportionately more native-born. Rates for some mental
illnesses were higher in central areas, but other diagnoses completely blurred this partial "pattern" of
geographic distribution.

274. PARSONS, Sydney J. (1955). A follow-up study of the
adjustment achieved by patients discharged from
the Toronto Psychiatric Hospital during the year
1946.
    Pre-morbid adjustment was noted from case re-
cords on, and 1951 conditions by interviews with families of, the 30 patients selected by accessibility
and according to proportionate distribution of diagnoses from the 333 who returned directly to the community of a total 567 discharged in 1946. Every case
is reviewed; personal, social, and vocational adjustment are thus assessed in the context of individual
life situations and norms. Among the 20 patients who
had adjusted "normally" by 1951 were 5 who had needed
psychiatric help since discharge and also the only 2
in the sample who were not "first admissions" during
their 1946 stay in hospital. The well-adjusted had
had the shortest average stay. Even the 10 patients
who made poor adjustments and suffered relapses nevertheless had managed to spend a total of 6,900 days
living as private individuals between discharge and
readmission. A parallel study is suggested after
1948, when the Social Service Department opened and
introduced more recording about, and involvement of,
relatives.

275. PRICE, Gifford C. (1950). A history of the Ontario
Hospital, Toronto; the development of institutional
care and treatment of the mentally ill in Ontario.
    The Lavell Manuscript (Ontario's Provincial His-
torian's record covering mental institutions up to
1932), sources there indicated, and official reports
and documents, provided material for this centenary
history. Until 1839 "care" was authorized only under
provisions for keeping the peace. The first separation

of mental patients, although in an adapted jailhouse on a regime of cupping and near-starvation, nevertheless meant notable improvement. Through a long period in the earliest buildings of the present institution good custodial care with entertainment and generous use of wines prevailed. Before 1900 mechanical restraints were disused, and open wards and some hydrotherapy were introduced. Gradually trained staffs, techniques like chemotherapy for neurosyphilis, netrozol therapy, and the use of electroshock and after 1946 group therapy, meant new emphasis on treatment. Overcrowding still persists; hence today's questions about training and research programs, segregating chronic and aged patients, and developing community care programs.

276. ROSS, Norman L. (1961). The interpersonal relationships of troubled school children.
This descriptive study focuses on 21 children referred during 1959-60 to the Child Adjustment Services, Toronto Board of Education — all whose files were available who had undergone diagnostic assessment in the Intensive Study Clinic and had been referred to another resource for continued special help. The mother who uses her child as a vehicle to bear off the resentments she fears might otherwise break her marriage, the ambitious father who pushes his son while jealous of his unusual abilities, the parents who in accepting a child's limitations "give up on him": such stressful and rejecting backgrounds were characteristic of the group. Exceptionally intelligent children were over-represented. One-third of the 21 children were schizophrenic, and almost as many had suffered physical illnesses earlier. The study suggests how school social workers can contribute to early recognition of mental illnesses, help children adjust to unusual circumstances, and promote mental hygiene in their homes.

277. SCOTT, Lorraine M. (1959). A follow-up study of the experiences after discharge of a number of girls who have lived in Warrendale, a residential treatment centre.
The 20 girls interviewed at least eight months after their discharge had all spent at least six months in the residence. All were disturbed at

admission, 16 having among them experienced a total
of 62 foster-home placements. Only 4 girls were still
communicating with one-time foster parents in 1958 --
many others welcoming the break. All but 3 girls were
by then managing independently and fairly successfully
in the community, 5 having married and 13 having taken
permanent jobs, in most cases after some academic or
training courses. Their social relationships seemed,
on the whole, satisfying. All but one girl said they
had found Warrendale helpful and, significantly, 14
had kept in touch with the centre. A graduate's residence in the city might help girls consolidate their
gains. Since 10 had left prematurely under family
pressure, and many had afterwards tried to sort out
family relationships, perhaps the centre should make
great efforts to involve families during the treatment
period.

278. SEIGEL, Mildred (1960). Emotional bonds between partners in cases of anxiety neurosis.
    Out of 23 closed cases studied here, all of par-
ents aged twenty to forty-five in intact households
who began continued service with the Toronto Psychiatric Hospital in 1956, only 5 patients' spouses were
interviewed, 3 by a psychiatrist and 2 by a social
worker, with 2 others who were referred for casework
refusing to involve themselves. These interviews,
patients' recorded perceptions, and psychiatrists'
summaries, convey that, seeking in marriage to satisfy needs left unfilled in parental homes, the patients were unprepared for and overwhelmed by the
roles involved in marriage and parenthood. The wives'
predominant problem was a sense of unworthiness, the
husbands', dependency. Patients' spouses may often
have been even more unwell, since withdrawal and inadequacy seemed the common response of those assessed.
Further study -- by interview, with other diagnostic
groups, and of repercussions on children -- is recommended, to clarify the implications of illness for
family well-being and for the treatment process by
the clinic team.

279. SHEPHARD, Barbara (1954). A comparison of adjustments
to stress: prewar civilian experience as compared
with battle experience.
    The scale for measuring adjustment in combat is
derived from the Department of Veterans Affairs'

186

unpublished survey of 1,271 neuropsychiatric casualties treated in Europe in 1944-45, as is the source material on prewar adjustments recorded then by treating psychiatrists. Ratings of prewar adjustment were made by the writer and checked against another social worker's assessments of sample case records. Study of recorded data on the 346 of the total 1,271 who could be reached and on the 169 who were infantrymen and unwounded, and comparative analyses of two groups of 16 cases each -- those who broke down early and those who lasted until stress was maximal -- support the hypothesis: ability to withstand battle stress is correlated with good adjustment in early life. Poor economic backgrounds were evident in equal proportions in both stress groups. Early family and social adjustment seemed most related to stamina; independent, ambitious, gregarious men were able to endure relatively high stress.

280. SINCLAIR, M. Elizabeth (1955). The problem of referring the hospitalized child to a psychiatrist.
Against background information in clinic records, parents' attitudes are here studied through scheduled interviews with the 35 available families whose children were inpatients in the Hospital for Sick Children when referred for psychiatric treatment between January 1949 and March 1953. Only 8 parents felt that family doctors or social workers adequately explained the referral. For 5 children tests and appraisal only were involved; 5 were given intensive therapy for severe behaviour disorders while parents participated simultaneously through casework; for 25, psychiatrists through limited contact tried to advise the parents, half of whom refused service. Most of the 18 children effectively treated had parents who could accept the diagnosis and become involved in the treatment. Procedures are recommended whereby social workers would explain to inpatients' families what the clinic offers and help them to use it. Understanding support of such families from hospital staff and home community should be encouraged.

281. SKELTON, Mora (1951). Social adjustment of patients discharged from Toronto Psychiatric Hospital.
This study was made just before an enlarged social service department and a follow-up program

187

were established at the hospital. Comparing hospital
records on condition at discharge in May, June, or
July 1949 with statements, in interviews during May
1950, by or about the 20 patients still available in
the community, the writer found that 6 had continued
improvements apparent at discharge, 4 had maintained
good recoveries, and two-thirds of the rest were unchanged. The accuracy of hospital prognoses for this
group suggests that diagnosis and treatment are primary determinants of patients' progress. All the
patients who had built on or held gains made during
treatment had support from relatives. All but 4
could function to some extent in occupations. Relatives, friends, and employers helped or hindered according to their understanding. To ease adjustments,
patients suggested group discussion beforehand in the
wards, and universal but voluntary and flexible follow-
up contacts with doctors and social workers -- someone
the patient already knew, whenever possible.

282. TAIT, Robert H. (1956). The leisure-time activities
of stutterers.
The Speech Clinic in the Toronto Psychiatric
Hospital tries to help patients towards improved speech,
better attitude to stuttering, and social adjustment.
Of the 44 who had "graduated", 2 answered questions by
mail and 30 in interviews. Only 3 recalled pre-
adolescent social difficulties. Apparently in adolescence all the stutterers tried "joining" but moved from
one group or activity to another, all but 3 feeling "un-
comfortable" with most people. After therapy 29 felt
greater social ease; the interviewer assessed 21 as
friendlier and more befriended as well, and all but one
of these were adjudged by the Clinic Director as "improved in social adjustment". Qualified therapists are
not yet widely available. Where rsources exist, social
workers should refer clients and collaborate during
treatment. Elsewhere they can offer some help through
casework, since patients who accepted their handicap,
and learned not to cover up or over-compensate, were
all socially freer and happier afterwards.

283. TURNER, Morley B. (1956). A follow-up study of the
factors in the adjustment achieved by a group of
patients with a diagnosis of reactive depression
who were discharged from the Toronto Psychiatric
Hospital.

From the hospital's records on 59 cases treated since August 1, 1952 for reactive depression and discharged to the community by May 30, 1955, 30 were found available for interview (22 directly and 8 through relatives). The 22 who accepted help from doctors and social workers after discharge were distributed throughout three groups: 12 improved; 12 maintaining discharge condition; 6 regressing. Although 5 mentioned occurrences which had proved disturbing, 2 cited similar occurrences which, by providing occasions for them to cope under stress, had had positive meaning. The 27 now working had responded to others' acceptance -- "When I relaxed and was able to admit that I had been sick for awhile, I found that the other fellows took their cue from this, and I have gotten along very well since then." Family support and understanding proved essential in convalescence. Besides efforts to ensure good home and work environments, social encouragement through former patients' groups is tentatively suggested.

284. WACKO, William J. (1951). Boarding-out care at the Ontario Hospital, New Toronto.
    Religious and welfare authorities in Europe and hospital administrations in North America have tried various kinds of family care for the mentally ill. New Toronto has Canada's most extensive home-care program, initiated for chronic cases almost exclusively, later serving mainly patients from northern counties who could thus be supervised through convalescence before discharge to far-off homes. Hospital records on 182 patients placed in eight different homes during 1945-49 show that placements per year increased from 21 to 55, and service shifted from chronically ill men to convalescent women with the predominant diagnosis manic-depressive phychosis. Of the 86 discharged, most had recovered after relatively short hospitalization and boarding periods, although some had responded under home care after long, apparently ineffectual, institutional care. Casework is increasingly emphasized to ensure good selection and safeguarding of homes used. Further study is urged of equivalent plans for male patients here; and of outcome for groups discharged directly and through boarding-out homes.

285. WALKER, Phyllis M. (1947). Graduates of the Haven;
     a follow-up study of the community adjustment of
     mentally deficient girls discharged from the Haven
     during the years 1931 to 1945.
        In the fifteen year period, 270 mentally defec-
     tive girls moved from Ontario Hospitals to the Haven
     for further training before employment. Data was
     collected on as many as possible (91 of the 60 per
     cent who could still be located) through interviews
     locally and questionnaires to out-of-town agencies.
     The 37 now well adjusted in the community had, on
     average, stayed longer and more happily in the Haven.
     Many more of the others had married and later found
     themselves unable to cope. Could the Haven offer
     some training for marriage as well as in domestic
     work, since so many girls become wives and/or mothers?
     Could universal lifetime supervision be arranged? If
     runaways were all traced and rehospitalized, and cases
     of delinquency and neglect prevented, both girls and
     community might feasibly benefit, especially in view
     of the encouraging percentage of Haven graduates who
     could be adequately "supervised" by only occasional
     friendly visits.

286. WALLACE, H. Ross (1959). Behaviour problems of boys
     separated from their fathers.
        Psychologists have indicated how sons grow by
     identifying with, depending upon, consulting and com-
     peting with, and following the example of, their fa-
     thers. Deprived of fathers, how do they react? Of
     98 cases opened for continued service with Toronto's
     Big Brother Movement in 1958, 60 concerned boys who
     had been separated from their fathers for at least
     three months. Eliminating 13 cases where the boy had
     left home and 2 uncompletely recorded, the writer
     noted, from the remaining 45 histories, that pre-
     adolescents predominated and that two-thirds were the
     oldest or only boy in the family. Incidence of con-
     flict with brothers and sisters or mothers, of steal-
     ing, or of withdrawn behaviour could be correlated
     with the boys' ages when separated and the degree of
     isolation from fathers or father substitutes. Fur-
     ther study might focus on boys whose homes were broken
     by marital conflict, or compare boys from broken homes
     with problem boys from intact families.

287. WEBB, Paul R. (1957). The vocational adjustment of
     patients discharged from the Toronto Psychiatric
     Hospital.
          Mr. Webb conducted interviews to discover how
     men feel about their progress, especially at work
     after at least six months in the community following
     hospitalization for mental illness. Only those able
     and willing to co-operate, of course, are represented
     in this study of 30 men discharged as improved in
     1953. Three outsiders who agreed to rate the inter-
     view findings evaluated the job adjustments as "poor"
     in 2 cases, "fair" in 14, and "good" in 14. Those
     who returned to their own jobs within a month after
     discharge fared best, most of them skilled workmen
     between thirty-six and forty-five with about fourteen
     years of education. Poor health was a factor in all
     less-than-good adjustments. Although relatively few
     felt concerned about employers' attitudes to their
     illness, acceptance of the hospital experience seemed
     part of good adjustment. Work was a central factor,
     for all these men, in recovering the self-confidence
     their illness had undermined.

288. WEST, Leslie A. (1954). The value of the post-discharge
     social service at the Toronto Psychiatric Hospital.
          Value is here assessed through the attitudes of
     the 22 patients (and 16 of their relatives) who had
     been discharged in 1951 or 1952, were still accessible,
     and had had at least three months' subsequent contact
     with the hospital's Social Service Department. The
     most negative attitudes were likely omitted with the
     11 families who refused the interview. Some patients
     found it hard to remember the period in question; for
     others attitudes were distorted by inner feelings.
     With due allowance for these imprecisions, an evalu-
     ation did emerge when interviews were analyzed (after
     study of hospital case records). Among relatives,
     dread of a recurrence of illness was the most acute
     concern at the time of discharge. Caseworkers could
     meet, define, and often relieve this dread. Patients
     had been most apprehensive about family relationships
     and their ability to work, and found help and reassur-
     ance mainly in the latter area. Further research may
     throw light on why the patients who were longest in
     hospital reported the service most helpful, and will
     assuredly help social workers to meet patients' and
     relatives' needs.

GROUP PROJECT. <u>Significant factors in the family</u>
<u>situations of children who come to the attention</u>
<u>of a Child Guidance service.</u>
The over-all objective was to explore the constellation of certain factors within the family situations and to study the impact upon parents' efforts
in child rearing. To ascertain what families come to
a Child Guidance clinic, their use of the services, and
the extent to which certain psychosocial, cultural, or
economic factors relevant to child rearing were present,
a group of students collaborated in a survey of 209 case
records of families who, during the calendar year 1961,
had initiated contact with the Toronto Psychiatric Hospital Child and Adolescent Unit, or the Toronto Mental
Health Clinic. Based on the findings of this preliminary investigation, a specific finding was chosen for
more intensive exploration by each student, who then
selected a sample of 10 to 15 cases appropriate to his
particular interest and supplemented the data already
collected with additional data culled from the case
records of the sample group.

The potential child patients in the over-all in-
ventory consisted of 147 boys and 62 girls, of whom
only 12 were under school age. A striking feature was
the predominance of the middle-class suburban family
with two or three children whose difficulty in child
rearing increases with the age of the child. Single-
parent families comprised 15 per cent of the total;
families with step-parent, adopted child, or adult
relatives were remarkably few. Unemployment was negligible, few mothers supplemented family income by
working. These families indicated stress and tension
in many areas of functioning, but somewhat less than
a third continued in treatment in these clinics, while
a similar proportion ended contact after the intake
interview.

289. CAMPFENS, Hubert (1961). <u>Effect of a large age dis-</u>
<u>parity between the spouses on child rearing.</u>
Assuming that an age differential of more than
five years between the spouses could be symptomatic
of attitudes and behaviour interfering with child
rearing, the 10 families in which the wife was five
to thirteen years older than the husband were selected
for intensive study. Marital tension, separation between spouses, mothers working, appeared more widespread in this group. There was insufficient data to

compare the mother's behaviour to children of each sex.
These women aged thirty-seven to forty-eight demonstrated a strong need to dominate husbands and children,
felt threatened by any loss of control, tended to suppress or deny difficulties in marriage and with children, and to blame others if problems could not be
avoided. They came to clinics when pressured by the
school, neighbours, or physician, and resisted involvement with clinic service. With 9 of the 10 potential
patients boys, and indications of difficulties with
other male children in the family, these mothers' inability to tolerate any aggressive behaviour in the
male child, and their prizing obedience and compliance,
seemed significant.

290. GIROUX, Joan (1961). A study of parental attitudes to-
     ward the male child in a sample of ten male chil-
     dren in treatment at a Child Guidance clinic, 1961.
          Fifty-eight per cent of the families expressed
     concern about the first-born child. To test the pos-
     sibility that in addition to inexperience, mothers
     have difficulty accepting the male child's masculinity,
     the writer studied the records of 10 of the 21 families
     with two or more children receiving intensive treatment
     at Toronto Psychiatric Hospital Child and Adolescent
     Unit. The bewildered withdrawn boys in the pre-puberty
     stage, still filled with intense jealousy of the first
     sibling, had parents who showed marked preference for
     the younger children, boys or girls, who were "easier
     to manage", and were unable to accept the first-born's
     performance. Disciplinary action was an infantile at-
     tempt to control, retaliate, or threaten withdrawal of
     love. Any expression of anger by the child aroused
     strong reactions and, for the mothers, fear of "the
     child becoming hard to handle". The parents insecure
     with themselves and the opposite sex, revealing strong
     dependency needs and difficulty in communicating af-
     fection, achieved a marriage which perpetuated neurotic
     reactions and impeded performance in the parental role.
     The writer concludes that the combination of personal-
     ities of the spouses, the marital interaction, and the
     potential to undertake child rearing gives significance
     to the ordinal position and sex of the child.

291. ROSINKE, Eleanore (1961). Factors which support or
     impede parents in responding to the offer of con-
     tinued service.

193

The writer examines the records of the 9 families continuing in treatment at Toronto Mental Health Clinic, with special emphasis on the stress elements in the presenting problem, the parents' judgment of their performance, the developing understanding of the nature of the problem, and their part in it. With the child presenting problems in school, these parents, in response to the referrals of physicians, friends, and schools, could seek help with long-established pervasive difficulties in the child, expose their feelings of inadequacy as parents and their anxiety in not meeting middle-class expectations for child performance. Insecurity in exercising authority in child rearing, usually symptomatic of uncertainty in other interpersonal relationships and areas of social functioning, nurtured readiness to acknowledge their problem as parents. Personal gains in marital and other relationships which derived from treatment enhanced motivation to continue. Strong dependency on families of origin, and lack of dependency gratification in marriage, were transposed to dependency on authority figures in the community for supportive sanction of treatment.

SEE ALSO Entries 31, 43, 298, 405, 411.

PUBLIC ASSISTANCE

292. FARINA, Margaret (1961). The use of community resources by families in receipt of public assistance.
     In the winter of 1960-61 Toronto's private
welfare agencies found their financial resources increasingly called upon by families in receipt of
public assistance. In order to investigate the degree of "adequacy" of this assistance, Mrs. Farina
interviewed 23 families in downtown Toronto, selected
from the city's Public Welfare files: how often did
they resort to community services, which ones, for
what kind of help, and what proportion of family income did this help represent? She found that city
rents, taking as much as 44 per cent of income, left
too little margin for other items needed, so that any
extra -- and even clothing fell into this category --
cut into the allowance for food. Political problems
arise when public assistance competes with low-level
earning; but human problems are aggravated when subsistence living is ill adjusted to community standards,
as Mrs. Farina's comparative budgets for the Toronto
area suggest is the case. She feels that Ontario's
General Welfare Assistance Act could be made more
flexible still to allow for local variations in cost
of living, individual variations in need, and a more
realistic margin for unexpected expenses.

293. MOORE, Arthur Murray (1958). The economic rehabilitation of former Mothers' Allowance recipients.
     At the time of this study, from records and by
interviews, of all 30 available Hamilton families who
had stopped receiving Mothers' Allowances between
April and December 1954 as cited by the Public Welfare
Department -- i.e., June-July 1955 -- allowances were
payable when needed for the care of children up to age
eighteen in homes with no employable breadwinner. In
19 cases the fathers had died, in 5 they were perman-
ently, and in 5 temporarily, incapacitated, and one
father had deserted his family. More than half the
families were still in need when allowances were dis-
continued because the youngest child was then of age
or employed, or the father was again employable. In
14 families without employable fathers the mothers
earned part of the income needed, and well over

three-quarters had children's earnings. Renting rooms helped 10 families. Emergencies hit low-income families hard, especially children who forego independence or education to help out.

294. SAVILLE, Hugh (1959). Families of offenders: the extent to which families of married men incarcerated in the federal penitentiary turn to public assistance for financial aid.
The 30 such families in 1957 with dependent children suffered all the psychological disadvantages of a "broken home" during the man's incarceration, some of the offender's isolation, the same stigma, and the full brunt of the economic consequences. Only an insignificant proportion of the families had been previously or persistently dependent on maintenance assistance. Even during the breadwinner's absence the majority were not registered as receiving public assistance or Mothers' Allowances; where help was recorded it was usually for brief periods, apparently as a "last resort". Some regulations are confusing: offenders' common-law wives who renounce their partners receive allowances as unwed mothers, whereas legally married mothers become eligible only after six months' waiting; under such circumstances as adultery, mothers become ineligible for allowances but no concomitant responsibility is acknowledged for their children's psychological, or physical, protection. These findings suggest the need for review of such rulings, provision of reports on offenders' families for sentencing magistrates, and fuller use of probation and parole.

295. THOMSON, David M. (1954). Some problems of deserted wives.
The writer interviewed 30 young mothers of pre-school and school-aged children, selected alternately from Toronto Department of Public Welfare (Central District Office) files of recipients of public assistance in March 1954. Welfare records supplied additional information. Twenty-four of the wives had been deserted at least once previously. Many showed confused reactions, hoping for a reconciliation at some moments and for a complete and final break at others. Only 8 reported that the children missed their fathers, although 18 now found their children hard to manage. Many families lived, cooked, and slept in one room. Some mothers were preoccupied with their own needs,

and others had no insight into the conditions necessary
for their children's healthy psychosocial development.
Many needed to turn to someone, but were cut off from
relatives and felt restricted by welfare eligibility
requirements. Casework services, better accommodation,
and a few ameliorations like babysitters and occasional
outings, could help to make their situations more tolerable.

296. THOMSON, Deryck I.A. (1950). Effects on family life
of chronic illness and unemployment relief.
    Records were studied on the 112 such families
on the Toronto Department of Public Welfare (Central
District Office) rolls in February 1950, and 30, selected by cross-stratification according to fathers'
age and type of illness and family size, were interviewed. Many had once lived comfortably, but when
illness cut them off from earning and unemployment
insurance (to which they had often long contributed)
their families were forced into overcrowded, prepon-
derantly sub-standard housing. Initial savings were
soon exhausted, especially where there were young
children. Almost half had struggled initially to a-
void medical expenses, often by costlier self-treatment.
Several found regulation care inadequate and humiliat-
ing. Distorted family relationships, deprivation, and
the stigma commonly felt, threatened children's lives
too. Strenuous efforts must be made to provide better
preventive and on-going medical care and healthier
maintenance grants and housing, and above all rehabilitation programs for these men who (28 out of the
30 interviewed) fiercely resent their dependent status.

SEE ALSO Entries 129, 187, 219.

297. BASSETT, Eva (1954). Social problems dealt with by
the guidance program in a secondary school.
     In the early 1950's the guidance program was
still in a formative stage in Toronto. To explore
the social aspect of its counselling services in the
context of the city's total welfare services, this
project presents the findings from 1950-51 records
on 221 junior students and from the statements (in
questionnaire responses referring to these same students and in interviews) of the guidance staff of 13
teachers at the Central Technical School (Toronto).
The problems encountered by guidance counsellors are
those familiar to caseworkers, but the teachers vary
widely in their training for this work, their interviewing techniques, and their opinions on the extent
of the school's concern with such matters as broken
homes or unsatisfactory housing. The use of the Child
Guidance Clinic and the appointment of a psychiatrist
for the city's school system indicate a reaching out
to other community resources. Education and social
work could profitably plan closer collaboration through
professional associations and specific joint projects.

298. CAMERON, Donald A (1961). Some social consequences
of reading disability.
     Although poor readers, once considered hopeless,
then often found to be normal or superior in intelligence, are today encouraged in Toronto under the supervision of two Reading Consultants, nevertheless the
dysfunction has social concomitants. This project was
based on interviews in the homes and schools of 15
children, selected by sex and geographic location from
the ten- and eleven-year-olds with English-speaking
parents, of average or better intelligence ratings but
retarded at least two grades in reading ability and
referred for that reason alone to a Consultant in the
Board of Education's Child Adjustment Services. Parents and teachers were not very sanguine about the
academic future of these children, who are generally
submissive and overzealous or a little withdrawn.
Remote home-school relationships -- parents perplexed
and often magnifying tensions by "helping", and
teachers too overburdened to explain or reach out to

parents — suggest that school social workers would make more effective the help being offered these children.

299. JOHNSTON, Ruth L. (1947). <u>An examination of the work of the educational social worker in York Township public schools.</u>
A social work function new in Canada is here described in the process of taking shape and gaining acceptance. An analysis of all the cases on file after the first two years of such work, and interviews — with 7 representative principals, one Attendance Officer, 2 nurses, and workers in 2 social agencies — showed that the work ranged from identifying a supposed case of neglect as a health problem and an alleged incorrigible as a foster child needing help, to attendance at court hearings on truancy, and that the community was finding useful the liaison work with schools, homes, and community services. One worker among 10,000 children could do little beyond diagnosis and referral, but 64 case records showed that the school or the home had registered improvement after "treatment" — most frequently talks with parents when a child's academic record indicated a problem. Although sharper definition of educational social work was needed even among school personnel, the community's concern about delinquency meant that there was ready sympathy with this type of preventive work.

300. SCHALBURG, Annette (1948). <u>School leaving at fifteen; a study of work permits issued by the Toronto Board of Education.</u>
In 1947, 1,274 of Toronto's fifteen-year-olds, about 15 per cent, on a parent's or guardian's statement that his "services are required for his 'necessary maintenance' or for the maintenance of 'some person dependent on him'", left school to work but agreed to attend evening or part-time classes until the legal school-leaving age of sixteen. A study of 200 of these, an alphabetical selection from Board of Education survey records, shows that 58 per cent left before completing Grade VIII, about 80 per cent came from families with less than the city's 1947 average industrial wage income, and almost half came from broken homes. Studies in two schools providing evening classes showed poor attendance records, with 86

per cent dropping out abruptly at age sixteen. About
140 of the children granted permits in 1947 had unusu-
ally high intelligence ratings. Scholarships where
indicated, help and counselling for families refusing
special classes for their children, more vocational
guidance work, and co-ordination of legislation on
schooling, employment, and child welfare, are recommended.

SEE ALSO Entries 246, 276.

TRANSIENTS

301. ASKWITH, Gordon Kingsford (1953). <u>Transient young men in Toronto.</u>
Out of the growing number of homeless youths aged sixteen to thirty who seek in public hostels or missions a night's shelter or a meal, Mr. Askwith talked with 100 men. He noted the anomaly that although Canada needs seasonal labourers, many men's needs off-season, when they drift into cities, are not met because of "residence requirements"; work is elusive in wintertime, and unemployment insurance benefits do not adequately cumulate on short-term jobs, many of which are not covered by insurance in any case. Although in grades completed and in age at school-leaving the group had slightly above-average records, skills were lacking. Disrupted domestic lives, ill health, low morale, and alcoholism were commonly associated with transiency even for this age group. "We stay in the shadows and become like animals," one respondent said. Good hostels and boarding houses together with skilled casework should be tried. Disorganized services now keep men walking all day from one office or mission to another for bare necessities, cut off from normal resources and contacts.

302. DUNN, Gladys (1949). <u>Homeless and transient men in Toronto: a study of the provisions available.</u>
Past needs and services were surveyed, persons at present trying to help transients were consulted in person or by letter, records were studied in the Central Bureau of Toronto's Department of Public Welfare, and 39 men registered there during one fortnight in April 1949 were interviewed. Certain relationships were traced with employment circumstances: transiency has increased steadily except during wartime; manpower needs, and services provided, both fluctuate with seasons; many non-resident applicants for help come from Canada's economically disadvantaged regions. The proportion of "professional drifters" and "drunks" betrays the long-standing inadequacy of services. In 1948 more transients applied at Toronto Police Stations for shelter than at the Central Bureau, notably in the under-thirty age group.

201

Better youth services, more lodgings, and separate
provision for the infirm, mentally unfit, and alcoholics, are needed and, above all, integrated services,
with public responsibility for material assistance
clearly defined, and private agencies planning together their respective supplementary roles.

GROUP PROJECT. A study of two hundred homeless
    transients in Metropolitan Toronto, 1960.
    The purpose of this study was to determine the
social and personal charateristics of 200 homeless
transients in Metropolitan Toronto and the classifi-
cations into which the transient population falls.
It was hoped that the results of the study would be
helpful in evaluating the present methods of dealing
with the problem and would provide a more informed
basis for the making of social policy. Each student
in the research group interviewed 20 men; the interviews were conducted at the single men's unit of
Seaton House, the Salvation Army Men's Hostel, the
Fred Victor Mission, and the Don Jail. Each member
of the team developed a special area of interest in
the subject as the theme for his or her report. The
study revealed that the homeless transient's failure
to achieve a successful level of functioning within
society at large cannot be explained merely by factors
in any one of the areas of education, employment skills,
age, or health. The evidence did show that a great
many came from socially and emotionally deprived homes;
had problems in forming and maintaining meaningful heterosexual relationships; showed symptoms of severe
over-dependency; and possessed damaged and weak personality structures.

303. DOUGLAS, Audrey M. (1960). Two hundred homeless
    transients in Toronto, with emphasis on their
    economic and citizen role performance.
    Is it enough for society to assume that homeless
transients are, by and large, poor role performers?
The author examined the citizen and economic role performance of a sub-sample of 20 men in the hope of
linking together personality, on the one hand, and
social structure, on the other. This was done in
order to gain some understanding, on an individual
basis, of the homeless transient's inadequate performance

of the citizen and economic roles. The results indicated wide differences in the role performances.
The well-known stereotype of the tramp cloaks a tre-
mendous variety of behaviour, and good economic role
performance did not always go side-by-side with good
citizen role performance, or vice versa. Homeless
transients present social problems of a quasi-medical,
quasi-criminal nature, with the consequences of personality and cultural and social pressures being
tightly interwoven to produce various modes of adaptation, and munificent varieties of economic and citizen
role performance. The help given by the missions and
hostels is not adequate in that it encourages rootlessness and mobility. Some type of residential treatment
with consideration given to individual needs is recommended.

304. LITTLE, William T. (1960). Criminality and personal-
     ity of the homeless transient.
         As a result of the interviewing in the Don Jail,
     the author postulated the following hypothesis: there
     are two separate personality types among homeless
     transients related to two definable patterns of illegal
     behaviour: (1) indictable (or serious) offences seem
     to characterize the aggressive, independent, capable,
     and relatively ego-defensive personalities; (2) non-
     indictable (less serious) offences seem to relate to
     the inadequate, retiring, unimaginative personalities
     who are lacking in ego-defensive persistence and have
     a tendency to break down easily under stress. In or-
     der to verify his hypothesis the author tested a group
     of indictable and a group of non-indictable offenders
     and obtained personality profiles for each group and
     for each individual offender. Grygier's Dynamic Per-
     sonality Inventory was used. The hypothesis was fully
     supported by the data, which showed statistically sig-
     nificant differences between the two groups. In the
     light of his own observations and experience, as well
     as his empirical findings, the author postulates a
     need for appropriate classification and treatment in
     the Canadian correctional system. The present system
     of classification is said to be ineffective as it does
     not differentiate the offenders according to their
     personality make-up and emotional needs.

305. LUMSDEN, Ross H. (1960). The problems, feelings, and
     dependency of homeless transients.

On the assumption that there is a desire and
potential for change on the part of some homeless
transients, the writer determined what homeless transients themselves believe are their special problems or
difficulties, and how they feel about their way of
life. A large number feel they have special problems
related to their social functioning, most often in
the economic and interpersonal relationships areas.
Contrary to popular thought, the majority do not like
their way of life. The tendency of a large number is
to project the responsibility for their failure in social functioning onto factors outside themselves. In
order to uncover some of the factors which appear to
have impeded their achievement of normal functioning,
the author examined the dependency in social functioning in a sub-sample of 20 men and analyzed the quality
of their parental relationships during their formative
years as a contributory factor. There is a marked
tendency to over-dependency among these men and 65 per
cent had experienced parental relationships characterized by deprivation, domination, or indulgence. Further research and a comprehensive program of
individualized-treatment services with provincial
leadership and interprovincial co-ordination are suggested.

306. NAKATANI, Ruth (1960). <u>Health and transiency</u>.
This study examines the health complaints as
reported by the homeless transients in the sample.
Although the complaints fell into nine categories,
traumatic orthopaedic, respiratory, and digestive
complaints were the most frequently stated. In comparison with the general population, the homeless
transients have better physical health. However, it
was the writer's view that the men understated their
complaints. Some reported complaints which related
to their mental state but the writer felt there was
a great understatement of mental disabilities by the
sample, perhaps because of fear of stigma and/or lack
of insight. Alcohol presents a problem to about one-
half the men. The medical service most frequently
used by the transients is the outpatient department
of hospitals, which report that the health complaint
often cloaks other underlying problems and conflicts,
such as alcoholism or a need for food, lodging, or
clothing. Health services could be channels for directing transients toward individualized services

aimed at treating their underlying problems, as well as a method of therapy for current sickness. A national health scheme, to cut across barriers of class and residence, is recommended.

SEE ALSO Entries 407, 409, 412.

307. BRETT, Fred W. (1953). A history of the Big Brother
     Movement of Toronto, Inc., 1912-1939.
     Both changing community and developing profession
are discernible through this history documented mainly
from minutes, reports, and correspondence. The agency
began under individual sponsorship as a laymen's movement to introduce wholesomeness into crime-breeding
environments. After World War I, with federated community support and boys' work specialists assisting
the volunteers, programs expanded and became diversified, as witness pioneering plans for "non-academic
children" and delinquents' foster care, and even group
work (although not so designated then). Anomalies
grew too: a non-authoritarian agency, it was closely
identified with the Juvenile Court; designed to service individuals, its programs overlapped "Y" functions
and service club operations. During the 1930's the
agency was reconstructed. The Board's responsibility
for administration and policy was defined; recruiting,
assignment, and functions of volunteers were clarified;
and professional staff functions were focused on casework and supervision. War deferred the co-ordinating
of youth services the agency saw as needed at that
turning point in its history.

308. BUDD, William (1950). The scholarship intake procedure
     of the Toronto Jewish Camp Council in 1950.
     Prior to the new admissions policy it had become
clear that need outbalanced resources and that, although individuals' obligations varied, every applicant's right to a place in a Jewish camp was absolute.
In 1950 parents were asked to bring proof of income,
and accept fee assessment according to a sliding scale.
This project describes the admissions procedure, and
the response, from interviews with 10 representative
Board members and the 7 intake staff workers and from
application records. Half of the Board members interviewed needed more information on and understanding
of the new policy, and 3 of the 7 workers interviewing applicants were competent to handle only a selected

minority of cases. Despite these symptoms of an overburdened senior staff, the "sliding scale" proved a
useful yardstick, parents participated in assessing
fees, and 89 per cent of them complied with the new
requirements. The record seemed to vindicate the
fairness and effectiveness of the policy.

309. CHELLAM, Grace E. (1956). Agency objectives and job
satisfactions in the Y.W.C.A.
Agency publications include under purpose: helping members to become "persons with a living relationship to God" and "responsible citizens". To see how
professional Y.W.C.A. workers in Toronto and in three
towns understood and responded to agency program, the
writer interviewed 40 of the total 42. Over 75 per
cent had more than three years' "Y" experience. In
qualifications the workers fell into three equal
groups: those with social work degrees; other specialist qualifications; and arts degrees. About one-sixth
were not church members, and 28 were not active in any
church program. All accepted agency goals as they
understood them and none saw conflict between personal
and agency values. Most program workers said their
greatest satisfaction arose from individuals' and
groups' development; most executives mentioned agency
teamwork and world-wide associations; others found
specific tasks most satisfying. Respondents almost
universally, though with uneasiness, reinterpreted
the agency's avowed evangelical purpose explicitly --
in terms of service.

310. CRAGG, Norman F. (1951). A study of movement out of
the Y.M.C.A. Secretaryship.
The viewpoint of Secretaries who remain should
next be documented, the writer suggests, to balance
this essentially negative study of the reasons men
gave for having resigned, between 1946-51, from sec-
retarial work in the Canadian Y.M.C.A. Out of the
total of 159, the 50 still traceable who had been in
the upper two executive groups received questionnaires,
and 45 responded; a one-in-two sample of the respondents was then interviewed personally. Many cited working hours, salaries, frequent moves, and so on, as
contributing factors. But most had felt dissatisfied
primarily with the lack of opportunity to grow personally and professionally, the lack of supervision and

staff co-operation, and what they saw as a gap between
the Association's avowed objectives and its actual
practices. Since dissatisfactions usually accumulate
gradually, early and responsive staff recognition of
them might obviate some resignations, and fuller interviews at separation might help the Association to keep
re-examining its purposes and means towards realizing
them in today's community.

311. DUFTY, Gene M. (1949). Supervision and training of
     staff in camping.
     Scheduled interviews were given to the camp di-
rectors of 33 (selected at random but roughly representative of various sponsorship) of the 63 camps in
the Ontario Camping Association which operated for
six to eight weeks in 1948 and drew their campers
mainly from the Toronto area. The method of providing help for program staff members, which they in
turn could pass on to staff members or campers in
their charge, was assessed against certain criteria
derived from the literature. Camps sponsored by agencies and organizations had almost as scant a framework as had private or even church camps, in preliminary
training in town and on the site, regular educational
meetings at all levels, the keeping and using of records,
and planning for and assessing improvement. There is
a clear need to set standards and explain to the camp
director his "responsibility to his staff for making
the camping experience a growing one".

312. FERGUSON, Audrey (1954). Staff perception of job sat-
     isfaction.
     With five agencies co-operating, the writer ex-
plored what sustained 50 of their social workers in
doing and continuing at their jobs. She gave them
scheduled interviews, questionnaires, and sorting
cards, and noted unsolicited comments on relevant factors, applying Guttman and Likert Scales in elaborat-
ing her method. Responses seemed not to vary according
to such factors as experience or age: workers of all
kinds contributed to the 28 references to "needing more
training", and group workers differed only in contributing all mention of "budget lacks". The morale-
building factors recently defined by a social psychologist were clearly identified here as: congenial agency
objectives, compatible fellow workers helpful

leadership, and organizational efficiency -- with intrinsic satisfaction in the nature of the job as an emphatic plus. Almost all expected to move to other jobs. Many indicated private reasons, but some complained of too much pressure, too little time, and of a feeling of being bogged down in procedural details and having too little say on policy decisions.

313. GARFIELD, Goodwin P. (1950). Methods of short-term staff training courses in social work.
Workers who have not had a full-time course of related theory and practice are the trainees considered in this project, although it is pointed out that professionals, too, profit from courses, as emphases shift and their own and others' experiences widen and change understanding and methods. Published discussions of the subject are the basis for this review of how to plan a course to make an agency's objectives clear to non-professionals and help them improve their performance. Democratic procedures should be used throughout training, with continuous as well as concluding evaluation. For conveying information, the lecture method proves effective, but discussion groups are more valuable where attitudes are involved, and where skills are to be taught, demonstrations and practice sessions. Three questionnaires which were used to elicit the evaluations of trainees in two local courses for camp leaders are appended, only one of which proved specific enough to yield what the writer considered supporting evidence.

314. GOODMAN, Marvin (1958). A study of leadership training.
This thesis examines practice (among voluntary leaders of recreational and informal education groups) in relation to theory. Group work principles were defined in 5 training sessions, each under a different special instructor, to 15 leaders of junior groups in Toronto's Holy Blossom Temple in 1957-58. Supervisors followed up with 13 conferences. The writer established "research units" from transcriptions of these sessions (some of which he attended as an observer) and then, in terms of the "units" analyzed the leaders' records of 27 group meetings each after the training sessions. The most effective teaching was direct and specific and concise, by methods involving demonstration and

student participation, reinforced in a later supervisory session. Most of the leaders had come wanting program suggestions; hence it was program suggestions they remembered and used. Had they shared in planning the course and thus been prepared, they might have learned and applied more of the group work methods that were presented.

315. JONES, Elizabeth Ann (1959). Staff concepts of the administrative component; a study of role perception within a social agency.
    The staff participating in this study all worked in a single voluntary private agency concerned with temporary child care and protection work. Aspects of the administrative process and staff involvement in it, derived from the literature, were the focus of the questionnaires administered personally to 11 caseworkers, 4 supervisors, and one executive. Respondents were also asked to appraise the degree of responsibility of these three positions. If staff members who are clear about their own and co-workers' roles are likeliest to fit harmoniously into a functioning whole, then the degree of agreement about roles in these responses was encouraging. However, viewpoints consistently differed between workers with training in social-work-degree courses, and those with other kinds of training. Supervisors tended to stress total context; caseworkers, particular skills and techniques. An extended and general educational effort will be necessary if all staff members are to accept the desirable maximum of personal responsibility and involvement in the administrative process.

316. LAMPE, Walter (1955). A study of job loads of seventeen group workers in ten recreational and informal education agencies in Toronto, 1955.
    To study job loads the writer had to devise a way of measuring them. First he established certain criteria— for example, assuming that a leader does not spend unnecessary time with a group, the addition of groups should mean an equivalent increase of time spent in direct leadership. Through Welfare Council lists he then identified the 17 trained group workers concerned with building-centred programs in Toronto in seven youth associations, two Settlements, and one family agency, and in consultation with them evolved

a schedule to test the allocation of their working hours during a two-week test period in the spring of 1955. Their impressions of how representative the test period was were given in interviews afterwards. Job loads apparently made for group work below professional standards, with too little time given to recording and planning. Administration was taking more time than group leadership. A further study should ask whether group work curricula should be redesigned to reflect this administrative emphasis or whether workers trained to lead groups ought to resist disproportionate administrative duties.

317. LIPMAN, Marvin H. (1956). <u>The administrative process of change from institutional care to foster-home care in the Infants' Homes, Toronto.</u>
     The need for institutional care was plain in 1875 when baby-farming, unsupervised, often meant drugging, brutality, and abandoning of infants if parents failed to pay or show concern. After fifty-one years the agency relinquished its last institutional premises. This change is documented from minutes, reports, and correspondence, especially for the period following World War I with its new awareness of the value of an individual life. Initially death rates were high, not only from epidemics but from marasmus (undernourishment and "nostalgia"). Nutritional and financial problems worsened when resident mothers rebelled against wet-nursing and housework duties. Board members, immersed in immediate pressures, felt strong identification with the agency. But in 1920 they began delegating responsibility to competent staff members. New Board members, administratively experienced through war work, showed energy and ingenuity in maintaining service while foster-home care was introduced, tried, and approved. Finally, self-evaluation and awareness of comparable efforts elsewhere developed as financial support broadened in the community.

318. McDONALD, Richard D. (1952). <u>An experiment in training camp counsellors.</u>
     The writer describes the process of following, in a camp setting, the Bavelas experiment --leaders developing their own training program from an initial defining of principles through successive practice,

211

observation, and evaluative sessions. He trained 4 observers to help him note all counsellors' performance before selecting 6 with comparable cabin groups; since all were eager to participate, he then chose experiment and control groups by lot. Discussions and group situations soon showed that, despite their convictions, counsellors had tended to meet actual difficulties with authoritarian methods and to gradually rationalize until they had formed such attitudes as considering ten-year-olds "too young to respect" or thinking, when they enforced a clean-up, that the boys thus "learned cleanliness". The method of training leaders, measured "before and after" on observation forms, was validated: as leaders developed liberating self-awareness and sensitivity to the meaning of boys' behaviour, they increasingly freed campers from counsellor-imposed wishes, and gave them the responsibility of choice.

319. MILNE, Donald R. (1950). Volunteer leaders in Scouting.
    The Boy Scouts, unusual in its use of supervisory volunteers and its system of group sponsorship, had 1,122 volunteer leaders in Toronto in 1949-50, about 10 per cent supervisory. From the Association's 1,034 available files key-sort cards were used to tabulate age, sex, marital status, education, and occupation in relation to the amount of training taken and the length of service. Other factors had no appreciable relevance, but clearly the more training leaders took the longer they had tended to serve. Those whose only prior experience had been as program members were, on average, least trained. The one-third with no formal training showed a disproportionate rate of turnover. Of 215 volunteer leaders resigning in the ten-month period, over 25 per cent gave as their reason conditions in the agency. In interviews with a 25 per cent sampling of this group the writer focused on perceived weaknesses, thus highlighting the new recruits' need for better orientation and support, and for inclusion in a progressive system of delegated responsibility.

320. MYLES, Jack S. (1951). The organization and administration of industrial recreation in Toronto.
    Increasingly over twenty years, as hours of work

have shrunk and mechanization has been extended, leisure of employees has been organized by their own representatives or by management. This project examines and assesses such programs in 25 plants with 250 or more employees each, representing seven industries in Toronto and its suburbs, through interviews with 32 informants and supplementary information from reading and discussion with spokesmen from 23 community organizations. In most cases employees shared administration and financing, with management providing facilities. Bowling, softball, quoits, golf, picnics, and dancing were most popular, with leadership usually volunteer and part-time. Plans for older workers or for those on shifts were as infrequent as provision for teaching beginners or for integration with community recreational projects. A co-operative scheme is recommended that would bring benefits to workers in small companies, as well as studies of methods of financing and broadening support for all the recreational activities.

321. PALMER, Jean (1950). The group process in a board of directors, Y.W.C.A., Toronto, 1950.
    At five meetings of a young branch's board, the writer observed and made coded notes on details relevant to a group evaluation. Unfortunately, the board proved atypical: at the second meeting a new chairman and ten new members were launched together; the ten old members were naturally more stable in attendance, more vocal in discussions, and more extensively involved in branch and agency activities. The fact that 87 per cent of interaction was focused on work demonstrated the group's concern with efficient functioning, and its membership seemed to co-operate harmoniously, although conflicts were avoided rather than worked through. However the members' services seemed often perfunctorily engaged: committee responsibility delegated without prior weighing of members' interests, reports delivered rapidly to inform members but not spark discussion, and so on. Better orienting of new members, preliminary circulation or a more selective agenda, and clearer definition of a board's program, planning, and policy-making functions, would make such a group's process more enriching and effective.

322. REID, Margaret L. (1948). A study of statistical recording systems in group work agencies in the Greater Toronto area.

To see what kind of statistical records were
kept and how they were used, the writer compared systems elsewhere with those of seven Toronto agencies,
all members of the Community Chest. She interviewed
administrative staff members in the agencies, studied
their procedures, and reviewed Community Chest practices here and elsewhere. All the agencies have forms
for collecting data. However, the criteria by which
they sort data are unsystematically designed and vari-
ously applied. Most agencies see statistics as a way
of enumerating work done and guiding supervisors.
Diverse understandings (for example, "members" may
mean a small club's elected quota or an institution's
annual registration, "services" may be applied alike
to babies examined in a monthly clinic and club members attending weekly) invalidate any comparative use
of records by the Community Chest. Standard forms
and definitions for agencies now reporting, and regular data collecting from others now not surveyed,
would help the Chest and the agencies to use records
as bases for intelligent action.

323. ROWLES, Jeanne (1952). The nature and adequacy of the
intake program at Central Branch, Young Women's
Christian Association, Toronto.
The writer recorded all this branch's front desk
activity from 9 a.m. till 9 p.m. daily through one
week of March 1952, studied records of the 80 membership applications received in that period, analyzed
the Membership Worker's process report of one interview, and herself interviewed 20 of the 62 applicants
who completed paid memberships. Almost half dropped
out after only three sessions, and few knew of any
activity except the one they had joined. Desk contact with newcomers took an average of two minutes
and even then space was congested and attention dis-
tracted by other calls. The Membership Worker had
met only 6 of the 80 applicants that week, but was
able to explain the agency's program and help individuals use it beneficially. Her position, created
only in 1950, already justified addition of a part-
time worker for peak hours, with a goal of staff
sufficient to make an interview available to everyone
seeking membership.

324. SHAPIRO, Seon (1956). A comparison of trained and untrained volunteer group leaders.

The writer acknowledges limitations in his comparative analysis of leaders' use of program: personal bias was possible since the setting was his own agency, Canadian Young Judaea in Toronto; 10 leaders had, and only 5 had not, training in the eight-week camp course at Biluim; and only trained leaders were involved with the groups who met regularly enough to report fully on their use of resources or to be observed adequately during the study period. However, it was possible to gather data on all 15 leaders through scheduled interviews and questionnaires on social and agency goals. The trained leaders appeared to have advantages in grasp of methods, educational techniques, relevant skills, and morale. When it came to defining group function and members' interests, those who had themselves been members for longer periods and had been actively involved in training courses and general agency concerns tended oftener to assert identification with the agency rather than with its objectives.

325. ZIMMERMAN, Louis (1947). Democracy in administration.
Recorded and recollected history since 1919, interviews with Board members, and interviews with 52 of the 1,291 adult members chosen at random from the four membership categories represented on the Board, show that the Y.M. and Y.W.H.A. of Toronto is designed for more thoroughgoing democracy than it so far practices. Attendance at 1946-47 Board meetings averaged only 52 per cent; the proportion of members who voted was even lower. Some members had joined to use athletic facilities. Even their Board representatives often felt identified with an activity rather than with the agency. Other influential agency spokesmen rarely participated in members' activities. Lay leadership and citizenship training might be further developed by such means as interviewing each new member, developing a club program for adults, promoting more effective committee work, training newly elected members for Board responsibilities, and perhaps setting up a separate Board of Trustees to bring in more community leaders and avoid giving businessmen disproportionate roles on the elected Board.

SEE ALSO Entries 2, 333.

326. LEE, Ormah (1956). The value of the psychological
report to the psychiatric social worker.
Psychology, emphasizing research, and social
work, emphasizing service, meet in complementary
functions in today's clinical setting. One aspect
of their interdependence is here explored in three
hospital departments. After their first interviews
with 40 beginning patients, 10 social workers assessed (in standard-scale ratings) their own understanding, using six questions appropriate to the
casework process. Two psychological tests chosen
for social relevance were then given to two of the
four patients interviewed by each social worker, and
reports were forwarded from the 14 psychologists to
the social workers concerned, who then gave second
interviews within a week to all 40 patients and a-
gain assessed their own understanding. Where psychologists had reported, social workers' understanding was significantly better of factors enabling a
good patient-worker relationship and of the patient's
ability to use help, and their understanding of emotional, sexual, and employment adjustments was somewhat improved, but of home environment virtually
unchanged.

————————

GROUP PROJECT. The intervention of social caseworkers
in crisis situations of clients and the outcomes.
The group undertaking this study developed the
conceptual framework and methodology of the research.
Two assumptions were basic to the project: (1) that
the social caseworker's intervention is purposeful
and directed towards positive outcomes; and (2) that
social casework records are adequate in terms of recording the sequence of critical situations, casework
intervention, and outcome for the client. The hypothesis, that the probable outcome of intervention of a
caseworker in a crisis situation of a client is positive for the client, was investigated by the group
as a whole. A random sample of 120 case records from
two family service agencies was studied. According to
the criteria established by the group, barely half of

these (61) resulted in positive outcomes for clients. Of the remaining, 36 were negative and 23 were classed as ambiguous outcomes. Hence the hypothesis was not supported. Yet the proportion of positive cases was double that of the negative cases. With a more refined technique for judging outcomes which would eliminate the large proportion (one in five) of ambiguous outcomes, a more conclusive result might be possible. From the tabulation of the data some relationships were suggested between: type of intervention; the timing and frequency of intervention; the nature of the crisis situations; and the outcome for the client. These suggested relationships were the basis for sub-hypotheses explored by each student on an individual basis.

327. BARTOL, Zlata (1962). Information giving as a mode of social casework intervention.
    This was the most frequent mode of social casework intervention. No significant relationship was found between the frequency of information giving as a recorded mode of casework intervention and positive outcome. In fact, further analysis of 15 cases in which information giving was the predominantly recorded mode of intervention showed that information giving is significantly associated with negative outcome. It appeared to make no difference to the outcome whether the crisis is "concrete" (based on tangible needs or problems) or "diagnostic" (based on relationship problems). Three possible influential factors were found in cases with negative outcomes: (1) the client's lack of understanding of the agency's function; (2) the client's lack of motivation for using casework help; and (3) the postponement of or delay in seeking help.

328. CRAIK, Mildred E. (1962). Communication as a factor in intervention by social caseworkers in crisis situations of clients.
    Analysis of the data revealed a statistically significant ($<.05$) relationship between information seeking as a mode of social casework intervention and ambiguous outcome in terms of the frequency and persistence of the social caseworker's questions. A random sample of 10 of the 23 cases with ambiguous outcome was investigated for evidence of poor communication. This evidence was abstracted from the records

on the basis of statements recorded by the social caseworker which were judged to indicate that communication
was not proceeding smoothly. Such evidence was found
in 9 of the 10 records studied. Three main conclusions
emerge from this study: (1) that high frequency and
persistence of recorded questions may indicate poor
client-caseworker communication; (2) that poor client-
caseworker communication as defined is associated with
ambiguous outcomes; and (3) that the data themselves
are subject to the hazards of communication between
the social caseworker and the researcher.

329. DEMETER, Steven (1962). The nature of crisis situations and the outcome of social casework intervention.
   Crisis situations were divided into two different
classes for examination: those crises which required
"concrete" services (financial assistance, placement,
etc.); and those which required "diagnostic" services
(clients with relationship problems, emotional problems, etc.). Two hypotheses were tested: (1) that
intervention in crises requiring "concrete" services
is more frequently associated with positive outcome
than crises which require "diagnostic" services; and
(2) those crises which require "concrete" services are
less frequently associated with ambiguous outcome than
those which require "diagnostic" services. While both
hypotheses were supported by the data, in neither instance was the support statistically significant. A
significant limitation of this study is the concern
with the crisis situation to the exclusion of any
underlying problem. A study focused on intervention
in client problems would possibly yield significantly
different results.

330. GIBBONS, Georgina J. (1962). The relationship of difficulty in obtaining information in relation to
environmental modification.
   If it is assumed that difficulties in communication are related to a high frequency of "information
seeking" as a class of intervention (see Entry 328
above), these difficulties will be reflected in other
areas of treatment. This leads to the hypothesis that
there is an inverse relationship between information
seeking as a class of intervention and environmental
modification as a class of intervention. A high frequency of information seeking and a low frequency of

environmental modification is associated with negative outcome. Conversely, a low frequency of information seeking and a high frequency of environmental modification is associated with positive outcome. All cases where environmental modification made up one-third or more of the total treatment interventions were examined. Over 68 per cent of these 47 cases revealed support for the hypothesis. Thus a statistically significant inverse relationship between information seeking and environmental modification was found. Further examination of a sub-sample of cases showed that in concrete crisis situations (see Entry 329 above) the most frequently used method of environmental modification was contact with and referral to other agencies. In diagnostic crisis situations the most frequently used method of environmental modification was contact with relatives. This suggests the hypothesis that in crisis situations of clients, contact by the social caseworker with relatives contributes to positive outcomes.

331. MABEN, David R. (1962).   A study of the effects of social work practice.
    From the findings of the group project two sub-hypotheses were derived: (1) "direction giving" interventions which occur early in the sequence of total interventions are more frequently associated with positive outcome than those that occur late in sequence; and (2) interventions that appear first in the sequence of total interventions and are directly related to the crisis are more frequently associated with positive outcome than those that are not directly related to the crisis. The first hypothesis was strongly supported by the data and found significant at the .01 level. The second hypothesis was not statistically supported, although there was a tendency for first interventions related to the crisis to be associated with positive outcomes. Conclusion can be drawn that "direction giving" interventions directly related to the crisis situation of the client, occurring early in the sequence of total interventions, are likely to result in positive outcome for the client.

SEE ALSO Entries 68, 90.

332. BLOW, John Needham (1951). <u>A study in co-operative recreation</u>.
    Although wartime's needs and drives make unique some features of the overseas experience of Canada's four national voluntary organizations (the Canadian Legion, the Knights of Columbus, the Salvation Army, and the Y.M.C.A.), this project searches the records on 1939-45 activities, and various leaders' comments, for principles applicable in peacetime. The wish to serve, voluntary unity rather than compulsory subjection to military command: these forces for co-operation felt by the voluntary organizations have their peacetime equivalents. War experience meant close association, adequate support without competing campaigns for funds, and planned apportioning of work. The techniques evolved can be instructive now. The many bodies co-ordinating special interests (e.g., camping, citizenship, youth hostels, adult education) need to work with governmental parks, fitness, and cultural programs, to develop leaders and plan for what the Recreation Division of the Canadian Welfare Council calls "the whole range of leisure-time interests" in Canada.

333. BOURKE, William A. (1953). <u>Principles of budget making</u>.
    Five of Toronto's Community Chest agencies, selected in consultation with the Welfare Council for variety of experience, are here studied primarily through interviews with executive directors. Since budget requests and operating budgets were involved among the five agencies, intricacies of procedure in all 16 cases are not detailed. Instead, six principles of budget making, derived from theoretical writings, are used to assess agency practice in general terms. Theoretical principles were all to some degree apparent in the practice assessed. But long-term planning was adequately carried out in only one instance (a well-anticipated postwar emergency), and the relating of plans to community cost structures, in only two instances. Only one agency carefully related costs and units of performance. Most curtailments were made under pressure rather than through forethought. Further study is recommended of the proportion of support

member agencies receive from public funds, private donations, and fees from members or clients.

334. BOYS, John F. (1953). The birth of a community mental health clinic.

To study the process by which a new need is recognized and met, Mr. Boys analyzed one instance using the files of the Toronto Mental Health Clinic, the Canadian Mental Health Association, and the Toronto Welfare Council. In wartime many social workers were absorbed by governmental welfare services, and the depleted staffs in private agencies were increasingly pressed for a new kind of casework service. Mental health authorities had been nationally oriented. In wartime they became active locally, first participating in federated fund raising and allocating, then in 1941 surveying mental health needs here. The Toronto Welfare Council, like a professional social worker with a client, stimulated the casework agencies and "enabled self-help". In response, agencies held lectures and workshops while permanent staffs were recruited, and by 1945 the needed courses and clinical training for psychiatric social workers and consultative services for caseworkers generally were provided.

335. CLEAVER, Frank A. (1949). An evaluation of admission procedures within the Community Chest of Greater Toronto.

In 1946 two agencies applied to the Chest for inclusion as beneficiaries of the annual campaigns and as participants in joint community planning, the Toronto Religious Education Council on behalf of its Boys' Work Board, and the Jewish Vocational Service; the first applicant was refused and the second accepted three years later. Also in 1946 studies of community organization began under a plan of the National Conference of Social Work. The standards adopted for those studies were used here to assess these two applications on the recorded evidence in Community Chest files. It was found that the procedure approximated accepted standards in only one applicant's case. In neither case was adequate research completed. Moreover some procedures authorized in the organization's constitution were omitted, delegation of functions was imprecise, and co-ordination seemed haphazard. The implications apply not so much to the instances

used in this exploratory analysis as to community organization structure and procedures in general.

336. DAVIES, Yvonne S. (1949). The participation of women
in the activities of the United Jewish Welfare
Fund of Toronto.
     Underlying this examination of one volunteer
organization is the larger question: how can an active,
continuing, and informed interest in community services
be encouraged? The history, as it is to be found in
memoranda, letters, and minutes from the organization's
files for the 1938-47 period, is assessed in terms of
the records of other comparable groups and elaborated
by interviews with three active participants in the
work of the Women's Division, three former participants, and three well-qualified but non-participating
women. A recruitment problem emerged as central: giving more women a greater share in policy making,
broadening the base of support, and attracting new
canvassers to keep pace with growing needs. Some educational projects had proved successful, e.g., training women to explain to invited groups the work of
affiliated agencies. More such projects, on a year-
round basis, were recommended, with whatever increase
in professional staff the volunteer group needed to
help them carry out their plans.

337. DEMPSEY, William A. (1949). Relationship between
government officials and citizens in municipal
recreation.
     Through records and participants' observations,
the organizational structure of the recreational program in Forest Hill Village (Toronto) is studied five
years after its inauguration and after the first provincial grants were made available for such municipal
programs on approval by the Minister of Education.
The local Board of Education was represented on the
program council and budgeting committee, as was the
Municipal Council which sponsored the undertaking.
Designated organizations were also represented, and
all these delegates together with program convenors
elected members-at-large. But volunteer participation
fell off when a recreational director was hired;
decision-making and fund-allotting devolved upon a
relatively constant and unrepresentative group which
gave priority to publicly-supported programs for the

young rather than to self-sustaining adults' programs.
If this recreational undertaking were essentially the
responsibility of area representatives, and authority
were delegated from municipal officials through executive members to individual citizens, community support might be broader.

338. GODFREY, Patricia (1952). Canadian Y.M.C.A. war services 1939-1946; a study in relationships.
Canada's six voluntary organizations, designated
after 1941 the "Auxiliary Services Organizations", each
representing a significant segment of the nation, re-
tained their identities throughout the wartime period
of semi-official co-ordination. The Y.M.C.A., in its
relations with its local supporters, with the other
five organizations, with Ottawa, and with the armed
forces, is described in this study. Specifically
based on wartime documents, Y.M.C.A. files, and on 30
interviews with persons connected with war services,
the study emerged out of the writer's work as a research assistant on a University survey, undertaken
by the School of Social Work on behalf of the Defence
Research Board, of "experience in meeting the social
service and welfare needs of the armed forces" during
World War II. Out of a welter of local committee projects, government grants and budgeting, uniformed private staffs and supervisors without rank but with
service status, overlapping functions and inter-
organizational jealousies, such co-operative ventures
as the centralized supplying of canteens in Italy
could still emerge. Administration by the forces
might make for more efficiency — in personnel, program, and equipment. But civilian organizations, albeit less readily manoeuvred into integrated activities,
perhaps provide the more flexible and varied welfare
services suitable for a citizenry under arms.

339. GREENE, Barbara H. (1948). The volunteer in community
service.
This primarily theoretical discussion includes
a survey of practices in three Toronto agencies: the
Y.W.C.A., Central Branch, with 64 volunteers drawn
largely from membership ranks and doing mainly administrative work; the Y.M.H.A., which used its 136 volunteers as much in program as on boards and committees;
and the University Settlement, where 112 of the total

133 volunteers were used in program activities. Most
social services were initially carried out by volunteers.
The continued support by and usefulness of volunteers
today depend on agencies' care in recruiting, selective
placing, orienting, training and supervising, and recognizing their contributions. The Volunteer Department
of the United Welfare Chest, established in 1945, provides central facilities and leadership in these methods.
Through interested lay participants the agencies can
learn more about the community and make agency services
more widely known.

340. JOLLIFFE, J. Paul (1948). The development of a community project: the North Toronto Memorial Gardens.
    The initial campaign to raise the community's
share for this proposed indoor ice arena reached only
one-third of its objective in three months. The writer
analyzes this experience for its theoretical interest
and its immediate relevance to many other projects being planned currently throughout the city. He interviewed participants, attended meetings, and read
minutes and records of administrative groups and consultants, and in the light of professionally-established
standards for a democratically planned and supported
undertaking he assessed the process in North Toronto
as follows: though the need was well explored the
feasibility of support was not; though planning was
vigorous at committee level the Community Council had
little share even in decisions; there was more promoting than informing; and co-operation was good with
municipal officials but not with organized groups in
the community. In sum, detailed plans were neither
formed early enough nor circulated widely enough, and
authority throughout was too centralized, too remote
from popular control.

341. LAPPIN, B.W. (Diploma 1947). Joint fund-raising in
Toronto: the role of the Jewish community.
    To trace the factors that led to community fund-
raising this study uses general histories and the files
of the Welfare Council and the United Jewish Welfare
Fund. Both the Council and the Fund were established
in 1937, at a time when immigration and the economic
depression had led to a proliferation of agencies.
The concern for agency autonomy operated in Toronto,
as it had elsewhere, to necessitate gradual, thoroughly

prepared steps until the United Welfare Chest (later
renamed the Community Chest) developed in 1944. To
record a representative range of Jewish views, informal interviews were held with 6 social workers and
6 leaders, and scheduled interviews were given to 20
canvassers and 100 citizens. All saw the Chest as
expressing the community at this stage of its development. To bridge the gap between leaders and contributors, better education is urged, especially more
balanced presentation of local as well as overseas
needs. As experience allays the doubts and insecur-
ities inevitable in a new venture, it is felt, inter-
cultural co-operation will strike deeper roots in the
community.

342. MACDONNELL, Katharine G. (1955). The Community Chest
     budgeting process.
        What did participants in the Community Chest
     think of the budgeting process? And did differing
     opinions reflect any divergent attitudes on the part
     of representatives of planners and recipients (those
     appointed by the Welfare Council of Toronto and Dis-
     trict) and contributors (the public representatives
     appointed by the Community Chest)? Questionnaires
     were sent in 1954 to the members of the local Budget
     Committee and of the eight sectional committees that
     assist by reviewing agency budgets in various fields
     — to 99 volunteers altogether, 85 of whom responded.
     Subsequently the members of two sectional committees,
     18 in all, were interviewed. Answers reflected no
     wide variation between the Council viewpoint and the
     public's. Budgeting procedures were generally con-
     sidered adequate and decisions equitable. Criticisms
     focused on the difficulties of matching figures and
     facts, and of making allocations that depend upon an
     understanding of agency policy. Some general defini-
     tion of "standards" is wanted for comparative use,
     and further education is desirable, especially about
     the Welfare Council in relation to the Community Chest.

343. McISAAC, James A. (1953). A study of lay participation
     in the Windsor Community Welfare Council.
        Were lay delegates active enough in the Council?
     Records of their attendance, proposing of motions, and
     chairing of committees, indicated that they were not.
     To see why, certain factors hypothetically associated

with active participation were isolated -- energy investment, knowledge about the organization, and so on -- as a basis for scheduled interviews. The interviews were given in July 1953 to the 33 available (of a total of 46) lay delegates and individual members. Responses conveyed that few delegates experienced power or prestige accruing from Council membership although they claimed a satisfaction from it that, hypothetically, would have led to more active participation. It is recommended that representatives should be selected for enthusiasm rather than for their sense of duty and that lay delegates should have more representation on the Board of Directors. Such devices for stimulating interest as an annual "parliament" instead of quarterly meetings, and special sections on programs for children, the aged, and recreation are suggested.

344. MELVILLE, Robert N.S. (Diploma 1946). A primary assessment of recreational needs in Edmonton.
In February 1946 a group of agencies gave questionnaires to the nine-to-eighteen-year-olds in all Edmonton public and separate schools; of the 78 per cent responses, 11,363 were usable. Findings were classified according to the students' home districts. Mr. Melville contributes to this survey additional data on each district: a delinquency rate (the number of probationers in 1945-46 per thousand schoolboys), and a dependency rate (the number of persons noted in various social assistance agencies' files as receiving service per thousand estimated population). He compares these combined ratings with each district's proportion to student population of club memberships, to indicate which areas most need additional recreational services. Finally he appends a close-range evaluation of one of the 22 neighbourhoods which the group survey had identified. The high delinquency rate there seemed related to inadequate programs for teen-agers, but facilities did exist where most of the programs the teen-agers said they wanted could be developed, as well as those pensioners needed.

345. OLYAN, Sidney D. (1951). Democracy in action; a study of the Co-operative Committee on Japanese Canadians.
The process by which the civil rights of Japanese Canadians were asserted began only after the forced

relocation in 1943 of those who had been West Coast residents. Relocated families in Toronto needed housing and recreational services. "Y" representatives, attempting to meet those practical needs, provided the nucleus around which the protest of many scattered groups and individuals was organized. Into the Committee thus formed information flowed, was verified and redisseminated. When the Committee saw certain coercive and undemocratic actions taken on the authority of federal legislation purportedly to "permit repatriation", it was able effectively to contest the government's power to enforce the legislation. But since the Committee's broad support included both the intransigent and others counselling compromise, what it primarily attempted and contrived was a watch-dog operation rather than forthright legislative action. The writer commends this example of co-ordinated action on a Canada-wide scale to the attention of social workers who also deal in sensitive areas within a varied community.

346. SHIFF, Murray (1952). The youth program of the Canadian Jewish Congress in Ontario.
The economic depression impelled youth to organize out of common concern for their future and need for social interchange. War turned Jewish organizations to work for servicemen and refugees and intensified their cultural awareness; but its passing enthusiasms and changing leaders meant, too, fitful growth. Mr. Shiff documents this history from Congress and Youth Council files since 1938. In Toronto delegates to the Council seldom took back to their constituent organizations ideas for enriching programs. Outside Toronto, lack of coherent, consistent support for city or temporary inter-city councils inhibited development. It is recommended that the Canadian Youth Commission, appointed by the Congress in 1951, should bear in mind this history in planning for the future: youth organizations need to avail themselves of help, and enlist support, from local and national adult groups, in order to profit from their experiences and to develop such program resources as leadership-training workshops, drama festivals, and courses in Jewish education.

347. SOLKIN, William W. (1948). A problem in Jewish community organization in Canada.

Thirty-eight communities were represented at the 1947 plenary session of the Canadian Jewish Congress: delegates from local organizations, groups' spokesmen, and key individuals. Simultaneously the Council of Jewish Federations and Welfare Funds, Inc., had 12 affiliated Canadian local Councils with 6 more participating informally. Yet of Canada's 21 organized Jewish communities, 14 were not fully centralized; and the 46 sizeable but still unorganized local communities represented about half of Canada's Jewish population outside the three major centres. Concentration on civil liberties, refugee and war work, and European and world Jewry's postwar needs had postponed the necessary local organizing that all groups wanted to see. However a jurisdictional dispute stalled negotiations between Congress and Council representatives in January 1948. The writer assesses pros and cons. He concludes that historical considerations argue for the Congress as the natural pivot for Canadian organizing, but that the professional skills and standards prevalent in the Council would be useful here and should be developed in co-operation with the Council.

348. TUDOR, Mary (1954). Community organization for hospital and medical care.

Although by 1953 some 250,000 Canadians had subscribed to consumer-sponsored health plans, the Co-operative Union of Canada knew of only 8 such organizations. The writer finally tracked down 48, wrote to 45, received replies from 39, interviewed persons concerned as opportunity offered, and closely analyzed one Ontario co-operative. Around 1900 Maritime miners' pay deductions were assigned to panel doctors chosen according to miners' proportionate preferences. This system, however, was superseded by a profession-sponsored scheme (similar to the B.C. doctors' alternative to an abortive government-sponsored plan there). Credit unions gave rise to most of the existing co-operatives in Quebec and Ontario. Wherever subscriber groups were too small or incomes too low to attract profession-sponsored or commercial plans, local organizations might plan for themselves. When members could scrutinize health records contributors appreciated why rising premiums were needed; open books sacrificed confidentiality but also prevented abuses. Lay control has proved

228

effective, offering fairly standard contracts usually drawn up by local doctors.

SEE ALSO Entries 402, 403.

349. BHATT, Perviz (1957). <u>A study of the admissions criteria of the School of Social Work, University of
Toronto.</u>
The writer examined files on 1950-51 enrolment
in the Toronto B.S.W. course and found that in 25
cases applicants were admitted despite relatively
serious reservations. An equal number of cases were
studied where no question of acceptability had been
raised, with the same number (13 of the 25) proceeding to the second-year M.S.W. course in 1951-52.
Background data from application forms, letters of
reference, answers to the questionnaire on social
work experience or aptitude, medical certificates,
and bursary applications provide the bases for faculty assessment and the Admissions Committee's decision. Where an applicant's ability to handle
stress, for example, or to take responsibility, or
his capacity to change was questioned, his Field
Work Supervisor's evaluations and the faculty's periodic grading conferences were consulted to see
whether these weaknesses persisted. The two groups
defined by different lay and faculty expectations
at admission were indistinguishable on the basis of
later performance reports.

350. COLLINS-WILLIAMS, Mabel (1952). See Entry 352.

351. SLADEN, Kathleen (1957). <u>The question arises; a
study on social work and religion.</u>
Drawing upon reading and discussions, the
writer observes that definitions of social work
commonly approach, through concepts like needs or
values or goals, a definition of man. Has man a
spirit? Religious and Freudian answers are summarized from D.R.G. Owen's <u>Body and Soul</u> and from C.
Hall and G. Lindzey's <u>Theories of Personality.</u> The
social worker, trying "to help effect the wholeness
of man", in theory usually defers to the first answer; the 1930 White House Conference, for example,
proclaimed every child's right to "spiritual and moral
training". However, in practice the Freudian, bio-
psychosocial view of man is taught in professional
schools and applied in non-sectarian agencies. Information about beliefs, the writer holds, may be essential

to an understanding of some clients, as about medicine of others. Therefore she feels that religion should be a collateral study in social work curricula. She also recommends that an interdenominational referral resource be developed and used in Toronto.

352. STEWART, Isobel, and COLLINS-WILLIAMS, Mabel (1952). Some common elements in the professional disciplines of school teachers and of social group workers.
    To develop individuals who can come to good terms with others in society is an objective in both schools and agencies sponsoring more informal group activity. Does professional training reflect this likeness of aim? The writers studied authorities to derive their categories, and then divided the work of analyzing procedures and courses in 11 schools: 4 teachers' training schools in Canada and 2 in the United States, and 2 Canadian and 3 American schools of social work. The phrasing of the questionnaire used caused some confusion, apparent especially in responses about the content of courses. Varied teaching methods and emphasis on practice work were found in both groups, with supervision more external and impersonal for teachers. By conforming to the standards of their professional association and admitting only graduates, the schools of social work ensured more consistent programing than did the varied state or provincial teachers' colleges. Although a common educational philosophy could not be traced in teachers' and group workers' preparatory courses, the interdisciplinary study provided interesting particulars and suggested new avenues for further investigation.

353. TEASDALE, Elinor Constance (1950). Graduates of the University of Toronto School of Social Work.
    Through questionnaires -- to all 161 university graduates who subsequently completed the two-year social work course during 1935-44 -- the formal education part of the profession's development is studied. Only one student in five had majored in social science as an undergraduate. First jobs were predominantly in child welfare and family service, 87 per cent with private agencies. By 1948 more workers were in public service, and a few more in new fields such as medical and psychiatric social work, although the number of group workers dwindled after the war. By then half

231

the graduates had withdrawn, mainly because of marriage and children, two-thirds of these after three years or more in social work. Of the remaining 53, 10 were employed outside Canada. Salaries here were low on the whole, with some gradual improvement evident. Perhaps review of professional education, selection, and field circumstances is needed if students are to be encouraged to commit themselves more enthusiastically to social work.

354. BRAITHWAITE, John Bismarck (1956). <u>Objectives of a</u>
<u>professional staff for competitive teams.</u>
The coaches of the two basketball teams studied
at St. Christopher Settlement House (Toronto) in 1955-
56 were volunteers, under professional supervision.
How far were group work principles operative among
the 22 boys under fourteen years of age who were
players there? Co-opting assistant observers the
writer gathered data on observation sheets for the
coaches during nine sessions and the participants
during thirteen practice sessions and five games.
He also gave the boys questionnaires, discussed a-
gency objectives with staff group workers and the
Athletic Director, and recorded proceedings at one
meeting of the Basketball Council, where team representatives learned citizenship by administering
their own affairs. In both questionnaires and observations one team's members showed more pronounced
reactions. Skill and experience in playing, as well
as personality, relationships, and leadership will
affect the usefulness of team membership for any
given individual. Coaches and staff all acknowledged
group work objectives, but one team seemed to serve
skilled players best, and in both "recognition"
seemed inadequate.

355. BUNDY, R.W. (1952). <u>To devise a method of testing</u>
<u>for a measurement of growth of democratic atti-</u>
<u>tudes in groups.</u>
This project's tests were devised for general
adaptability as well as to trace one quality among
33 boys at Camp Northland over a three-week period,
and for 6 of them through a further camp period.
Each weekly test described familiar camping situations, offering five choices corresponding to a
scoring-range from the most democratic to the most
laissez-faire and the most authoritarian preferences.
An accompanying sociometric enquiry asked campers to
choose preferred associates in typical undertakings.
Finally attitudes as expressed in behaviour were observed and recorded on prepared charts. Despite
prior explanations, the first test answers seemed
attempts to please, judging by subsequent scoring.
After one poorly handled camp-out, attitude scores

dropped. Although these tests indicated considerable instability of attitude, the close relationship between test scores, interaction scores, and change scores suggests that they provided indications of attitude growth and, most usefully perhaps, reflected the leaders' qualities.

356. CRITCHLEY, David M. (1949). The impact of the community services upon a youth group.
The writer consulted available records in the eleven agencies in contact since 1939 with members of a group known as the "Harrow Street Eagles", also drawing on his own experience as leader of the 11 "Eagles". Their escapades on Y.M.C.A. premises had led to the club's formation. Although the boys' difficulties corresponded with the areas of concern of the agencies involved, individually the boys were not assured of continuous help: schools tended to work in isolation, nurses on a short-term basis, welfare agencies on only part of a family situation, and the group work agency without adequate facilities or casework consultants. Rarely did one agency refer a boy to another. Very few workers who checked the Social Service Index followed the leads indicated. Integration is urged to ensure total service. Preparatory research is suggested into: intelligence ratings of all children on a street like Harrow Street; schools' dealings with maladjusted children like the "Eagles"; and whether delinquents' clubs are advisable within a general building-centred program.

357. ENGLANDER, Rhoda (1954). Change in children as perceived by parents in groups led by trained workers and in groups led by volunteer workers.
With the help of the Director of York Community House the writer selected 24 sets of parents from eight groups in the two leadership categories, and interviewed in each home three times between February and May 1954. Parents tended to assess a child's relationship with siblings in terms of peace and quiet, his behaviour in terms of respectfulness and obedience, and so on. Within their terms of reference most perceived changes clearly. Where leaders were trained, more parents reported children talking about the club and bringing home things made there; and often what parents perceived as interest in the club, group workers perceived as development in some

234

other area. Since children under volunteers were
markedly younger and less experienced club members,
the two categories could not be compared instruc-
tively. Despite uncertainty about the agency's objectives, many parents had welcomed contact and
hoped for more projects that would involve family
participation.

358. GIMA, Anne (1957). <u>Some factors affecting the
    decision-making process in social group work.</u>
        The writer's observations of individuals' be-
    haviour at three meetings each of two groups, and
    the group workers' records and comments, are here
    analyzed in relation to the members' share in decid-
    ing on a program for a next meeting. The groups,
    each of 8 girls of limited intelligence aged ten or
    eleven, met during 1956-57 in two Toronto Settlement
    Houses. After summarized background and behaviour
    reports, the worker's rating of every girl's status
    in her group is charted beside the writer's notes of
    how many relationships the girl had with other chil-
    dren and how often this member contributed to the
    group's decision-making. A correlation between status
    and relationships appeared for only one of the groups,
    and none was apparent between status and number of
    contributions to decision-making. However, four
    emotional needs -- for self-expression, recognition,
    security, and acceptance -- were identified by the
    writer as governing, according to their intensity,
    the girls' capabilities for making decisions.

359. GRAHAM, Glenna M. (1959). <u>What are the policies in
    Toronto leisure-time agencies concerning referrals
    to casework services and to what extent are they
    being carried out in practice?</u>
        The writer interviewed all 14 trained workers
    giving direct leadership to anywhere from one to seven
    groups each in the ten agencies. During 1956-57 they
    had referred a total of 35 clients, most commonly to
    mental health agencies, with counselling the service
    most frequently recommended; in 22 cases the worker
    knew a staff member in the agency suggested. Dis-
    turbed behaviour occasioned referrals, as did such
    problems as trouble between parents and children, or
    illness in the family. Prospects seemed good in the
    17 cases where the group member had approached the
    worker for help -- all 7 completed referrals were in

this category. Despite the theoretically close relationship between worker and group member, many of
the interviewed workers felt that their limited contact with members inhibited referrals. Public awareness of agencies' services would help people to accept
workers' suggestions, especially in a context of informed and confident relations between casework and
group work services.

360. LANG, Norma C. (1955). Common factors producing in-
       digenous leadership.
       To test the hypothesis that the leadership role
will be shared, but among high-status members in a
group, the writer studied 35 girls in four groups of
day-campers aged nine to twelve in West Toronto during the summer of 1952. Using the Moreno sociometric
test, she attempted to assess the leadership component
in the psychological structure of the four groups.
Leadership was shared among 10 highly chosen campers,
and each group showed different patterns of variation
in individual scores and status positions. In three
groups personality factors were mentioned most often
as the basis of choice, in the fourth, members' contributions to the group. Counsellors' assessments,
agreeing with group scores in first choice of leader,
gave a high proportion of negative items in describing
non-leaders. Counsellors often seemed struggling for
"tolerance", and popular campers, struggling to meet
needs to control, win approval, etc. Analysis of this
kind, therefore, should prove useful to planners of
counsellor-training and group service programs.

361. LEAROYD, Margaret A. (1952). Group-work--casework
       co-operation in a recreational agency.
       Relations between the Counselling and the Pro-
gram departments of Toronto's Y.W.C.A., negligible
before 1947, were stimulated by a series of joint
conferences and, after additions to professional
staff in 1949, became increasingly extensive. The
writer observed these developments as a staff member
during 1948-51. Through agency records and interviews
with various directors and staff social workers, she
studies the interdepartmental experience from the
group worker's viewpoint. Group leaders in the Central Branch sometimes referred individuals to caseworkers, and sometimes consulted with them about
individuals. Although the other branches seldom

236

referred individuals for counselling, they did bring
in caseworkers to lead discussions, and thus put them
in contact with branch members. Since girls who spon-
taneously sought counselling often belonged to a group
already, or else were too disturbed to join one, re-
ferals from caseworkers to group workers were fewer
but often involved more intensive co-operation. One
experiment, offering individual vocational counselling
to members of a branch club on dance nights, proved a
novel and successful joint project.

362. LEMMON, Walter (Diploma 1948). The use of group work
methods in Boy Scouts Associations.
In theory both group work and Scouting stress
the same structural and control techniques of creat-
ing a social climate wherein an individual can develop
into a responsible citizen. However, recording, although part of Scouting procedure, is not clearly
enough defined towards any end; and supervision, although provided for in Scouting's structural hierarchy,
is not close and regular enough for effectiveness. To
assess actual practices the writer sent 53 questionnaires to all trained Scoutmasters in Ontario, and
analyzed the responses of the 53 per cent who participated. Large Troop meetings apparently tend to swamp
small Patrol meetings, and classroom instruction, to
replace the self-education prescribed in the book.
Scoutmasters, in the main, apply modern Scouting
principles. However, when 70 per cent of boy patrol
leaders are selected on criteria other than members'
choices, and when 65 per cent of Scoutmasters chair
executive meetings (Courts of Honor), with 57 per
cent of them planning the programs, an over-directing
tendency is apparent.

363. McDONALD, Roma F. (1953). Group process in the program planning of a dance committee, Y.W.C.A.,
Toronto, 1949-50.
The dance committee, which arranged all-
association weekly dances, was made up of representatives appointed or elected in all affiliated clubs.
The social evenings planned had attracted great numbers almost from the outset. But success had led to
sameness of program and over-weening autonomy among
committee personnel. To correct these difficulties,
the committee's function within the agency was clarified; thereafter finances took less meeting-time, and

better managing of mechanical details permitted a shift of attention to program planning. Gradually the committee became more receptive to new ideas which varied sources began to contribute. In this thesis the focus was explicit (program) and the method scientific (correlating age and attendance, or timing items on agenda). However, the writer was the staff leader who did the process recording on the committee meetings studied. She feels that group process might be studied more objectively by using several groups and some very specific focus, such as implemented program ideas in relation to their source.

364. MACFARLANE, Margaret Ann (1950). The efficacy of the group work method in achieving the objectives of a religious agency.

Only the writer was both trained and active as leader of a pre-adolescent group in the Anglican Church where this study was made. To minimize personal bias she instructed two volunteers from the Anglican Women's Training College in group work principles and asked them to evaluate her group's functioning (a third neutral observer, fuller instruction, and more observation periods, would have made this technique more useful, she felt). Comparative study of her own and a similar group, through records and questionnaires completed by members at the beginning and end of the spring term, was obscured by differences in the groups' programs and members' maturity. All sources agreed that under the trained leader the girls' participation and democratic responsibility improved. Since lively new methods are welcomed by religious educationalists, group work should be applicable to an informal religious setting. Its effectiveness with this test group, the writer notes, might have been greater had agency limits been consistently borne in mind.

365. MAGDER, Beatrice (1953). An examination of the extent to which the group work method can be used with six- and seven-year-olds.

This study is based on agency records of two beginners' groups in downtown Toronto -- 9 girls in the University Settlement and 14 boys at St. Christopher House -- and on the writer's observations of the girls' group for six weeks in early winter, 1952. Routines and the constant presence of the group worker

238

provided continuity. The program, initially centred around arts and crafts where children could take part but remain individualistic, could be guided towards co-operation by gradual sharing of tools, for example, or by making articles for a parade or circus. A child's proposal to add ticket-selling to the circus project instances the form of participation in planning which is characteristic in such an embryo group, where experience is limited and attention spans are short. Workers could use an active and varied program to help one child to join in and another to accept second place, until all were having a good time.

366. MARKUS, Elliott J. (1958). <u>Attitudes of practitioners to the essentials of social group work.</u>
    To find out what is professionally acknowledged as the core of group work knowledge and skills, the writer extracted propositions put forward in 10 publications, consolidated and revised these to a list of 211, and asked 40 trained practitioners in Toronto to tally each as "indispensable", "important", "relevant", or "not social group work". Agreement with authorities was substantial. Two items about <u>esprit de corps</u> were roundly rejected, perhaps because ill-favoured words were used. Neither relations with the community nor "formed groups" were commonly classed as indispensable, and "group feelings" were recognized least by those working with primary groups. These workers most consistently defined group work as helping individuals. Those remotest from practice most fully endorsed the theory, with disagreement sharpest where propositions were most specific. Principles of action and thought about group living as a new way of helping people have been defined. Now further research is needed to provide an adequate scientific basis for social group work.

367. NOWLAN, Nadine M. (1962). <u>A study of the relationship between the "Prescriptiveness of the Pattern of Constituent Performances" of arts and crafts projects and the participation of a group of disturbed girls.</u>
    Do emotionally disturbed girls prefer projects involving several options among procedures, or projects where all operations are essential? The 9 youngest residents of Warrendale, a treatment centre for emotionally disturbed girls, participated in an

experiment. Choice (or no choice) was kept, as far
as possible, the only factor influencing preferences,
which were measured by duration of performance. Twelve
arts and crafts projects were introduced to the participants, six high-prescriptive activity-settings and six
low-prescriptive. Each girl was free to choose if and
for how long she wished to participate in any of the
projects, each of which could be completed in about
an hour. The length of time each girl did participate
was carefully measured. Previous speculations in the
literature suggested that durations would vary, and
preferences would thus be indicated, according to the
"prescriptiveness of the pattern of constituent performances". However, no such variation appeared in
the Warrendale experiment.

368. PEAL, Nancy A. (1955). Culture and program in group
       work.
       Out of her experience in the York Community
House of the Neighbourhood Workers Association the
writer postulated "a difference between working-class
children and middle-class children in their attitudes
toward, and interests in, the tools of program used
in social work groups". She used fathers' occupations
for class grouping, re-examining agency registration
data when another staff worker challenged any child's
identification, and then studied answers to interviews
she had previously conducted with 36 children around
eleven years of age. The neighbourhood's high mobility and the children's prior group membership notwith-
standing, emphatic differences did emerge in experience
and preferences. Most working-class children, for example, liked the idea of visiting a bakery or dairy
while a middle-class choice would be the museum; creative outdoor play predominated in working-class experience, whereas middle-class children used more play
equipment. Both groups responded to what they found
"realistic". Group work clearly involves awareness
of cultural values in community and individuals, and
conscious use of program to convey, and encourage,
acceptance of differences.

369. ROGERS, Joyce Patricia (1952). The correlation be-
       tween attendance of group members and educational
       qualifications of group workers.
       A method is tried here of assessing techniques

and insights developed at random in comparison with those professionally developed in recent years. Through scheduled staff interviews about, and study of, records on 44 active teen-agers' clubs with stable leadership in eleven Toronto agencies during the program year 1951-52, the writer compiled two sets of tabulated "scores". Attendance figures were derived from monthly summaries for the clubs, since unfortunately individuals' records, which would have reflected membership turnover as well, were not part of the statistical information compiled in most agencies. Leaders' professional or relevant education and experience, the frequency of supervision, and recording practices were scored according to a set-points system. The resultant correlations proved insignificant: 28 volunteers, 12 salaried workers, and 4 student leaders, scoring averages of 10, 32, and 23.8, led groups scoring averages of 72.6, 70, and 73.9, respectively. Apparently some variable, such as group feeling or leader's personality, affects attendance more than any of the qualifications studied.

370. STEIN, Morris A. (1953). Methods used to introduce Jewish content in the program of the Toronto B'nai B'rith Youth Organization and the relationship of these methods to social group work.
     The agency studied included members representing a variety of Jewish viewpoints and staff trained or undergoing training in social group work. Information was gathered through social work students' records, official files on chapter meetings since September 1950, and annual staff summaries, by interviewing executive and group leaders, and by observing 1953 meetings of three groups, two special programs, and two regional conventions. Twenty-five programs with Jewish content showed the agency's firmly defined policy, reinforced by structures (publications, committees, project designs) and by staff commitment to agency objectives. Religious and interfaith projects and discussions and fund raising were all used, perhaps more effectively than direct teaching or prescribed oratorical contests. Members were told before joining about the agency's Jewish emphasis. Their programs were freely, democratically planned, and the writer — holding that "group work cannot proceed in a vacuum" after all — feels that individuals' needs could be and were met through groups also meeting content requirements.

371. STEWART, Kenneth B. (1957). <u>An examination of the decision-making process as method by professionally trained group workers and untrained workers.</u>

The Neighbourhood Workers' Association staff chose eight of its children's groups, four in each leadership category, for systematic observation by visitors who sat in on weekly meetings and kept records on detailed observation sheets which the writer had developed. Records showed that trained workers allowed members more opportunities to make their own decisions than did the untrained workers. Both used verbal influences more than gestures and direct action. Both directed their help primarily towards individuals, and acted oftenest in the advising role, although untrained workers tended to be controlling, to police or instruct, except when members explicitly asked for their opinions. Trained workers intervened less and gained more response, using the decision-making process as method more effectively than did the untrained workers. Despite some workers' unallayed awareness of the observers' presence, and some particulars which the recording sheets might have defined more precisely, the data-collecting method proved workable and fruitful.

372. TAKEDA, Ken (1958). <u>Status and role of individual members in small groups.</u>

The writer used sociometric tests, questioned group leaders, and observed sessions of two formed groups of boys aged eight to eleven, with 6 and 7 members each, in York Community House, Neighbourhood Workers' Association. Correlated ranking and scoring results indicated that relationships in one group were stable, in the other less so. Although the boys explained their psychosocial and functional preferences on different grounds, their test answers did not reveal the anticipated "differences in status between psychosocial choices and functional choices". And only in one group was the hypothesis borne out that members with high sociometric scores would take a higher proportion of functional roles than the low-scoring members. However, the members taking influential and constructive roles were the ones given higher status by fellow members. Such relationships might be restudied through repeated tests, or in terms of members' needs and outside influences, and so on, or through greater emphasis on origins and reciprocating of choices.

SEE ALSO Entries 314, 316, 318, 404.

373. FINE, Charles (1959). <u>Examination of an aspect of the social-work--social-science relationship.</u>
The cultural anthropology section of social science has studied what happens when people are uprooted and transplanted. Do social workers avail themselves of the major insights gained? Using explicit references to Italy in case records as an indication of workers' awareness of ethnic factors, the writer assessed all 34 instances in four diverse agencies where first- or second-generation Italians received continued service from qualified workers between January 1956 and mid-May 1959. Explicit references occurred oftenest where clients were first-generation Italians or social workers were of non-British origin. Neither cultural stress nor Italian tradition was mentioned in records on 42 per cent of first-generation and 64 per cent of second-generation clients. In 15 cases given close reading, workers had made 23 attempts to relate social work goals to the clients' ethnically-conditioned perspective. To apply current psycho-cultural insights even more sensitively may involve fuller differentiating of ethnic factors, and overcoming of language barriers -- by caseworkers training interpreters or themselves knowing or learning their clients' tongue.

374. LAIDLAW, Kathleen M. (1953). <u>An experiment in the use of the Hunt Movement Scale.</u>
Although evolved to standardize judgment of family welfare casework, this technique is here applied to psychological counselling and psychiatry. An attempt is made to measure change in the cases of 25 disturbed children and accompanying parents who made five or more visits to the Toronto Psychiatric Hospital Outpatient Department between September 1948 and April 1950. Cases used to anchor the rating scale are described and assessed in detail. The degree of improvement of 20 children and 16 parents, examined beside certain additional factors, indicates correlation between parental acceptance and degree of involvement in the treatment plan, and patients' positive movement. Despite limitations -- a writer untrained in the technique; records sometimes unexplicit about categories used; subjects too diverse

because severity of disturbance was not initially
taken into account -- the correspondence between these
results and clinical reports differently evaluated
elsewhere suggests that the Hunt Movement Scale might
usefully be applied in this field.

375. MOHR, Johann W. (1959). <u>Evaluative research in social</u>
<u>casework</u>.
Through an extensive bibliography and summaries
of eleven cogent studies Mr. Mohr surveys the prelim-
inaries, accomplished over the past fifteen years, to
the establishment of a conceptual framework and a
methodology which would alleviate social caseworkers'
concern "to know better what we are doing in order to
do it better". He analyzes the selected evaluative
studies in terms of the source and arrangement of
data and the measuring techniques applied. The inter-
play between developing experience and epistemology is
illustrated: for example, if casework interviews could
be transcribed verbatim the distress-relief-quotient
method of measuring change might prove valid; or, in
reverse, the evaluative technique of follow-up has
incidentally revealed that ex-clients, instead of
feeling the anticipated resentment, welcomed follow-
up as evidence of continued interest. Since casework
deals with multi-dimensional human situations, research
must formulate its frames of reference accordingly.
Large-scale agency and educational research projects
should be planned within one unified design.

376. PURDY, Phyllis M. (1955). <u>Growth and movement in</u>
<u>adolescent girls; an experiment in the use of</u>
<u>the Hunt Movement Scale</u>.
Can the Hunt Movement Scale, developed in a
family agency, be used to measure change in clients
(adolescent girls) in a casework agency (the Big
Sisters Association)? The test cases were those of
50 girls, selected at random from 150 continued service cases which were closed between January 1954 and
June 1955. Two-thirds of the girls were between fourteen and sixteen years of age, 88 per cent came with
problems involving personality or behaviour, and 40
per cent lived at home with both parents. Significantly
varied rates of change emerged only when second ratings
applied special criteria adapted to adolescents' uneven
development and contradictory patterns of adjustment
and relationship; five interviews proved minimal for

establishing an effective client-worker relationship. Ratings were made for the 33 parents involved, out of a potential 77. Children's positive movement ratings tended to correspond with positive parental movement and with early, prolonged agency contact. The findings suggest how important to adolescents are parental support and time to grow.

377. WEYMAN, Robert M. (1955). Factors associated with movement in a casework service for boys.
 The case records of the Big Brother Movement (Toronto) on all 67 clients under age sixteen coming in 1951-52 for casework provided data for assessing the amount of change in each boy according to the Hunt Movement Scale, and for noting factors hypothetically associated with such change. Ten factors were considered — age, schooling, home interest, and so on — for each of four groups graded according to assessed change. The chi-square test of the data led to the conclusion that none of the factors was significantly related to movement, although there was some support for correlating greatest progress with frequent and numerous interviews, and a parent's intelligent initiative. Perhaps factors not in case records governed individuals' responsiveness. Perhaps a more precise instrument for considering both the change and associated influences needs to be devised. Meanwhile a non-statistical study, of individual cases most and least improved, for example, would be more instructive.

SEE ALSO Entry 355.

378. BROWN, Katharine A. (1961). Lawyers' attitudes to-
     wards social workers.
          It is not uncommon for two professions to ap-
     proach the same client or problem, but from different
     viewpoints and with different resources. Effective
     collaboration depends upon clear mutual understanding
     of functions and skills. This writer, with another
     student, examined the attitudes towards social work
     held by 30 lawyers in general practice. The writer
     suggests a possible connection between the generally
     unfavourable attitudes found and the relatively poor
     status of domestic relations work in the legal pro-
     fession. Personal contact with social workers ap-
     peared not to improve these attitudes. The Family
     Court provides the main source of contact. Most
     lawyers referred clients to the Family Court or other
     social agencies in spite of their low expectations of
     counselling. Perhaps legal training engenders a more
     volitional concept of human motivation than that ac-
     cepted by social workers. Further research might show
     whether self-confidence in the counselling role affected
     lawyers' perceptions.

379. CHETKOW, B. Harold (1955). The rabbi and the social
     worker.
          The writer interviewed all the permanent heads
     of Jewish congregations in Toronto who upheld a recog-
     nized theological position — 18 rabbis altogether,
     serving about 40 per cent of Toronto's Jewish popula-
     tion. All would have agreed with the 1952 Institute
     on Church and Social Welfare Service that "without
     the adjustment of the individual to the Spiritual
     reality of the Divine Will, any other adjustments are
     incomplete". All liked to handle some problems them-
     selves, e.g., those involving family relationships.
     Non-Orthodox denominations were more fully informed
     about local resources and applied more casework and
     group work skills and insights in synagogue programs.
     The European Orthodox rabbis in particular defined
     areas where the rabbinate and social work are funda-
     mentally incompatible (in attitudes to common-law
     unions, for example), indicating the importance to

co-operation of thorough mutual understanding. A similar survey in a smaller city or town is suggested,
another from the agency viewpoint, and an exploration
of leadership patterns in the Jewish communities of
larger and smaller centres.

380. GARDNER, Douglas G. (1958). The clergy and social
work.
Using questions like those Miss McLean asked of
parish priests (Entry 384) or Mr. Chetkow of rabbis
(Entry 379), the writer interviewed 30 of the 90 United
Church ministers in charge of congregations in Greater
Toronto. Small and large congregations in downtown,
"fringe", and suburban locations were all represented.
Despite other available services, most notably those
offered through schools, all the clergymen had been
consulted frequently for counselling during the previous
year, with marital difficulties and the needs of transients and the aged the commonest occasions, alcoholism
and financial problems most often referred to social
agencies, and mental health problems most inconclus-
ively handled. All clergymen on agency boards referred
people to social workers (but no clergymen reported
referrals from social workers). Local meetings and
joint projects are needed to build more mutual understanding and co-operation.

381. GUILD, Marian B. (1961). Lawyers' help with social
aspects of socio-legal problems.
The lawyer accepts responsibility for protecting
the client's legal rights and improving his position
vis-à-vis others; but by virtue of professional standards he also owes a responsibility to the common interest and to principles acknowledged in his culture.
What should the lawyer do, and what does he do, to
help his clients as human beings in trouble? On this
question the writer, with another student, interviewed
30 lawyers who work alone or with one partner in seven
Toronto neighbourhoods. Their group characteristics
— such as ethnic background, social class of district
served, attitude to domestic relations work, and knowledge and opinion of social work — could be here
correlated with four typical responses to clients' social problems: counselling only, counselling and referring to other sources of help, referring only, and
accepting no responsibility for other than strictly

legal services. A more inclusive sample might test
these tentative conclusions and explore the bases for,
and intensity of, the responses here apparent.

382. JELINEK, Dagmar M. (1956). The attitudes of Anglican
clergymen toward the new approach in treatment of
sex offenders.
By present Canadian laws long sentences are prescribed for sex offences; for the offender classified
as a sexual psychopath an indeterminate sentence (often
in practice lifelong) is mandatory. The laws do not
provide for universal psychiatric examinations in sex-
offence cases or for psychiatric treatment for those
convicted. Does this "old" approach diverge from that
of a representative 40 of Toronto's 75 rectors? There
is no "official opinion"; 24 had counselled offenders,
and although only 4 mentioned referral to psychiatrists
as part of their counselling procedures, 13 when asked
specifically reported at least one such referral.
Usually the counsellor's experience fostered understanding or deepened his sympathy. Most saw the offences as
symptoms of emotional sickness rather than as conscious
evil-doing, but lacked knowledge of the etiology or of
psychiatry's therapeutic techniques. Despite some evidence of punitive feeling there seemed general awareness
of the new approach, if not of all its legal and social
implications.

383. LAZARUS, E. Joseph (1957). Some community attitudes
to social work and social workers.
This study is based on data gathered between 1952
and 1956 by the Sub-Committee on Attitudes of the Committee on Interpretation of the Toronto Branch, Canadian
Association of Social Workers. The Sub-Committee arranged for eight discussions on the topic "What do you
think of social work and social workers?" by a labour
group, a church association, one home and school and
two service clubs, a gathering of newsmen, and two
groups of young adults who had had some contact with
social workers. Mr. Lazarus analyzes the tape record-
ings that were made at these discussions, sorting 456
positive or negative opinions into 36 areas of reference. Positive comments predominated, with child welfare services particularly approved; most of the
criticisms were in the areas of fund-raising or government regulations. This way of testing community opinions
was found promising. Judging from the 90-odd persons

who participated in the discussions, the community
accepts social workers, but needs more specific information about agencies and services.

384. McLEAN, Catherine D. (1955). The Catholic parish
   priest's use of community resources.
   The writer interviewed 33 of Toronto's 45 Catholic
   pastors (2 of the 10 of these who serve ethnic minor-
   ities were interviewed indirectly through English-
   speaking curates). All 33 said they were consulted
   about problems of financial need and family problems,
   the categories which, respectively, they were most and
   least likely to refer to social agencies. Alcoholics
   Anonymous was the agency most widely praised, and recreational community centres perhaps the least known or
   accepted. All parish priests wanted the help of social
   workers, although some equated social work with the
   work of St. Vincent de Paul Societies; very few had
   knowledge of what was involved in professional training;
   and the Welfare Council was less clearly understood than
   the Community Chest. Parishes and pastors showed wide
   individual variations in parishioners' problems, lay
   organizations' help, and attitudes towards and experience with social agencies. Further study — of inter-
   relations from the social work side, and of the apparently
   inadequate representation of pastors on Welfare Council
   volunteer committees -- is recommended.

385. MESSINGER, Lillian (1959). Marriage counselling: a
   study of the attitudes of thirty doctors to marriage
   counselling services.
   As the number of troubled or broken homes increases, specialists in counselling in America, in
   state- or UN-supported guidance centres in Europe, and
   in scattered local casework services in Canada have begun offering preventive or remedial help. In Toronto
   counselling is offered under church and family agency
   sponsorship. Is this service adequate? In interviews
   with 30 doctors selected at random from four lists
   supplied by three hospitals and the telephone book, the
   writer found that all had patients consulting them because of marital unhappiness. Almost all felt that
   disproportionate and inappropriate claims were thus
   made on their time. Pre-marital education and well-
   publicized, fee-charging marriage clinics geared to
   all classes would satisfy a need many doctors noted.
   The 1955 Welfare Council survey indicated that marital

counselling inside family agencies seemed to provide service adequate to community needs. The present study suggests that a separate, distinct agency might better develop the service and better reach the public wanting it.

386. WINKLER, Doreen (1961). <u>The obstetrician-gynecologist as marriage counsellor</u>.
Assuming that their patients sometimes discuss non-physiological problems with these specialists, the writer interviewed 17 (as available, from hospital listings of names) about this part of their practice. Five respondents were predominantly concerned with objective, physiological data and obstetrical work, referring patients to lawyers and clergymen oftener than to social workers and psychiatrists; 12 had a psychophysiological orientation and defined their area of competence more inclusively. Both groups said sexual maladjustment was the commonest problem encountered, but the latter -- younger practitioners on the whole -- also mentioned alcoholism, financial worries, poor communication, and often counselled husbands too. On the whole this younger group was readier to use psychiatrists and more familiar with social work. Such specialists, calling in other existing community resources on occasion, can provide adequate marriage counselling in Toronto, the writer feels. Further study is suggested of where physicians learned their counselling techniques, and how and to what effect they use them.

GROUP PROJECT. <u>Diverse conceptions of the skills, activities, and competences of social workers: a study of one crucial aspect of interdisciplinary practice</u>.
In an increasing number of agencies social work is carried out not as an isolated professional activity, but in conjunction with other disciplines. In such circumstances the mutual attitudes and expectations of colleagues, and all aspects of intercommunication, are of first importance. A group of students studied concepts of the social worker and his profession held in such multi-disciplinary settings. Two agencies of each of the following types participated: general hospitals, psychiatric hospitals, mental health clinics, treatment centres for the

mentally ill, rehabilitation centres, nursery centres, and religious centres. Seventeen disciplines were involved. Each agency nominated representitives of at least three disciplines. In all 151 respondents were given scheduled interviews in which open-end questions were directed to the respondent's conception of his own job, of the social worker's job, and of teamwork. The following reports draw on all or parts of the material thus acquired.

387. APPLETON, Joy Louise, and SMEDLEY, W. Mary (1960). Doctor's and nurses' perceptions of the social workers' activities and competences.

The responses obtained from the 27 doctors and 23 nurses were examined by these writers in the light of their general hypothesis that perceptions of social work are affected by the setting in which the respondent works, irrespective of his discipline. Fifteen physicians and 14 nurses worked in non-psychiatric settings, the remainder in psychiatric settings. Material was classified by two categories: first, perception of services rendered directly to the client by the social worker; second, services indirectly rendered through collaboration with the medical team, and with the community. The writers produce evidence to suggest that the physicians and nurses in a psychiatric setting were less inclined than their non-psychiatric counterparts to see the social worker as providing mechanical or social services rather than psychological services. They also had a greater awareness of her skills, knowledge, and training, and her competence, not merely with the patient, but also with family and community. A need is indicated for more interpretation of allied professional roles to be included in the teaching programs of medical and nursing schools. In addition, the social worker herself is responsible for making her work intelligible to her colleagues.

388. BROWN, Mary Kay (1960). Colleagues' education and their conception of the social worker.

Starting from the assumption that education furthers mutual understanding and harmonious interaction, this writer examined the relationship between the educational level of respondents and their perceptions of the social worker, her function and skill. Four educational levels were defined (high school,

institutional, university, and post-graduate) and
represented by a random sample of 22 respondents drawn
from all the agencies. It is suggested that within
an actual working situation the respondent's perceptions of the social worker were not affected by his
educational level. Such an effect was discernible,
however, on all concepts concerning the social worker's
function and skill when seen abstracted from the real
work setting. Further research is suggested, using a
larger and more diversified sample with particular
reference to the social worker and the psychologist
in a teamwork relationship.

389. CHAKRABARTY, Donna Jean (1960). <u>Perceptions of social
    work by non-professional staff</u>.
        Expansion of ancillary non-professional services
has gone hand-in-hand with the development of the helping professions, notably in institutional services. A
sample of 22 non-professional staff was selected by
educational and occupational criteria. They were employed in the general hospitals, rehabilitation centres,
and treatment centres as nursing attendants, house parents, clerical workers, technicians, or domestic workers. The employing agency's main function, the attitude of superiors, and the amount of contact with the
social worker appeared to be directly related to the
respondents' perceptions. The function of the social
worker was seen to concern concrete, or vaguely defined, social problems rather than psychological problems. Almost one-third of respondents had no conception
of social work skills, while as many identified skills
of understanding and relationship. In general the
prestige of the profession was high, but was not seen
to include the power to make decisions. Non-professional
staff have intimate contact with patients and with the
general public; they represent a channel of communication that may warrant closer study.

390. HAMILTON, Madeleine E. (Non-degree Candidate, 1960).
    <u>Communication and teamwork in multi-discipline
    settings</u>.
        Considerable variations in each of these factors
were reported. Are they interdependent? Do patterns
emerge common to certain agencies or professions? The
writer used material from all 14 agencies, but made an
intensive study of the 2 mental health clinics and the
2 treatment centres. Teamwork was most frequently

mentioned in the four-agency group where a greater amount of formal and informal contact took place, including the sharing of records. The social worker's involvement was greatest where she and the psychiatrist appeared to form the basis of the treatment team. A unit's autonomy and physical contactness seemed to increase awareness of teamwork. In the ten-agency group little contact with colleagues led to fewer acknowledgments of teamwork. This situation usually reflected the attitude of the agency's administrators rather than its administrative structure. The type of service given did not appear to be relevant. The conclusion drawn is that the highest order of teamwork is created by mature, professionally-secure individuals.

391. KROEKER, Henry J. (1960). <u>Interdisciplinary variations in concepts of the skills, activities, and competences of social workers</u>.
   What similarities and differences of concepts do respondents in any one discipline or agency portray? Are patterns of concepts distinguishable, and if so, do they reflect professional or agency orientation? The writer drew his sample from five professional disciplines operating in eight agencies: in all 8 nurses, 5 occupational therapists, 6 physicians, 7 psychologists, and 7 psychiatrists. Differentials of focus and nature were used to construct profiles and variations of the sample as a whole, of the individual professions, and of four agencies selected for a comparative study. Results suggest a shift from the historical concept of the social worker giving material assistance to needy families, to one of a variety of services being offered to the primary client. Work with colleagues or the community was rarely mentioned. The psychiatrists and, to a lesser extent, the nurses showed the soundest over-all orientation towards social work, while the physicians were more vague. The psychologists were outstandingly aware of service to clients' families. The occupational therapists were without clear concepts of social work. It is noteworthy that the concepts prevalent in inpatient agencies corresponded most closely with those of the psychiatrists, and in each agency the chief administrator was a member of that discipline.

392. SANDERS, Lorraine J.V. (1960). <u>The social worker and the dynamics of intra-team relationships</u>.

The writer attempts to identify the concepts held by team workers and pays particular attention to the influence exercised by the type of agency concerned and by the presence of professionally-trained social workers. The data were supplied by the 41 respondents employed in the day nurseries, the rehabilitation centres, and the religious institutions. The quality of team relationships was found to relate more closely to the type of administration and patterns of communication than to the type of service given, or to the discipline in charge. The physical setting was important to informal communication, and so was long tenure of office. There was a direct relationship between favourable concepts of social work and the respondent's level of education; also the frequency of contact with a professional social worker. Where no professional social worker was employed, concepts of social work skills and training were hazy. Further consideration could be given to establishing efficient channels of communication, interpreting social work to non-professional staff, and strengthening social workers practising without professional training.

393. SMEDLEY, W. Mary (1960). See Entry 387.

UNCLASSIFIED

394. DANSKY, Karl, and LAWSON, William T. (1949). Three
types of leadership in adult education.
     The basis of this descriptive field study was
non-participant observation of the learning process
in three lecture-and-discussion courses under auto-
cratic, democratic, and laissez-faire leadership --
mainly a measuring of the quantity and direction of
verbal contributions. The quality of the group experience was indicated by students' answers to brief
questionnaires. The courses' effects on attitudes
and opinions were assessed very generally through
students' answers ("before" and "after") to test questions designed by instructors. The authoritarian
leader lectured, following his prearranged outline,
allowing only residual time for questions which were
not forthcoming on three of the ten occasions. The
laissez-faire leader's group was the most vocal, but
had the highest incidence of domineering or submissive
student expressions. In the democratic group students
directed comments to one another oftenest, and showed
the highest percentage of change in attitude on the
tests. The study thus offers clues to effective use
of lecture-and-discussion courses, and to techniques
for evaluating effectiveness.

395. EMERY, Edward C. (1955). A study of the out-of-school
activities of a group of first-form high school
boys and girls.
     Mr. Emery tabulated returns - on two forms, and
a time-sheet of out-of-school activities throughout
one week in March 1955 - from 119 boys and girls between thirteen and sixteen years of age in the George
Harvey Vocational School; the Guidance Department
chose the classes tested and explained the forms.
Television, radio, and movies absorbed the most hours
although few students considered that the programs
"influenced" them. Over half the boys and almost one-
third of the girls had part-time jobs and about the
same proportion belonged to clubs. Most seemed to
follow whatever opportunities opened up in their home
neighbourhood, even though these were not meeting
some needs of maturing young people -- boys especially
appeared to find little help with forming their phi-
losophies of life. The writer feels that the technique

for assessing needs which he has tested here should
be complemented by talks with students and should
lead to community planning for new resources to enrich these relatively barren leisure-time interests.

396. LAWSON, William T. (1949). See Entry 394.

397. TYLER, Frederick H. (1952). Application of group
education characteristics in a Farm Forum group.
     UNESCO was sufficiently intrigued by the Cana-
dian Farm Forum's technique of adult education (combining nation-wide broadcasts with local discussion
groups) to undertake a survey of the total program.
The present project was concurrently undertaken to
study one individual group through observations on
five meetings, questionnaires (which 87 per cent of
members completed), and post-meeting evaluations on
three sessions (by some 80 per cent of attending members). Despite a friendly, democratic atmosphere,
those most active in community affairs tended to be
active in the group but passive individuals tended
not to develop confidence there. Negative comments
in discussion were rare; yet many who had not contributed to the discussion said, on evaluation forms,
that they "disagreed with the group's conclusions".
Discussion guides and forms for reporting the group's
conclusions to central headquarters sometimes focused
and sometimes inhibited discussion. Greater stress
on local implications of topics discussed would
heighten members' interest. Trained group workers
might enhance such benefits as members already noted,
predominantly "learning to understand and accept
others".

398. WOLFE, Gordon (1961). A study of the Jewish upper-
middle-class adolescent girl through her use of
time.
     Questionnaires to 38 available of a 50-member
Confirmation Class in Holy Blossom Temple ascertained
how hours had been allotted in the previous week. In
separate interviews later 10 representative girls and
their parents elaborated on their preferences. Over
40 per cent of the time for grooming, meals, homework,
and chores, in that order, reflects both developing
self-awareness and continuing parental influence.
Despite lip service to individuality, group conformity

was apparent: parents usually regarded the much telephoning as a substitute for visiting, the girls as a way of keeping informed (to "keep in the swim"). Half the girls were taking lessons, (dancing, music, etc.) and despite complaints about homework many mentioned self-improving activities as desirable. Dating concerned both girls and parents. Pressure to be both popular and academically successful, to qualify for both university and a good marriage, created some anxieties and imbalances. Recommended to supplement casework are more emphasis on specific household management skills, and group discussions of general community concerns.

REPORTS   NOT   ABSTRACTED

Following is a list of titles of a limited number of reports for which abstracts are not available:

399. ARMSTRONG, Geraldine Anne (1960). Significant rela-
     tionships in the environment of the unmarried
     mother.

400. AXMITH, Gail Maxine (1962). Sexually promiscuous
     juvenile girls in Galt Training School.

401. CHEOW, Josephine (1962). The marital interaction as
     found between the spouses of the multi-problem
     families at London, Ontario.

402. DAVENPORT, Gwen M. (1962). From District Association
     to Area Council: a study of change.

403. GIBSON, Helen (1956). A study of District Associations
     of the Neighbourhood Workers Association.

404. HARMAN, E. Mae (1955). Use of group work method in
     working with delegate councils.

405. LUNDY, Lawrence Allen (1962). A follow-up study of
     ex-patients referred by the Ontario Hospital,
     Toronto, to rehabilitation services of the Ontario
     Department of Public Welfare.

406. MEDJUCK, Marilyn (1962). A study of fifteen children
     who had early life experience in Neil McNeil In-
     fants' Home.

407. MELLOW, J. Rodger (1962). Employment characteristics
     of the homeless transient man in Toronto.

408. PAK, Po Hi (1962). Marital conflict.

409. ROBINSON, W. Kenneth (1962). Public attitudes towards
     the criminal transient.

410. STEPHENS, Mary (1950). Membership fees and payments
     in recreation and informal education agencies in
     Toronto in 1950.

411. STRINGER, Helen E. (1962). The family background of
      the manic-depressive patient.

412. TOUMISHEY, T. George (1962). Homeless transients: a
      study of the characteristics of a group of two
      hundred homeless transients, with special emphasis
      on the educational and vocational experiences of
      these men.

INDEXES

INDEX OF AUTHORS

(Numbers refer to listings in Compendium)

Aaron, J.S. 146
Abrams, P. 198
Albert, S.J. 107
Alderwood, J.A. 179
Aldridge, G.J. 243
Alexiade, H. 199
Allen, D.R. 143
Amos, J.L. 218
Anderson, F.W. 108
Appleby, E.E. 109
Appleton, J.L. 387
Archibald, H.D. 110
Armstrong, G.A. 399
Askwith, G.K. 301
Atkinson, D.E. 111
Axmith, G.M. 400

Bain, I. 33
Barnes, J. 34
Barrass, D.F. 112
Bartol, Z. 327
Bassett, E. 297
Bauman, C. 113
Baumgartel, B.W. 114
Bear, M.L. 200
Bell, M.M. 35
Bellamy, D.F. 187
Bhatt, P. 349
Blackburn, W.W. 115
Blezard, R.J. 244
Blow, J.N. 332
Boes, L.F. 87
Boeschenstein, G.M. 191
Bojovic, N.S. 68
Bourke, W.A. 333
Bouschard, P. 9
Boyce, W.A. 219
Boys, J.F. 334
Braithwaite, J.B. 354
Brant, M.J. 36
Brett, F.W. 307
Briault, M.A. 245

Brock, M. 220
Brown, D.F. 116
Brown, J. 246
Brown, K.A. 378
Brown, M.K. 388
Brown, R.I. 221
Browne, H. 222
Budd, W. 308
Bundy, R.W. 355
Burgess, B. 192
Butkevicius, S. 247
Byles, A.J. 180

Cameron, D.A. 298
Cameron, E.H. 170
Campbell, C. 248
Campfens, H.L. 289
Castellano, V.G. 249
Chakrabarty, D.J. 389
Chandler, R.G. 181
Chatterjee, P.K. 171
Chellam, G.E. 309
Cheow, J. 401
Chetkow, B.H. 379
Clark, D. 88
Clark, D.C. 250
Cleaver, F.A. 335
Coleman, H.E. 71
Collins-Williams, M. 350
Cooper, V.E. 155
Couse, A.K. 117
Cowan, L.D. 223
Cragg, N.F. 310
Craik, M.E. 328
Crane, E.L. 149
Critchley, D.M. 356
Culham, L.J. 37

Dansky, K. 394
Dastyk, R. 3
Davenport, G.M. 402
David, R. 224

Davies, Y.S. 336
Davison, A.M. 201
Dawson, H.P. 58
De Marsh, H.R. 251
Demeter, S. 329
Dempsey, W.A. 337
Dingman, F.S. 118
Dorgan, H.J. 20
Dorricott, W.M. 182
Douglas, A.M. 303
Duffy, E. 72
Dufty, G.M. 311
Dunlop, J. 73
Dunlop, J.E. 10
Dunn, G. 302

Edmison, E.A. 172
Ellis, B.L. 119
Emery, E.C. 395
Englander, R. 357
Eno, E.E. 94
Erwin, R. 59
Ewald, F.E. 147

Falconbridge, J.A. 21
Farina, M. 292
Farry, J.B. 11
Feldbrill, Z. 202
Felstiner, J.P. 120
Felty, I.K. 225
Fenemore, R.S. 74
Ferguson, A. 312
Ferguson, M. 22
Fields, B.P. 156
Fine, C. 373
Finlay, D.G. 252
Foster, A.E. 157
Friesen, D.H. 226
Friesen, M.A. 12
Fulton, E.C. 95

Galleazi, M.J. 158
Gamble, J.E. 227
Gardner, D.G. 380
Garfield, G.P. 313
Gendron, P.V. 175

Gibbons, G.J. 330
Gibson, B. 121
Gibson, H. 403
Giles, H.A. 150
Gillen, D.M. 159
Gima, A. 358
Giroux, J. 290
Glassco, L.H. 122
Godfrey, P. 338
Goodman, M. 314
Goodwin, W. 69
Gordon, C.M. 96
Gordon, D.A. 75
Graham, G.M. 359
Graham, L.B. 1, 151
Grant, C.L. 203
Grant, J. 253
Greene, B.H. 339
Griffith, G. 38
Gripton, J. 39
Gross, D.P. 123
Grover, I.E.H. 13
Guild, M.B. 381
Gunning, D.L. 97

Haddad, J.N. 183
Hahn, E.B. 23
Hamilton, M.E. 390
Harman, E.M. 404
Harrison, C.M. 76
Headrick, M.E. 160
Hertzman, P. 254
Hetherington, E.S. 228
Hicks, P.P. 98
Hindley, J.D. 255
Holgate, E. 4
Holmes, L. 161
Holmes, R.F. 256
Hopwood, A.L. 188
Howden, G.N. 99
Howson, C. 40
Hunsberger, W.A. 24
Hunter, T.J. 229
Hutton, M.B. 70

Iwasaki, E.M. 257

Jackson, E.B. 60
Jackson, J.D. 124
Jackson, M.J. 5
Jaffey, A.D. 258
James, A. 212
Janes, W.G. 41
Jarvis, D.L. 259
Jelinek, D.M. 382
Johnston, R.L. 299
Jolliffe, J.P. 340
Jolliffe, R. 42
Jones, E.A. 315
Judd, F. 125

Kagan, G. 25
Katz, B. 162
Katz, S. 26
Kay, M. 260
Kaye, E. 261
Kemp, B.D. 61
Kennedy, M.F. 27
Kileeg, J. 262
Kinzie, D.M. 230
Klein, I.M. 126
Kobayashi, J.H. 43
Kohn, R.G. 204
Kroeker, B.J. 213
Kroeker, H.J. 391
Kulys, R. 193

Lacey, W.R. 127
Laflamme, K.J. 205
Laidlaw, K.M. 374
Lampe, W. 316
Lang, N.C. 360
Lappin, B.W. 341
Latham, C.R. 206
Latimer, E.A. 89
Lauder, E.G. 194
Lavender, J. 263
Law, H.B. 163
Lawson, C.A. 264
Lawson, W.T. 396
Lazarus, E.J. 383
Learoyd, M.A. 361
Lee, O. 326

Leia, S.F. 14
Lemmon, W. 362
Leppanen, A.E. 265
Lesser, S.M. 266
Lichtenstein, D. 144
Lindenfield, R. 77
Lipman, M.H. 317
Little, W.T. 304
Lowery, R. 28
Lucas, J.I. 128
Lugsdin, M.I. 267
Lumsden, R.H. 305
Lundy, L.A. 405
Lustgarten, P. 268
Lutes, J.R. 195

McClelland, P.R. 269
McClure, K.H. 44
McConney, D.M. 184
McCool, M.E. 231
McCorkell, E. 63
McDonald, R.D. 318
McDonald, R.F. 363
Macdonnell, K.G. 342
McEachern, W.D.C. 232
McFarlane, G.G. 129
Macfarlane, M.A. 364
Macfarlane, P.O. 270
McGrath, W.T. 130
McGuire, J. 100
McIsaac, J.A. 343
McKenzie, J. 78
McLean, C.D. 384
McLean, E. 233
MacLeod, A. O. 62
Macmillan, E.J. 234
MacQuarrie, L.B. 152
McRae, M.A. 164

Maben, D.R. 331
Macklin, O.M. 29
Maeers, D.D. 15
Magder, B. 365
Maier, A. 235
Main, S. 131
Main, W. 30

Mann, W.I. 79
Margulies, L. 207
Markus, E.J. 366
Marshall, H. 271
Medjuck, M. 406
Melichercik, J. 132
Mellow, J.R. 407
Melville, R.N.S. 344
Mendel, A. 272
Messinger, L. 385
Milne, D.R. 319
Mohr, J.W. 375
Monson, I.A. 236
Moorby, K.V. 237
Moore, A.M. 293
Morley, M. 45
Myles, J.S. 320

Nagel, H.N. 133
Nakatani, R. 306
Naundorf, R. 177
Neilson, J.A. 6
Nevidon, P.T. 16
Newbury, M.A. 238
Newton, M.J. 208
Nichols, L.N.M. 273
Nichols, M.D. 64
Noell, M.A. 239
Norman, A.C. 214
Nowlan, N.M. 367

O'Brien, M.T. 80
O'Connor, C.J.M. 46
Okam, M.O. 185
Oke, J.K. 178
Oldham, H.P. 240
Olyan, S.D. 345
Outerbridge, W.R. 134

Paget, N.W. 47
Pak, P.H. 408
Palmer, J. 321
Palmer, S. 165
Parlee, M.J. 101
Parsons, A.F. 48
Parsons, S.J. 274

Peal, N.A. 368
Peebles, J.M. 166
Posen, M.M. 65
Price, G.C. 275
Priestman, R.W. 102
Purdy, P.M. 376

Ramsey, D.P. 49
Reed, M.P. 17
Regier, O. 153
Reid, D.C.S. 135
Reid, M.L. 322
Rich, M. 81
Robinson, J.A. 173
Robinson, M. 50
Robinson, R.B. 136
Robinson, W.K. 409
Rogers, J.P. 369
Romkey, L. 103
Roseman, R. 167
Rosinke, E.R. 291
Ross, N.L. 276
Rousell, C.T. 241
Rowles, J. 323
Rudney, B.D. 82
Russell, D.A. 51

Sanders, L.J.V. 392
Saville, H. 294
Schalburg, A. 300
Schlesinger, B. 90
Schmidt, W. 7
Schreiber, M.S. 189
Schwalbe, A.L. 83
Scott, A.M. 18
Scott, E.J. 104
Scott, J.A. 137
Scott, L.M. 277
Seigel, M. 278
Shapiro, S. 324
Sharpe, M.J. 174
Shaw, R.C. 91
Shephard, B. 279
Shiff, M. 346
Sibbald, P.A. 209
Sinclair, M.E. 280

Singer, C.B. 168
Skelton, M. 281
Sladen, K. 351
Smallman, M.M. 84
Smedley, W.M. 393
Smith, M.R. 186
Smith W.R. 52
Sohn, H.A. 215
Solkin, W.W. 347
Splane, R.B. 2, 53
Stanley, W.L. 92
Stein, M.A. 370
Stephens, M. 410
Stern, W.I. 8
Stevens, F.L. 54
Stewart, I. 352
Stewart, K.B. 371
Stoneman, A.L. 66
Strathy, P.A. 138
Stringer, H.E. 411
Summers, G.M. 93

Tait, R.H. 282
Takeda, K. 372
Taylor, D.E. 139
Taylor, E.D. 31
Teasdale, E.C. 353
Tela, C. 19
Tessaro, A.F. 140
Thomas, F.G. 105
Thomas, M.R. 55
Thomas, M-C. 242
Thomson, D.M. 295
Thomson, D.I.A. 296
Thuringer, H.P. 196
Thurlew, S. 210

Tiessen, L.H. 154
Toews, H. 190
Tonogai, S.L. 197
Toumishey, T.G. 412
Treen, H.W. 85
Tudor, M. 348
Turner, M.B. 283
Tyler, F.H. 397

Veitch, B.A. 176
Vine, W.G. 141

Wacko, W.J. 284
Wakabayashi, A. 86
Walker, P.M. 285
Wallace, H.R. 286
Walsh, N.M. 145
Ward, B.M. 67
Warriner, W.L. 32
Wass, D.K. 56
Wasteneys, H. 211
Webb, P.R. 287
West, L.A. 288
Weyman, R.M. 377
Whaley, B. 216
Wilson, E.A. 148
Wilson, H.L. 142
Wilson, N.R. 106
Wing, D.M. 217
Winkler, D. 386
Wolfe, G. 398
Woodsworth, J.E. 169

Ziemann, A.M. 57
Zimmerman, L. 325

INDEX OF AGENCIES

(Numbers refer to listings in Compendium)

Adult Probation Department, Toronto 139
Alcoholism Research Foundation 3,4,5,6,7,9,12,14,17,19,34
Association for Emotionally Disturbed Children 260

Banstead Hospital, England 272
Big Brother Movement 262,286,307,377
Big Sister Association 262,376
B'nai B'rith Youth Organization 370
Board of Education, Toronto 246,276,298,300
Boy Scouts Association 181,184,319,362

Camp Northland 355
Camp Tamakwa 318
Canadian Arthritis and Rheumatism Society 242
Canadian Association of Social Workers, Committee on
  Interpretation, Subcommittee on Attitudes 383
Canadian Jewish Congress 346,347
Canadian Mental Health Association 334
Canadian National Institute for the Blind 229,234
Canadian Young Judaea 324
Catholic Children's Aid Society of Toronto 62,80,104,170,
  171,172,173,174
Central Technical School 297
Child Guidance Clinic, Kingston 244
Children's Aid Society of London and Middlesex County 175,
  176,401
Children's Aid Society of Metropolitan Toronto 34,36,37,
  39,40,41,42,43,50,51,52,56,57,58,59,60,63,65,66,71,72,
  73,74,75,76,79,81,83,85,86,95,96,99,100,101,102,105,121,
  157,170,171,172,173,174,251,263
Community Chest of Greater Toronto 335,341,342
Council of Jewish Federations and Welfare Funds 347

Department of Citizenship and Immigration 203,206
Department of Labour, Ontario 212,213,214,215,216,217
Department of Public Welfare, Hamilton 293; London 175,
  176; Ontario 53,67,102,405; Toronto 20,48,69,70,187,219,
  292,295,296,302
Department of Reform Institutions, Ontario 115,127
Department of Veterans' Affairs 29,149
Don Jail 10,11,12,13,15,16,18,19,113,303,304,305,306,407,
  409,412

Earlscourt Children's Home 92
East End Day Nursery 358

Family Service Association of Metropolitan Toronto, see
  Neighbourhood Workers Association
Farm Forum group 397
Frank Oke School 259
Fred Victor Mission 303,304,305,306,407,409,412

George Harvey Vocational School 395

Haven (The) 285
Holy Blossom Temple 314,398
Hospital for Sick Children 222,231,237,261,280

Infants Homes of Toronto 84,94,97,103,317

Jamaica Children's Service Society 78
Jewish Camp Council 308
Jewish Community Centre, Hamilton 198
Jewish Family and Child Service 162,168,202
Jewish Home for the Aged 22,23
Jewish Vocational Service 207,335
John Howard Society 117,124,133,135
Juvenile and Family Court of Hamilton 125; of Metropolitan
  Toronto 107,111,114,115,121,122,126,128,136,140

Mercer Reformatory 143,144,145
Metropolitan Toronto Association for Retarded Children 43,
  257,269
Metropolitan Toronto Housing Authority 191,192,193,194,
  195,196,197; see also Toronto Housing Authority
Multiple Sclerosis Society of Canada 241

National Employment Service, Counselling Service for Older
  Workers 153,154; Youth Employment Centre 150,151
Neighbourhood Workers Association 158,159,160,163,164,165,
  166,225,357,368,371,372,403,408
Neil McNeil Infants' Home 88,406
New Mount Sinai Hospital 25,220,235

Ontario Camping Association 311
Ontario Hospital, New Toronto 284,411
Ontario Hospital, Toronto 31,247,249,273
Ontario Medical Association 20
Ontario Reformatory, Guelph 110,131; Mimico 143,144,145

Ontario Society for Crippled Children 230
Ontario Training School for Boys, Bowmanville 115,141,146,
   147,148; Cobourg 146,147,148; Guelph 146,147,148
Ontario Training School for Girls, Galt 112,119,146,147,
   148,400

Protestant Children's Homes 54,77,82

Sacred Heart Children's Village 91
Ste. Anne's Hospital, Ste. Anne de Bellevue, Quebec 266
St. Christopher House 200,354,358,365
Salvation Army Men's Hostel 303,304,305,306,407,409,412
Seaton House 303,304,305,306,407,409,412
Second Mile Club 21,27,28
Shaughnessy Hospital, Vancouver 240
Social Planning Council of Metropolitan Toronto 402; see
   also Welfare Council of Toronto
Sunnyside Children's Centre, Kingston 255

Toronto General Hospital 233,236
Toronto Housing Authority 187,188,190; see also Metropolitan Toronto Housing Authority
Toronto Mental Health Clinic 245,252,256,289,291,334
Toronto Psychiatric Hospital 161,243,248,253,254,258,264,
   265,267,268,270,271,273,274,278,281,282,283,287,288,
   289,290,374

Unemployment Insurance Commission 152
United Jewish Welfare Fund 336,341
University Settlement 8, 179,182,339,365

Victoria Day Nursery 68

Warrendale 277,367
Welfare Council of Toronto 334,341; see also Social Plan-
   ning Council of Metropolitan Toronto
Women's Patriotic League Emergency Workroom 26
Workmen's Compensation Board, Ontario 226

York Community House 357,368,372
Y.M. & Y.W.H.A. 325,339
Y.M.C.A. 150,310,338
Y.W.C.A. 150,186,309,321,323,339,361,363

INDEX OF SUBJECTS

(Numbers refer to listings in Compendium)

Adjustment: of discharged mental patients,274,281, 283; vocational,203,226, 239,265,287

Adolescents: measuring change in,376; mentally ill,270; Negro,83; as unmarried mothers,100, 101; use of time,395, 398; as wards,56,75

Adult education,394,397

Alcoholics: cultural factors relating to,16; drinking patterns of, 3,8,15; employment of, 3,10; interpersonal relations of,4,12; marital relations of,19; motivation for treatment of,6, 13; as offenders,18,113, 117,127; parent-child relationships of,5,9,17, 34; relatives of,11; social adjustment of,7,14

Anti-discrimination,212, 213,214,215,216,217

Attitudes: democratic,355; of practitioners towards group work essentials, 366; of public towards transients,409

Beech-Hall Housing Project,189

Big Brother Movement,307

Blind,223,229,232,234

B'nai B'rith Youth Organization,370

Boarding home care: for children,86; for mentally ill,284

Boy Scouts: drop-outs in, 184; group work methods

in,362; volunteers in, 181,319

Boys' Work Board,335

Brief service,162,268

Budgeting,333,342

Camp counsellors,318

Camping: admissions to,308; for diabetics,225; for handicapped children,230; staff,311,318; testing attitudes in,355

Canadian Jewish Congress, 346,347

Case conferences,155

Casework intervention,327, 328,329,330,331

Casework services: as seen by clients,163; division of,40

Catholic Children's Aid Society of Toronto, Board of Directors,46

Catholic Welfare Bureau,35

Cerebral palsied,222

Change, measurement of,355, 374,376,377

Child Guidance Clinic, Kingston,244

Child guidance clinics,45

Children of Unmarried Parents Act,53

Children's aid societies, 47,49,53

Children's Aid Society of Toronto,42,44,64

Children's Protection Act, 57

Chinese immigrants,201

Clergymen,380,382

Closed foster homes,79

Common-law unions,157

Communication,328,390

Community services: child
care,169; participation
of women in,336; use of
by public assistance re-
cipients,292, by a youth
group,356; volunteers
used by,339
Co-operative Committee on
Japanese Canadians,345
Council of Jewish Federa-
tions and Welfare Funds,
347
Counselling services,150
Crisis situations,327,328,
329,330,331
Cultural factors,16,36,368

Decision-making,358,371
Delegate councils,404
Deserted wives,295
Diabetics,225,233
Divorce,55
Doctors,385,386,387
Drinking patterns,3,8,15

Edmonton: recreational
needs of,344
Ethnic factors,373
Evaluative research,375
Extramural permit system,108

Fair Employment Practices
Act,212,213,214,215,216,
217
Family agency: financial
assistance in,160; re-
ferrals to,164
Family allowances,47
Family life: effects of
illness on,296; effects
of unemployment on,159,
296; immigrant,205; of
disturbed children,262
Father role,145,286
Fees,410
Forest Hill Village recreational program,337

Foster parents: interpretation of their job,80; at-
titudes towards agency,85
Fund-raising,341

Gastrointestinal illnesses,
235
Greek immigrants,199,205
Guidance program in a
school,297

Hard-to-place children,58,
67,83
Health and housing,190,194
Health plans: co-operative,
348
Heise, B.W.,49
Home finding,76,84
Home teaching,223
Homemaker service,156
Hunt Movement Scale,374,
376,377

Imprisonment,116
Indian Placement Program of
the Indian Affairs Branch,
Department of Citizenship
and Immigration,206
Indians, North American,36,
206
Infants' Homes of Toronto,
89,317
Information: giving,327;
seeking,330
Institutional care: children
needing,91; effects on
children,88,406; for un-
married mothers,98; fric-
tions in,92; use of social
worker in,90
Intake,168,323
Inter-country adoption,1
International Social Ser-
vice,1
Interpersonal relations: of
alcoholics,4,11,12; of
school children,276; of

unmarried mothers,104,399
Intervention of social workers,327,328,329,330,331
Italian immigrants,200,209,
  249,373

Jamaica: child welfare in,78
Japanese immigrants,1,210
Japanese in Canada,210,345
Jewish Camp Council,308
Jewish content in program,370
Jewish immigrants,198,202,204,
  207
Jewish Vocational Service,204,
  335
Job loads,316
Job satisfaction,309,312
Juvenile and Family Court,
  Hamilton,125
Juvenile delinquents: children's aid wards,121;
  community services for,
  356; immigrant,114; in
  training schools,115,141;
  incorrigible,107; mentally
  retarded,122; recidivist,
  126; separated from fathers,
  286; sexual,111,140; truant,
  136; unmanageable,137

Kelso, J.J.,33,49

Lambert Lodge Home for the
  Aged,30
Langmuir, J.W.,2
Lavell, Alfred E.,108,275
Lawyers,378,381
Lay delegates,343
Leadership,360,394: train-
  ing for,314,324,357,369,
  371
Leaside,177,178
Legislation for child wel-
  fare,49,53,55,57,87
Legitimate children: adop-
  tion of,63
Leisure-time activities,178,

282,395

Manic-depressives,264,411
Marital conflict,19,165,408
Marital relations,220,278,
  401
Marriage counselling,166,
  385,386
Matrimonial Causes Act,55
Measurement of change,355,
  374,376,377
Mentally ill: adjustment
  and rehabilitation of,
  265,267,274,281,283,287;
  adolescents,270; breaking
  treatment,268; children,
  244,246,251,252,255,256,
  260,261,262,263,276,280,
  289,290,291; ecology of,
  254,258,264,276; elderly,
  31; employment of,250,
  287; readmission of,272;
  relatives of,271,272;
  value of social service
  for,248,288
Mentally retarded,43: community adjustment of,285;
  delinquent,122; families
  of,253,257,269; psycho-
  social patterns of,259;
  unmarried mothers,103
Midland Park, Scarborough
  Township,177,178
Mother-child relationship,
  252
Mothers' Allowance recip-
  ients,293
Multi-problem families,155,
  167,175,176,401
Multiple sclerosis,241
Music School in University
  Settlement,182

Negroes,83,214
Neighbourhood Workers Association,155,403
North Toronto Memorial Gardens,340

Nurses,387

Offenders: alcoholic,18,113, 117,127; chronic,18,143, 144,145; employment of, 132,133; families of,129, 294; female,109,111,112, 119,128,148,277,400; recidivist,131; sexual,382, 400; transient,304,409
Old age pensioners,20,32
Older children, adoption of,59
Older men, employment of, 153,154
Ontario: social welfare history of,2
Ontario Adoption Clearance Service,67
Ontario Charitable Institutions Act,87
Ontario County Home, Whitby, 24
Ontario Hospital, Toronto,275
Ontario Medical Welfare Board,32
Ontario Training School for Girls, Galt,123
Ontario training schools, 120,146,147,148,400

Parent-child relationship,5, 9,17,34,104,252
Parents: age disparity of, 289; attitudes towards leaving child in hospital, 237, male child, 290, psychiatric treatment of child,280,291; of mentally retarded,253
Parole,133,138
Permanent wards,51,57: adjustment to wardship of,37; adolescent,56; adoption of, 58,59; delinquent,121; education of,39; impressions

of agency service,44; Indian,36; meaning of wardship for,38; mentally ill, 263; unmarried mothers,96
Poliomyelitis,224,239
Portuguese immigrants,200
Priests,384
Private placements,66,78
Prerogative of mercy,142
Probation,116,134,139
Program planning,363
Psychological report,326
Punishment,110
Putative fathers,99,102,105

Rabbis,379
Reactive depressives,283
Reading disability,298
Receiving Centre of the Children's Aid and Infants' Homes of Toronto, 90
Recording systems,322
Recreation: co-operative, 332; for the aged,27,28; for mothers,185; in Edmonton,344; industrial, 320; municipal,337
Referrals from group work to casework,359,361
Regent Park (North),187,188, 190
Regent Park (South),191,192, 193,194,195,196,197
Rehabilitation: blind,223, 232,234; handicapped,218, 219,236,405; mentally ill, 265,267; offenders,109, 116,124,135; paraplegic, 239; tubercular,227,228; vocational,218,232,265
Rejected foster homes,74
Religion and social work, 351,364
Rent,188
Replaced foster homes,72,73
Rheumatic fever,231

Rheumatics,342
Role perception,315,372

Sacred Heart Orphanage,93
Schizophrenics: home care of,
260,266; in school,246;
post-hospital adjustment
of,247; social characteris-
tics of,264
School social work,299
Sentencing of offenders,125
Sheltered workshops,26
Single males,4,13
Social science and social
work,373
Social Planning Council of
Metropolitan Toronto,402
Social welfare in Ontario,2
Sole-support mothers,70
Special Placements Section of
the Women's Division,
National Employment Service,
221
Staff training,311,313,318
Status,372
Stress,279
Stutterers,282
Successful foster homes,71,
77,81
Sunnyside Children's Centre,
Kingston,255

Teaching and social work,352
Teen-age canteens,183
Telling child about adoption,
62
Time variations in adoption,
60
Toronto Mental Health Clinic,
245
Toronto Psychiatric Hospital
Outpatient Department,243,
251
Trained leaders,324,357,369,
371
Training School Act,120
Truancy,136

Tubercular,227,228
Two-generation families,
170,171,172,173,174

Unemployment: effect on
family,159; and older
men, 153,154; and public
housing,187; relief,296;
social consequences of,
152
United Jewish Welfare Fund,
336
University of Toronto
School of Social Work:
admissions to,349;
graduates of,353
Unmarried mothers: adolescent,101; age of,100;
disposition of children
of,94,95,103; institu-
tions for,98,106; legis-
lation for,53; mentally
retarded,103; repeater,
97; in two-generation
families,173; wards be-
coming,96
Untrained leaders,324,369,
371

Values,147,176
Veterans: domiciliary care,
29; social services for,
238,240; widows of,149
Victor Home for Unmarried
Mothers,106
Visiting Homemakers Association,156
Volunteers: motivations
of,179,181; training of,
314,319,324,357; use of,
180,339

Wellington County Family
Court,118
Windsor Community Welfare
Council,343
Work permits for school
children,300

Workmen's Compensation Board,
   Ontario, 218

Y.M. and Y.W.H.A.: administration of,325
Y.M.C.A.: secretaryship of,
   310; war services of,338
Y.W.C.A.: job satisfaction
   in,309; objectives of,309
   program for mothers in,185;
   results of experience in,
   186

www.ingramcontent.com/pod-product-compliance
Lightning Source LLC
Chambersburg PA
CBHW021855020426
42334CB00013B/338